Dreamworlds of Shamanism and Tibetan Buddhism

Dreamworlds of Shamanism and Tibetan Buddhism

The Third Place

Angela Sumegi

State University of New York Press

Cover photos of Bhutanese masked dancers by the author.

Published by
State University of New York Press, Albany

Printed in the United States of America

For information, contact State University of New York Press, Albany, NY
www.sunypress.edu

Production by Diane Ganeles
Marketing by Susan Petrie

Library of Congress Cataloging-in-Publication Data

Sumegi, Angela, 1948–
Dreamworlds of Shamanism and Tibetan Buddhism : The Third Place / Angela Sumegi.
p. cm.
Includes bibliographical references and index.
ISBN 978-0-7914-7463-1 (hardcover : alk. paper)
ISBN 978-0-7914-7464-8 (pbk. : alk. paper)
1. Dreams—Religious aspects—Buddhism. 2. Buddhism—China—Tibet. 3. Shamanism—China—Tibet. I. Title.

BQ4570.D73S86 2008
204'.2—dc22 2007033165

10 9 8 7 6 5 4 3 2 1

To my husband, Zsolt

This talk is like stamping new coins. They pile up,
while the real work is done outside
by someone digging in the ground.

—Rumi

Now, this person has just two places—this world and the other world. And there is a third, the place of dream where the two meet. Standing there in the place where the two meet, he sees both those places—this world and the other world.

—Bṛhadāraṇyaka Upaniṣad 4.3.9

Contents

Tables

Preface

It was dusk when the shaman's assistant led me along a footpath winding down the mountainside. We were going to the house of a Bhutanese *pawo* (Tib. *dpa'bo*), who would call his spirits to answer my questions. Facing his altar and a small window that let in the very last of the evening light, the shaman began his performance. I watched and listened with his family and neighbors as he began a slow chant to the beat of his drum, culminating after an hour or so in a deafening crescendo and a wide-eyed, shaking, growling, whirling dance.

The shaman's altar was laid with Buddhist ritual objects; he wore a monk's robe over his formal Bhutanese dress, and on his head was the five-pointed crown that adorns many Tibetan images of buddhas and bodhisattvas. His drum was the same type as those used in monastic rituals, and his eerie cries and movements seemed echoed by the lama dances that I had heard and seen in the Buddhist monasteries of Bhutan. According to his own identification, he is a "Buddhist" pawo, and the spirit that possessed him was Gesar of Ling. Fittingly so, I thought, since Gesar is a legendary warrior hero of ancient Tibet reconstructed in Buddhist terms and claimed by Buddhism, but whose origins are hidden in the complex interweaving of shamanic and Buddhist religious systems. In this encounter, which took place after the research for this book was done, I found renewed evidence of the continuing interaction between Buddhism and shamanism in Himalayan cultures. It also confirmed for me the importance of studying this relationship in order to understand the ways in which shamanic and Buddhist worlds have, over centuries, both contested and enriched each other.

In exploring the relationship between culture and dream, the anthropologist Barbara Tedlock suggests that the emphasis in dream studies should shift from psychoanalytic dream-content analysis to dreaming as a "psychodynamic communicative process"[1] to be studied within the dream interpretation and classification systems of the cultures themselves. With regard to the Tibetan Buddhist context, contradictions surrounding the approach to dream have previously been interpreted as arising from distinctions between the categories of popular and elite religion. This book questions the usefulness of these categories, and looks at the role of dream as a mediator in the dialogue between shamanism and Buddhism in Tibetan culture.

Acknowledgments

I would like to express my appreciation and gratitude to friends and family who have supported me throughout the endeavor of completing this book. My friend and mentor Dr. Nalini Devdas took time from her own work to read, search out references, and offer much-appreciated advice. Dr. Marie-Françoise Guédon guided my introduction to shamanic worldviews. From far-off Bhutan, Chris Fynn shared his considerable knowledge of Tibetan thought and literature and provided invaluable bibliographic references. I would like also to thank Mary Finnigan for permission to use excerpts from a taped interview with His Holiness the Dalai Lama, and James and Tsering Mullens for permission to use their translation of a Tibetan dream manual. My thanks also to Dr. Eugene Rothman, Ryszard Cimek, Claire Bélanger, and all those who offered their time, thought, and advice throughout the writing process. I am also very grateful for the professional assistance of my copy editor, Wyatt Benner and for the guidance offered by the editorial and production staff at the State University of New York Press.

I would like to acknowledge a debt to two authors whose work had a strong influence on this book. Geoffrey Samuel's analysis of cultural patterns or modalities and his theoretical framework for Tibetan religion helped me greatly to situate dream in the Tibetan context; and Serinity Young's work on dream in Buddhist biographies not only supplied a wealth of insight into Buddhist dreams and dream theory, but also provided a starting point for my own thoughts on the subject.

I thank His Holiness Pema Norbu Rinpoché, Khenchen Tsewang Gyatso, Lama Lhanang, Jurme Wangda, the monks of Namdroling monastery, and the many residents of the fourth camp at Byla Kuppe, all of whom have generously shared with me their learning and their experiences of Tibetan life and culture. Finally, I wish to thank my daughter Ildiko whose careful work in editing and proofing various versions of this manuscript allowed me to see the task through to its completion. The merit in this work reflects the contributions of many people; the faults are my own.

Introduction

All experience is lost. What we know of our world and ourselves is constructed from records preserved in words and formulas, in wood or stone, in body, bone, and memory—but records are problematic; they must be confirmed, interpreted, and constantly reevaluated in order for us to maintain confidence in our creations of world and self. Dream narratives with their attendant theories, practices, and interpretations are an especially difficult type of record to work with, because it is not at all clear exactly what type of knowledge they can be used to construct, or that they support any structure at all. A single dream can be made to bear a multitude of interpretations,[1] while the theories and methodologies utilized in understanding dreams and the process of dreaming are equally numerous. However, despite the diversity of paths taken to explore what Kelly Bulkeley calls the "wilderness of dreams,"[2] they all begin with the fundamental question—Do dreams and the activity of dreaming have any meaning or purpose? Do dreams signify meaningless chaotic mental activity during sleep, to be dismissed upon waking, or are they meaningful, though enigmatic, manifestations of our deepest self-awareness, to be pondered and interpreted upon waking?

Although there are those who take their stand firmly on one side or the other, contemporary dream researchers have worked to mediate the stark dichotomy that such a question poses. In his book *The Wilderness of Dreams*, Bulkeley seeks to provide an approach that, as he says, "accounts for both the interpretive and the natural scientific aspects of dreams."[3] To support his argument that dreams have religious meaning, Bulkeley employs two guides: the hermeneutic theories of the German philosopher Hans-Georg Gadamer to resolve divergent views on the basic question of whether or not dreams have meaning; and the concept of "root metaphors," personal and cultural metaphors that deal with existential concerns. Owen Flanagan, who argues from a neurophilosophical standpoint that there is no physiological or evolutionary value to dreaming, offers a different kind of resolution. Dreams, he proposes, can be thought of as the "spandrels of sleep,"[4] a mere side effect of the way in which the brain functions during sleep. In his view, however, this fact does not render dreams entirely meaningless. Flanagan suggests that just as humans have discovered a decorative use for spandrels, so some dreams can be employed creatively and meaningfully to illuminate aspects of human well-being and identity. Another contribution to the debate on the nature and value of dreams comes from an anthropological perspective. Current research has underscored the importance of the cultural context in which dreams are theorized and interpreted; it emphasizes the role of the dreamer's world and the cultural discourse that reflects the dream and is reflected in it.[5] This model further implies that a cultural framework could also apply to the significance of the question itself. In other words, why ask that question? Why does the meaningfulness or meaninglessness of dreams concern us? Do we seek knowledge about the physiology of sleep, the nature of consciousness, the function of the brain, the experience of dreaming, our relationship to gods and spirits? One could entertain many possible answers. In this book, I examine questions and answers related to dream as they are situated in the context of Tibetan Buddhist culture.

My interest in the questions that dream raises in Tibetan Buddhism was initially stimulated by the dreams and visions of the Fifth Dalai Lama (1617–82) recorded in the *Sealed and Secret Biography*, published in 1988 by Samten Gyaltsen Karmay along with the related texts and illustrations of the Gold Manuscript.[6] Ngawang Lobzang Gyamtso, known as the "Great Fifth," was one of Tibet's most powerful spiritual and political leaders, and as the head of the dominant Gelug school[7] he oversaw the transformation of Tibet into a Buddhist ecclesiastical state. It is with regard to the Dalai Lama as the state's chief embodiment of the Buddha's teaching that the dream images in these texts interested me. They portray ritual implements and magical charms, wild animals, fearful birds of prey, effigies of tormented human figures bound and shackled; they are images dedicated to the exercise of spiritual and political power, the exorcism of evil spirits, and the defeat of enemy forces. What is to be made of such "Buddhist" dreams? I was struck by the incongruity that this imagery focused on practical ritual purposes emerged from the mind of one steeped in the study of a philosophy that emphasizes the empty and illusory nature of self and ritual.[8]

The world of dream in Tibetan Buddhist narratives occupies a conflicted and ostensibly irresolvable space. Dreams are said to be unreal and deceptive, a profitless pursuit; nevertheless, they constitute a magical art to be mastered by the yogi, and their meaning is of supreme value. The response of Tibet's great yogi Milarepa (1052–1135) to his student's request for an interpretation of his dreams is typical of the attitude toward dream found in Tibetan biographies and religious literature. Milarepa's reply to Gampopa begins with a stern admonition:

> Have you not read Sūtras and many Tantras?
> Dreams are unreal and deceptive, as was taught
> By Buddha Himself, in the Final Truth of Pāramitā.
> To collect, supply, and study them
> Will bring little profit.

Still, he goes on to validate his student's interest in dreams and to elaborate on them:

> And yet, your dreams were marvelous—
> Wondrous omens foretelling things to come.
> I, the Yogi, have mastered the art of dreams,
> And will explain their magic to you.[9]

The basic contradiction between dreams as worthless and dreams as valuable has not gone unremarked by scholars of Tibetan Buddhism, but neither has it been granted much significance beyond being an example of the difference between elite religious philosophy and the practical folk religion of laypeople. However, as a way of understanding how competing religious worldviews manifest in the daily lives of a particular group, the popular/elite model has been reevaluated. Current scholarship has moved away from measuring one against the other, and toward the analysis of religious behavior and ideology in terms of internal cultural principles. In her monograph on the relationship between Buddhism and Shan religion, Nicola Tannenbaum questions the various meanings of "Buddhism" in Shan culture and proposes that the label obscures more than it reveals when used as the central or key element in understanding their religion. Tannenbaum suggests that the cultural principle of power-protection explains Shan religion better than Buddhism, despite the fact that Shan people identify themselves as Buddhist.[10] Ethnographical research has also brought new insights to bear on other religious systems that identify themselves as Buddhist.[11] With regard to dream as an aspect of Tibetan religion, however, the model has prevailed with no reevaluation of the popular/elite dichotomy.[12]

According to the popular/elite model, the monastic elite holds the view that dreams ultimately represent confusion and deception whereas the popular approach values dream as the bearer of prophecy and omen. Clearly this is not true in an absolute sense. In my research among contemporary lay Tibetans, they repeatedly stated that dreams are a product of mental confusion, and are therefore unreal, insignificant, and not to be dwelt upon. But might the popular/elite model still work in a relative sense? In other words, might the elite be more likely to view dreams as not worth pursuing and ordinary people more likely to regard them as practically useful? If we think of popular and elite as the poles of a continuum, then the following picture could be expected according to the model: At the extreme popular end, there might be a strong attachment to dreams and other omens as prophecy and direction for everyday life. In the middle, there might be the same ambivalent views on dream held by monastics and ordinary folk alike. Finally, among the most elite there might be a complete disinterest in dreams and omens. Yet even this is not the case. In the world of spiritual adepts and esoteric rituals, there is an overwhelming interest in dream as prophecy and direction for life, albeit from a religiously educated and informed point of view. And while I did not find anyone who held such extreme attachment to dreams or omenology as I have allocated to the popular pole above,[13] the spiritual elite, as we will see, are in fact more likely to be interested in the practical use of dream signs than ordinary lay people are.

The popular/elite divide, then, does not provide a satisfactory explanation for the underlying causes and significances of the contradictions inherent in Tibetan religious attitudes to dream. In seeking for a fuller understanding, it seemed to me that the Tibetan Buddhist emphasis on dream and visionary experiences corresponded to a similar emphasis in the religious complex of shamanism. Much of the imagery in the Fifth Dalai Lama's secret biography resonates with shamanic themes of struggle with disease, death, and malefic spirits. In one dream, he sees a large scorpion penetrating his body and devouring him from the inside; then, emitting flames, it burns away all remaining body parts.[14] The Dalai Lama observes that he was suffering from an illness but felt better after this dream and shortly thereafter recovered completely. This gruesome dream and its association with healing calls to mind the visions of dismemberment and death that mark the initiatory healing of a Siberian shaman. In light of research that supports the existence of a relationship between an indigenous shamanic heritage and the development of Buddhist practices in Tibet,[15] I chose to explore dream in Tibetan Buddhism as a site of the encounter between shamanism and Buddhism: a third place, so to speak, from which to appreciate the dialogue between these two worlds, and from which to contemplate the significance of divergent approaches to dream in Tibetan Buddhism.

Buddhism and shamanism—both of which are more accurately described in terms of constellations of belief and practice rather than as monolithic isms—represent religious complexes whose fundamental stances appear, if not opposed to each other, then at the very least oriented in quite different directions. Shamanism rests on the belief that the universe consists of seen and unseen dimensions, that it is animated by spirit forces, and that suffering is a result of disharmony or negative interactions between humans and their social and natural environment. The goal of the shaman is to acquire the power residing in the unseen dimension of reality and mediate it for the practical benefit of the community. Alternatively, basic Buddhist teachings emphasize that the universe arises and ceases according to the principles of causality and conditionality, that it is impermanent and without essence, and that human suffering is a result of self-oriented desires and ignorance. The religious goal is nirvāṇa—freedom from all ignorance and grasping, and the cessation of the cycle of rebirth and redeath called saṃsāra. Whatever Buddhist ritual experts do for the practical or mundane benefit of their community is carried out in the context of this ultimate goal. In contrast, shamanic activity, whether pertaining to this world or the world of the spirits, is primarily oriented toward serving individuals in a defined communal context in whatsoever practical ways they may demand, and is generally unconcerned with concepts of ultimate liberation or salvation.

The shamanic perspective maintains that harmony implies a balance of power in the universe—in other words, evil and darkness have a place in the cosmos that is to be upheld as fearlessly as light and goodness.[16] Johannes Wilbert's study of the Warao Indians of Venezuela illustrates this view very clearly. The magic arrows of the dark-shaman seek out human victims to provide sustenance for the spirits of the underworld, and for the Warao, it is unthinkable that the shaman should be prevented from doing his work: " 'One cannot imagine what would happen if our dark-shamans were to stop providing nourishment for the spirits of the west,' is a common reply to a field-worker's query. 'The world would probably come to an end. All children would die and so would the gods.' "[17] What are the dynamics, then, when such a perspective encounters a soteriologically driven vision of the universe that aims to eradicate evil and achieve the ultimate good? In the following pages, I will consider this question in relation to the shamanic use of dream in order to determine what significance can be attributed to the contradictory attitudes evident in Tibetan Buddhism toward the phenomenon of dream.

The anthropologist David Gellner proposes that religion in general and rituals in particular can be analyzed in terms of their primary purpose: soteriological, concerned with ultimate liberation from the ills of the world; social, concerned with the solidarity of the group; and instrumental, "the attempt to make specific things happen within the world."[18] With regard to the social dimension, shamanic activity generally serves the practical needs of individuals belonging to a specific group or community. Although Buddhism (in its emphasis on monastic values and renunciation of the world) upholds detachment from society, the Mahāyāna Buddhism of Tibet is inseparable from its social context, since it seeks the universal salvation of sentient beings.[19] Both shamanic and Buddhist traditions, therefore, share a social purpose, even if the community of those to be served is understood differently. Similarly, shamanic methods and Tibetan Buddhist rituals equally provide for the practical needs of their communities in terms of healing, divination, or protection.The third category then remains: ultimate liberation from the ills of the world. The Buddha's first teaching laid down the eightfold way, the path to nirvāṇa and the complete cessation of suffering; however, no comparable doctrine of ultimate salvation from the ills of the world *as the goal of religious life and behavior* appears in shamanic ritual complexes. Shamanism generally emphasizes a balance of power and holds to the idea that evil cannot, and indeed should not, be ultimately eradicated. The significance of this divergence will be investigated in a later chapter, but we can note here that the distinction constitutes an important divide between shamanism and Buddhism, one that supports and maintains the integrity of their views on dreams and dreaming.

In engaging with the subject matter of this book I have taken a multidisciplinary approach, using whatever tools furthered my understanding and insight into the relationship between shamanic and Buddhist perspectives as manifested in their approaches to dream. A variety of methods, therefore, were used in the research for this work, including informal and unstructured conversations and interviews with lay and monastic Tibetans, participant observation, textual analysis, as well as reference to travelogues and the contemporary writings of shamanic and Buddhist practitioners. My intent was to trace themes of tension and resolution in shamanism and Buddhism that coalesce in Tibetan attitudes toward dream. Chapter 1 offers a working definition and discusses the characteristics of shamanism and the role of dream in such a system. Chapters 2 and 3 examine the attitudes to dream present in Indian Buddhism and its Vedic heritage. Although the early propagation of Buddhism in Tibet is linked with both India and China,[20] I will be concerned in these chapters only with the Indian connection, since my aim is to establish that conflicting attitudes to dream were present within the cultural matrix of Buddhism, and expressed in its foundational texts. Chapters 4 and 5 take up the significance of dream in the Tibetan context as it relates to the religious orientations of Tibetan culture and as it manifests the ambiguity and unease characteristic of religious encounters.

Despite frequent references in this book to "Buddhism" and "shamanism," I am aware of the differences that each term embraces and the disputed nature of such categories. Indeed, contemporary scholarship eschews the notion of a singular "tradition." However, it is not clear to me that the shortcomings of an essentialist approach are overcome by addressing oneself to smaller and smaller units, whether of time, culture, or philosophy. Although there is no Buddhism apart from particular beliefs and behaviors designated as such, it is the fiction of identity and essence that allows for vision beyond the truth of description. With regard to dream, I have sought to determine and trace relationships between disparate texts, historical periods, and cultures in order to perceive certain patterns and to note how they are reconfigured in Tibetan culture.

Although I have used data drawn from Tibetan culture as well as from a wide range of shamanisms to explore the processes that inform the relationship between shamanic and Buddhist worldviews, this is neither an ethnographical nor a Tibetological study. My aim has been to understand the ways in which dreams and dreaming act as a site of cultural dialogue between shamanism and Tibetan Buddhism, a site that accommodates both dissonance and harmony, where resolution does not efface the tensions that provide an impetus to creativity. A comparative approach, therefore, allows me to discuss Tibetan perspectives on dream by comparing them to Indian Buddhist views, on the one hand, and shamanic attitudes, on the other. In this endeavor, Jonathan Smith's reminder is worth noting: "Comparison does not necessarily tell us how things 'are' . . . like models and metaphors, comparison tells us how things might be conceived, how they might be 'redescribed.' . . ."[21] This book, then, is an enterprise in the redescription of the role of dreams and dreaming in the complex interface between Buddhism and shamanism played out in the Tibetan context.

A word on Bön. The Bön religion of Tibet has been variously portrayed: by Buddhist polemicists as anti-Buddhist folk magic and superstition; by Western scholars as a poor copy of Buddhism; and by contemporary Bön practitioners as the indigenous religion of Tibet.[22] The pre-Buddhist religious background of Tibet, however, is difficult to determine with any great accuracy—as far as we know, record-keeping and writing came to Tibet from India along with Buddhism only in the seventh century CE. The documents discovered by Aurel

Stein and Paul Pelliot during their expeditions in 1907 and 1908 to the Buddhist cave temples of Dunhuang indicate that pre-Buddhist Tibetan religion was intimately related to the activity of priests known as Bön.[23] This term has occasioned much confusion, since it refers not only to pre-Buddhist ritualists but also to a religious tradition that developed in close association and competition with Buddhism.

The present-day religion known as Bön presents scholars with great challenges in deciphering its relationship both to Buddhism and to the pre-Buddhist religiosity of Tibet. Per Kværne outlines three general ways in which Bön has been understood: as the shamanic religion of early Tibet, polemicized by Tibetan historians; as the organized religion of today that appeared around the tenth century and is barely distinguishable from the Buddhist traditions of Tibet; and as referring to the practitioners and wide range of practices of magic and divination that characterize Tibet's folk religion.[24] According to David Snellgrove's summation of the confusions that have proliferated with regard to Bön and Buddhism,

> *Bön* (meaning "priest who invokes") is one thing, and *Bönpo* meaning "follower of BÖN" ("Tibetan religion") is another. The early Buddhists certainly came into conflict with the *Bön* ("priests who invoke") who were active in Tibet long before Buddhist doctrines were introduced, but their real long-term rivals were the *Bönpos* who were busy constituting their BÖN ("Tibetan religion") while the Buddhists (*chos-pa*) were busy constituting their CHOS (*Dharma*). The development of BÖN and CHOS were parallel processes, and both *Bönpos* and *chos-pas* were using the same literary language within the same cultural surroundings.[25]

Scholarship initiated by Snellgrove shows that the organized living tradition of Bön is neither merely a copy of Buddhism nor an unbroken continuation of the pre-Buddhist religion of Tibet, but a distinct soteriologically oriented spiritual tradition in its own right.[26] The modern Bön tradition, along with Tibetan Buddhism, draws on the same complex matrix consisting of the indigenous foundations of Tibetan culture and worldview intermingled with ideas and imagery from surrounding cultures. Therefore, although the Bön religion has a strong shamanic component, I do not look to it as the indigenous precursor to Buddhism.[27]

That being said, however, there are contending voices; and the relationship between Bön, Buddhism, and the indigenous beliefs and practices of Tibet is still far from clear. John Vincent Bellezza's research on the spirit-mediums of Upper Tibet provides strong evidence for the role of Bön in the survival of ancient shamanistic practices bound to the local geography of Tibetan communities.[28] Shamanism in Tibetan culture has been overlaid with both Bön and Buddhist traditions; nevertheless, it makes itself known through correspondences that can be drawn between elements of Tibetan religion (whether Buddhist, Bön, or folk practices) and other, more clearly defined shamanic complexes.

Chapter 1

Shamanisms and Dreams

As a field of study, shamanism continues to inspire vigorous debate concerning its parameters. There are those who argue that the terms "shaman" and "shamanism" do not properly apply to the phenomena of possession or spirit mediumship and should be limited to the religious complexes of Siberia and related cultures.[1] However, in this book I follow the lead of scholars who work with a comparative and analytic use of the terminology related to shamanic studies.[2] As I have used it, "shamanism" is a convenient label for a variable constellation of religious beliefs and practices grounded in an animistic worldview that ascribes intentionality and the capacity for communication to a vast range of phenomena. In addition, shamanism is focused on mechanisms believed to enable persons to mediate power and protection for the benefit of a particular group,[3] although techniques for accessing power do not always include states of ecstatic trance, and those who "shamanize" may or may not do so in the capacity of a specialist.

I accept Michel Perrin's analysis that a shamanic belief-system functions according to three basic characteristics: first, the belief in the double nature of persons and their environment—the person consisting of body and separable soul or souls, the external environment consisting of "this" world of materiality and the "other" world of spirit; second, the belief in the shaman's ability to communicate intentionally with the spirit world; and third, the relationship between the shaman and the community, meaning that the shaman acts in response to social demand.[4] To expand on Perrin's threefold analysis, I also accept the following ideas drawn from the work of Vladimir Basilov. Shamanism implies a worldview that regards the universe and all its parts as interconnected and imbued with spirit forces that can interact with human beings in positive or negative ways. Human beings, therefore, have no innate superiority over nature and participate in the complex interactions of the universe in the same way as all other beings. The cosmos consists of various levels or dimensions of existence other than the visible world of humans—dimensions that are permeable and accessible by humans. Ordinary people can unintentionally access these other places or states of existence, but the intentional work of a shaman requires the assistance of spirit forces.[5] Within these broad parameters, small-scale tribal communities around the world engage in distinctive methods through which they meet their particular needs regarding the protection or restoration of life force, of property, and of personal, social, economic, and environmental well-being. In this working definition, then, shamanism refers both to elements of specific indigenous religions analyzed by scholars in the field as well as to a belief system that appears cross-culturally, though not uniformly.[6]

The processes of dreaming and dream interpretation are vital components of the religious practices and beliefs of many societies; however, in themselves, dream and religion alike manifest a particular approach to the world and to human existence. In this chapter, my aim is to draw the reader's attention to those aspects of a shamanic worldview that support and validate the world of dream as an arena of human activity, both ordinary and extraordinary, and to show that they are present in the Tibetan context.

THE WORLD AS BEING

Peter Furst says, "In general shamanism expresses a philosophy of life that holds all beings—human, animal, or plant—to be qualitatively equivalent: all phenomena of nature, including human beings, plants, animals, rocks, rain, thunder, lightning, stars and planets, and even tools, are animate, imbued with a life essence or soul or, in the case of human beings, more than one soul. . . . The origin of life is held to lie in transformation. . . ."[7] This describes what Furst calls an "ecological belief system." It is an approach to being and beings that resonates throughout the folk culture of the Tibetan region until today.[8] The sacred mountains and lakes of Tibet are powerful beings who are kin to its people from primordial times.[9] Indeed, in Tibetan traditional history, the dominion of Buddhism over their world is portrayed in the image of the land itself as a great demoness captured and pinned by twelve "limb-binding" temples.[10]

The multiplicity of being manifests in shamanic cultures around the world where there is a shared belief in various types and classes of spirits or nonhuman beings who interact with humans. *Lha*, the Tibetan word for such spirits, has wide-ranging connotations. *Lha* can refer broadly to benevolent sky gods, the gods of ancient Buddhist cosmology, the spirits associated with a particular locality, nature spirits, and the ghosts of certain people, as well as to the deities, enlightened and unenlightened, who are the focus of tantric Buddhist practice.[11] The different kinds of lha are classified in a number of ways. According to one analysis, three classes of spirits are related, respectively, to the three cosmic zones. The benevolent gods (*lha*) occupy the upper world of sky or heaven, mountain spirits (the *nyen* and *tsen*; Tib. *gnyan* and *btsan*) and the "earth-lords" or "soil-owners" (the *sadak*; Tib. *sa bdag*) dwell in the middle zone of earth, and the water-serpent spirits (*lu*; Tib. *klu*) make their homes in the lower realms under the earth and in the depths of lakes and rivers. Most of these spirits are thought to be easily angered or disturbed by human activity, the result of which is disease and misfortune. The water spirits who appear as snakes are said to send leprosy when angered; others are thought responsible for plague or cancer. Commensurate with such a worldview, popular religious activity is primarily defensive and centered around propitiating those spirits who are powerful and temperamental, and who can be vindictive in their dealings with humans.[12]

Bellezza notes that one of the most important functions of the present-day spirit-mediums (*lha-pa*) of Upper Tibet is their specialized ability to restore harmony between humans and their living environment, thereby pacifying and healing the diseases that result from disharmony. The following excerpt from a Bön text attributed to the eighth century lists the kinds of activities that can elicit the anger of the *yul-lha*, the protector deities of the locality. It reveals the anxieties inherent in all human activity that disturbs or impinges on the natural world.

> (iv) Listen to my speech . . . In the event that we did upset you let us be peacefully reconciled. We reconcile you by offerings of jewels and incense.
>
> If we screamed on the mountaintops,
> and irrigated with water channels and reservoirs,
> and excavated at your mighty springs,
> and accidentally lit big fires on mountains,
> and killed your mighty deer and hunted your wild ungulates . . .
> [If we] molested the mighty *yul-lha*, rendered them unconscious, upset them, startled them, made them ill, and injured them, whatever transpired; we offer . . . these offerings of various kinds of herbs and medicines.

> (v) . . . If you are angry may you be pacified. If you are quarrelsome, we will reconcile the contention . . . May all your grudges be pacified. May all our infectious diseases and ailments be pacified. May your hatred and malice be pacified . . .[13]

In Tibetan folk religion, the most easily angered spirits are the *sadak,* "masters of the earth," "lords of the soil," who are disturbed especially by such invasive activities as building, digging, or any form of pollution of the earth. Religious acts of constructing stupas or temples were thought no less immune to the anger of the spirit owners of a place than secular activities of house building, hunting, or irrigating the fields. Concern with the vagaries of the spirit world is also expressed in Buddhist rituals, which commonly include the propitiation and domination of the local deities. The offering of *torma* (Tib. *gtor ma*—a ritual cake broken and scattered about for spirit beings to enjoy) is intended to pacify the local gods. It is presented in some rituals with pleasing words such as:

> I offer this torma of a nectar-ocean
> To the lords of place and soil.
> Please accept it, and without malice
> Be my good and steadfast friends.[14]

Other liturgies evoke a much stronger sense of control and command. "The entire assemblage of obstructors consisting of gods and so forth who stay on the grounds of the great maṇḍala listen! . . . [B]e content with these tormas and go each to your own place. If you do not depart, with the vajra of the knowledge of the wrathful ones, blazing as fire (your) heads will be shattered into a hundred pieces, no doubt about it!"[15] Every step of practical or religious life could potentially anger the local deities and bring about misfortune or illness. Therefore, the ability to pacify or control the local spirits would be an important aspect of religious activity, one that is linked in many forms of shamanism with the ability to work with dreams.

In contemporary Tibetan life, the primal anxieties related to the interaction between humans and the spirit inhabitants of the environment can still be observed. Sudhir Kakar relates the story of a young monk from the diaspora Tibetan community of Dharamsala, India, who fell on the hillside, bruising his face and cutting his palms and elbows. He washed off the blood in a stream where a couple of Westerners were also washing clothes and dishes. The next day, his face swelled so grotesquely that he could not perform his duties in the monastery. Upon consulting a lama specialist, he was told that it was a spirit attack from the angered *lu* deity of the stream. As a remedy, the monk was advised to take offerings to the stream, apologize, and request forgiveness. The swelling soon receded, and life returned to normal. In response to the question of why the lu did not attack the Westerners, the monk had several answers. First, they were washing clothes, which results in external dirt—blood is internal impurity and much more polluting to the *lu*. Second, their personal energy and fortune (*lung-ta*; Tib. *rlung rta*) may have been higher than the monk's; finally, they probably did not believe in the lu, and knowing this the lu did not waste time in attacking them, but turned on the one who feared him.[16] This last explanation might bring to mind Lévy-Bruhl's analysis of so-called primitive mentality, according to which the conceptualizations or "collective representations" that constitute the worldview of a group follow their own laws, and reflect a social reality that is not expected to apply to outsiders.[17] However, for the purposes of this book, it is more important to note that such an explanation implies the understanding that reality is a function of the particular view that one holds. It underscores the notion that the world arises and interacts with a person according to how it is perceived and appropriated. This principle can be recognized in the Tibetan method of working with dream—once the dream perceptions are appropriated as dream and not as the reality they appear to be, they become subject to the control of the dreamer. The relationship between communication with deities and control over dream perceptions is found in both shamanism and Tibetan Buddhism but, as will be discussed later, a soteriological framework effectively separates the Buddhist from the shamanic approach.

Allied with the belief in a plurality of spirits inhabiting and enlivening the world is the shamanic view that the human body is inhabited and animated by one or more souls or aspects of soul—a word that encompasses a wide range of indigenous concepts regarding the various dimensions of personhood.[18] "Soul" in Tibet's folk culture is captured in the concept of *la* (Tib. *bla*). The la has left the body when someone falls unconscious, is extremely ill, or suffers a severe fright. The permanent separation of the la from the body signifies death. The la has shape and mobility, and although it is intimately associated with the life force of a person, it can also dwell outside the body in any aspect of the environment, such as trees, rocks, lakes, or animals.[19] Samten Karmay cites the following passage from a ritual text, in which the shamanic idea of a "soul" that wanders about separate from the body is integrated with the Buddhist body/mind analysis of a person. "If one practices magic what does one kill, the body or the 'mind'? The body is made of matter. Even if it is killed, it does not die. As for the 'mind,' it is empty and therefore there is nothing to kill. Neither the body nor the 'mind' is killed. It is the *bla*, which wanders like a sheep without a shepherd that must be summoned."[20] As this passage indicates, the landscape of soul journeys is a dangerous one; during its wanderings the soul can be seized by a demon or spirit of some kind, in which case a complicated ceremony to recover it is required.[21] Although Tibetan rituals of ransoming the soul are found in Buddhist texts, the basic principle and elements of the ritual can easily be recognized in shamanic practices of soul recovery.

In the Tibetan folk tradition, the idea of multiple souls, common in shamanic systems, is reflected in the belief that a person has five protective spirits (*gowé lha*; Tib.*'go ba'i lha*) that come to be associated with the child at birth and that reside in different parts of the body. Among them are the life force deity at the heart, the "man's god" or protector of men in the right armpit, the "woman's god" or protector of women in the left armpit, the "enemy god" at the right shoulder, and the deity who presides over the locality on the crown of the head.[22] These spirits are regarded as internal aspects of a person's life force or soul, but at the same time they are propitiated externally as separate beings. The ambiguity supports the shamanic belief that personhood is a pervasive principle of existence. In other words, just as the various spirit energies that populate the external environment are regarded as discrete persons, so too the internal dimensions of a human being, the various souls, can be perceived as substantial "beings" who possess agency to act in different ways and fulfill different functions.[23]

ANIMATE AND INANIMATE BEINGS

In shamanism, the souls of humans and the spirits associated with natural phenomena are interrelated, but the exact nature of that relationship is not easy to determine. The label "animistic" is commonly applied to cultures that engage in a particular way with their environment—as persons interacting with persons. Although this does not mean that animistic societies are ignorant of the difference between animate and inanimate, neither are these categories regarded as complete opposites. For example, studies of Ob Ugrian groups like the Daur Mongols indicate the use of different verbs to distinguish between things "with a soul" and things "without a soul."[24] Yet, there is also the belief that the shadow soul, which resides in people and animals, is, paradoxically, also present in things "without a soul."[25] What constitutes the animate, then, is somewhat more complex than might be understood from the stereotypical notion imposed on animistic cultures that "everything is alive." This position is elaborated by Nurit Bird-David, whose study of the Nayaka, a south Indian hunter-gatherer community, resulted in her reevaluation of animism and a more nuanced understanding of this complex worldview.[26] She emphasizes the prominence of kinship in the Nayaka definition of "person" as "one whom we share with" and concludes that for the Nayaka, personhood is not a given characteristic of inanimate things but an expression of relationship. "As and when and because they engage in and maintain relationships with other beings, they constitute them as kinds of persons: they make them 'relatives' by sharing with them and thus make them persons."[27]

A similar dynamic appears in Caroline Humphrey's study of Daur Mongol shamanism. She relates a story in which a man who had recently moved to a barren, stony place thought that the single beautiful tree growing there was worthy of worship. The author notes that this tree was not outstanding in any magical way, nor did it contain a spirit; however, *subsequent* to being brought into a relationship and ritually worshipped as a sacred tree, it was regarded as having an indwelling spirit.[28] Jean-Guy Goulet's work on the North American Dene Tha also substantiates this constitutive aspect of animistic societies. He writes of the self-validating nature of the Dene Tha reality, in which the various elements "elaborate each other in a back-and-forth process."[29]

In the Tibetan context, Bellezza also notes a strong sense of kinship with the indigenous mountain and lake deities; and in titles like "grandfather," "mother," "elder brother," and "elder sister" he sees the vestiges of a genealogical relationship.[30] The strength of this link with the gods and the essential mutual support between the people and the spirit powers of the landscape—the way in which they "elaborate each other"—is brought out in a Bön supplication to Targo, the deity associated with the sacred snow mountain range of the same name in northern Tibet: "We fulfill the wishes of the lions, tigers, leopards, iron [-colored] wolves, black bears, boars, *mi-dred*, soaring winged creatures, and wild yaks, and your entire manifested entourage. If there is no one to offer to the gods how can the magical power of the gods come forth? If humans do not have vigilant deities, who will be the supporter of humans?"[31]

Such examples highlight two important characteristics of a shamanic worldview: one, that relationship signifies communication, which takes place between persons; the other, that certain realities are constituted, not given. In the Mongolian case cited above, the reality of the tree-spirit emerges through the relationship between man and tree, through the intention of the ritual and the action of worship. In the Tibetan text, the power of the gods manifests through their relationship to humans. People and their environment are perceived as belonging to an ecological whole in which relationship between "persons" is the dominant mode of existence. The creative transformation that is at the heart of shamanic ritual and dream work is dependent on this view of the organic nature of being and beings. The transformation of human to animal, or from ordinary tree to sacred tree, is not merely the process of one thing becoming another, but an unceasing unfolding that is the very nature of existence. As rain unfolds into the trees and trees into the wood and the sacrificial animal into the fire and the chants of the shaman into the smoke and the sky, so the ritual or the dream unfolds into reality.

The relationship between human beings and their environment reveals worlds within worlds, where the inner realm of the soul appears in the guise of the external world and vice versa. In Tibetan folk religion, a lake, stone, or tree can be the dwelling place of the soul and equally the dwelling place of a deity; the protector god of the locality has his seat on a mountain, but also on the crown of one's head. The "man's god" dwelling in the body is worshipped externally in a pile of stones on the roof of the house, and, likewise, the "woman's god" is worshipped in the central pillar of the house.[32] From this perspective, macrocosm and microcosm form a single continuum folding in upon itself; the traditional Tibetan house ladder made of a single notched tree trunk connecting the floors from top to bottom is, in the same moment, the primordial pillar of the sky that connects the sky to earth.[33] Similarly, waking reality and dream reality are recognizably distinct, yet they enfold one another. Dependent on the characteristics of his world, the shaman is able to fulfill his role and manipulate the diverse realities of his universe for himself and his audience.

CONTRACTS AND NEGOTIATION

The replaying of original promises, negotiations, and agreements is as integral to shamanic methods of establishing harmony and dealing with the needs of the various beings of the universe as the spells and incantations that bind the spirits. In his chants, a Nepali shaman recounts the original negotiations with animals that establish the contract between humans and chickens as the sacrificial animal for the ritual, along with the well-known characteristics of chickens. The song petitions the elephant, horse, buffalo, cow, goat, sheep, and pig, all of whom refuse to "go in place of man." It concludes:

"[I]f man will grant our sacred promise, then we will go,"
said the old cock, the old hen.
"So, just what is your sacred promise?" he asked.

The old cock and hen request that until midday they be rightfully allowed to stay in the corner by the door, to defecate on clean floors, to upset filled pots, to peck around the hearth, and scratch for food.

"[U]ntil midday is our promised time,
for all this, in place of man,
for untimely deaths, untimely crises,
with our blood we will satisfy the Time of Death, the
  Messenger of Death, . . .[34]

Apart from the etiology expressed in the song, I wish to draw attention to the consensual, contractual nature of the relationship between the various beings of the world; here, mankind does not hold a place of natural authority. All participants have an equal voice.

The theme of permission and consensus between humans and other beings appears in many cultures as an important aspect of shamanic activity.[35] Vilmos Diószegi's description of a ceremony among the Soyots of Siberia in which a staff is prepared for a new shaman further demonstrates this idea. The old shaman first selects the birch tree from which the staff is to be cut and asks the consent of the birch to be made into the staff. After the staff is carved, its consent to serve the shaman must also be obtained.

White birch-staff: be my horse, be my friend!
Again the shaman gave the answer: [on behalf of the staff]
I agree.[36]

Another kind of pact is described in a Nepali story of the mythical battle between the first shaman and nine witch sisters, whereby the shaman spares the life of the last evil witch in return for her agreement to obey his commandments when he performs the witch-removing rituals.[37] The roles are clearly defined as the witch pleads for her life:

I will cause illness, you will cure it,
you will receive wealth, you will receive grain,
I will apply reversed knowledge,
you will apply straightened spells,
I will obey your assigned times and assigned cures,

I will put frogs and turtles into victims,
you will cure them . . .
throughout the world, I'll cause illness,
you'll cure it, don't kill me.[38]

The emphasis on negotiation and consensus further implies that in a shamanic worldview all parties have a role to play and, indeed, *must* be allowed to play their part. A Daur elder puts it succinctly: "The fact is: all the things in the world and the people exist in their own way. We cannot and must not win over everything, but we must fight. Fighting is balancing. *Shurkuls* [devils] were never killed. You don't get the idea? If a shaman could completely get rid of *shurkul*, everything would lose balance. *Shurkul* has to be there."[39] Harmony is achieved through the public agreement or contractual arrangements between all participants, human and nonhuman, animate and inanimate, good and evil. But harmony and balance cannot be achieved or maintained without effort. Shamanizing and dreaming alike are manifestations of the ongoing struggle for equilibrium.

JOINING HEAVEN AND EARTH

In his wide-ranging study on shamanism, Mircea Eliade emphasized the role of the mountain in central and north Asian cultures as a cosmic link between the planes of earth and sky, human world and spirit world.[40] Heissig notes that in Mongolian religion, the reverence for sacred mountains was so great that in ordinary speech the name of the mountain was taboo, and euphemisms such as "the beautiful," "the holy," or "the high" were used.[41] The mountain summit, enveloped by sky, also serves as the throne or seat of mighty beings, as well as the place from where great shamans or ancestor kings descend, bringing their protection to the people.

The following Mongolian myth describes the origin and descent of such protectors and their relationship to the deities of the mountain. A son petitions his father to become a protector for all creatures because he has developed such great occult abilities.[42] The father agrees, but only if he, the father, is buried in the right place and worshipped. The son takes his father's body to the Red Cliff Mountain and worships him with offerings of tea, water, and milk-wine brandy. The spirit of the dead father allies with the nature spirits who are the "masters of the place" and grows more and more powerful, capable of creating hail, lightning bolts, and all kinds of terrible phenomena. In the same way, the mother's spirit also becomes extremely strong and feared by the people. Protection comes about when the spirits of the dead parents possess a man and a woman who are to become the first shamans. In their ecstatic state, they travel to the burial place on the Red Cliff Mountain, where they find drums and headdresses made of the feathers of the Yellow Bird; finally, they descend from the mountain, beating their drums and coming to the aid of the people.

In this shaman origin story, apart from the role of the mountain as a place of power, there are two themes common to many shamanisms: the recognition that the power to protect is inseparable from the power to destroy, and the idea that creative energy is generated by worship—that passionate attention to an object articulated in ritual. Through worship, trees and groves become beings of power; through worship, the spirits of the dead grow great.

In Tibetan culture, a similar reverence for mountains is observed, and the legends of the divine origin of their first king reiterate the theme of the descent of protectors from a special mountain. Tibetan mountain-gods are related to a category of warrior gods that hark back to the beginnings of Tibetan military and political strength. According to Tucci, "The attire and the mounts of these gods indicate unmistakably the pastoral and warlike nature of the corresponding social strata; . . . they wear armour, often a copper helmet or a felt hat (*phying zhwa*), with bird feathers on the hat and a mirror in their hand. This latter of course belongs among the essential items of equipment of the shaman."[43] The enduring bond between a particular group or village and their mountain protector is expressed by Thubten Norbu, the eldest brother of the Fourteenth Dalai Lama, who remembers how the sight of Kyeri, "this majestic glacier mountain, which was the throne of our protective deity Kye, always made our hearts beat higher."[44] In his description of the worship of the deity, he recounts that "[o]n a small hill not far from [the village of] Tengster there was a labtse, that is to say, a heap of stones dedicated to the protective deity of the village. . . . Here you offered up white quartz, coins, turquoises and corals, and prayed for rain, or for sun, or for a good harvest, or for protection from bad weather."[45] The villagers' worship of Kye reflects the popular and very likely pre-Buddhist cult practice focused on the propitiation of local protector deities, the *yul-lha* (god of the locality), for the sake of personal and community well-being. The worship of these local gods should not be confused with Buddhist (or Bön) traditions of circumambulating great pilgrimage mountains, like Mount Kailash; nevertheless, many similarities and overlapping elements suggest that the popular reverence for mountain deities was a principal vehicle through which Buddhism bound itself to the indigenous layer of Tibetan religion.[46]

The earliest version of the legends of Tibet's first king dates to the fourteenth century,[47] but elements of the story are found in songs from the eighth and ninth centuries that refer to the descent of a divine being from the sky onto the sacred protective mountain of the Yarlung Valley tribe.[48] This was King Nyatri Tsenpo,[49] who descended from the summit of Mount Yar-lha-sham-po to be greeted by twelve tribal chieftains or sages. They acclaimed him as their king and gave him his name, "Neck-Enthroned Mighty One," by hoisting him onto a palanquin supported on their necks.[50] In some versions of the narrative, the mountain is represented as a ladder—a tree trunk with seven or nine notches cut into it, each notch representing a level of the heaven worlds.[51] According to legend, the first king and his six descendants, known as the "Seven Heavenly Thrones," returned each night to their divine home in the sky.[52] Upon death, they were said to have returned permanently to the heavens, having no need for earthly tombs.[53] Their travel to the heaven worlds was by means of the *mu* rope or "sky-cord" attached to the crown of the head. This is the Tibetan version of the primordial connecting rope or ladder between earth and heaven common to many shamanic myths.[54] A Mongolian source of the same legend states: "When it was time to transmigrate, they dissolved upwards, starting from the feet, and, by the road of light called Rope-of-Holiness which came out of their head, they left by becoming a rainbow in the sky. Their corpse was thus made an *onggon* (saint, ancestor and burial mound) in the country of the gods."[55] Mortality finally came to the kings of Tibet when the sixth successor after Nyatri Tsenpo, brandishing his sword in battle, accidentally severed his mu rope—another example, like the relationship between waking and dream, where material and immaterial intersect without losing their individual properties. Thereafter, the kings were buried in earthly tombs.[56]

The ancient mu rope signifying the connection between earth and heaven maintains its presence in numerous Tibetan folk and religious practices. The rainbow-colored wings attached to the headdress of spirit-mediums (*lha-pa*) represent, according to Bellezza's practitioner interviewees, the link between the medium and the possessing deities, as well as the belief that after death, superior spirit-mediums dwell in the palaces of the mountain gods.[57] In popular rituals of birth and marriage the primordial bond between heaven and earth is expressed in the form of a multicolored string attached to the crown of the head.[58] And the rainbow path of the early kings who had no need of mortal tombs finds an echo in the Tibetan Buddhist belief that certain meditation practices result in the utter dissolution of the physical body at death into a body of light (*'ja'lus*). As Tucci notes, "The connection between heaven and earth is a primeval article of faith for the Tibetan."[59]

The image of a rope that joins the worlds features also in the beliefs of the Tungus, who tie a rope between trees to represent the path of the spirits as well as communication between humans and spirits.[60] Similarly, the Buryats in their initiation ceremonies tie colored ribbons between trees to symbolize the rainbow road of the spirits.[61] The ribbons stretch from the top of the tree that emerges from the smoke-hole of the yurt to a birch tree outside. According to legend, their ancient shamans were said to be powerful enough to walk on those ribbons—it was called "walking on the rainbow."[62] A contemporary Mongolian shamaness suggests that the relationship between the shaman's use of dream and the rainbow path of the spirits is hinted at in the Mongolian word for rainbow (*solongo*), similar to the word for shaman power dreams (*soolong*).[63]

In sum, traditional Tibetan culture shares many aspects of a worldview common to other shamanic religious complexes. There are also similarities between the religious implements and practices of Tibetan ritual practitioners and those of related central and north Asian cultures;[64] however, I have foregone discussion of these features in favor of emphasizing the correspondences in underlying attitudes. The world and human life is a network of relations and interactions among a great variety of persons, seen and unseen. Similarly, in microcosm, individuals function as a dynamic interplay of persons or "souls." Worship is both a mode of communication and a vehicle of creation. Through ritual, the world is consulted, hidden correspondences emerge, and deities are born; reality is created and transformed. Ritual is the process by which a person defines, empowers, and engages with the various beings and realities of the universe. Finally, in the imagery of mountains, connecting ropes of light, and the rainbow path between heaven and earth, Tibetans, like other shamanic cultures, access their primeval origins, ascend to the realm of the gods, offer themselves as vehicles for the descent of the gods, and pay homage to the ancestors who bind generation to generation and death to life. I have dwelt on these characteristics of a shamanic worldview in order to provide the necessary context and support for the following section on the shamanic use of dream—as a mode of communication, as a journey to other worlds, as creating reality, as revealing knowledge, and as bestowing power.

SLEEP AND DREAM AS SHAMANIC ACTIVITY

The nature and role of dream in traditional cultures, especially among Arctic and Central Asian peoples, has remained largely in the shadow of the more dramatic and overt elements of their shamanic practice and ritual. The darkened séances, ecstatic dancing, singing, drumming, and trances in which the shaman speaks with the voices of the visiting spirits or enacts a journey to another world, like the sacred implements of the shaman, or songs, myths, and stories, are outward manifestations of the shamanic complex that a researcher can hope to elucidate with some confidence of accuracy. However, I propose that it is in the ethereal domain of personal dreams and subjective visions that the nature of the shamanic healer is forged. From that place where, in the words of Jean-Guy Goulet, "the scope for empirical investigation is nil,"[65] the shaman reemerges into public life with the power to confirm the cosmos and draw the community into a dynamic of protection, of healing, and of destruction of opposing forces. Dreaming, in its widest sense, is the very foundation of shamanic activity. For many cultures, spiritual power is inextricably linked with a capacity for working with nonordinary states of consciousness that are closely related to sleep and dream.

Although researchers in the field have, for the most part, rejected Mircea Eliade's narrow definition of shamanism that focuses on "techniques of ecstasy," scholars continue to regard the presence and use of altered states of mind, actual or simulated, as a crucial component in defining shamanism. According to Geoffrey Samuel's broad statement on the subject, shamanism is "[t]he regulation and transformation of human life and human society through the use (or purported use) of alternate states of consciousness by means of which specialist practitioners are held to communicate with a mode of reality alternative to, and more fundamental than, the world of everyday experience."[66] In a shamanic context, however, what exactly are alternate states of consciousness? Anna-Leena Siikala explores this question in a study that compares shamanic forms of trance to specific features of altered states of consciousness. She defines shamanic trance states as "forms of behaviour deviating from what is normal in the wakeful state and possessing a specific cultural significance, typical features being an altered grasp of reality and the self-concept, with the intensity of change ranging from slight modifications to a complete loss of consciousness."[67]

With regard to the range of deviation from the waking state, Brian Inglis argues that the states of ecstasy, trance, and possession commonly associated with shamanism are part of a larger complex of mental states. He proposes that at one end of this continuum is possession, a condition where the person's normal self seems completely displaced; at the opposite end is sleep, a state of unconsciousness; and, in between, there is a range of conditions "in which consciousness is maintained, but the subliminal mind makes itself felt."[68] Inglis's suggestion is supported by the language of shamanic cultures that connect sleep and dream to ecstatic states of possession, waking visions, and various hallucinations, as well as the visions or mental panorama induced in both the shaman and the audience through songs and chants. In her study of a North American Dene community, Marie-Françoise Guédon notes that the same linguistic terms are used to designate dreams, spontaneous apparitions, and visions arising through voluntary trance states.[69] This is not to say that a dreaming person is necessarily in a shamanic trance or that the Dene do not differentiate between dreams and other visionary experiences, but it does resonate with the argument that trance and dream states provide a similar space-time context in which the shaman's activity can take place.

Nevertheless, a consciously induced condition of possession or trance is an extraordinary state, not experienced by everyone, whereas dreaming is reported by most, if not all, people. Indeed, Mihály Hoppál draws attention to a number of everyday activities that take on particular significance for shamans: sleeping, which is related to the beginning or ending of a ecstatic trance; yawning, which is related to the taking in of helping spirits; dreaming, which is related to soul travel and the acquisition of knowledge; and fasting, which is related to the preparation for trance.[70] Shamanic activity, then, makes use of the ordinary (that which is available to all) in extraordinary ways. From this perspective, anyone can be involuntarily subject to spirit possession and all people dream, but a shamanic use of these states involves a measure of intention and control over them, and is associated with the assistance and power of the spirit world. My focus here is not on the shaman's ability as a specialist within the community, but on what constitutes a shamanic use of so-called alternate states of consciousness.

The poles of the continuum outlined by Inglis come together in the association of sleep with the states of unconsciousness, or apparent unconsciousness, that are a particular feature of Siberian shaman séances, but that appear also in other shamanic cultures. An early Christian missionary to the Lapps provided the following description of a séance: "As if he had been possessed by falling sickness (epilepsy), so there does not seem to remain any breath in him and no sign of life, but it seems as if the soul has left the body. . . . When the spirit finally returns, the body wakes up as from a deep sleep."[71] In another case, a seventeenth-century Italian bishop observing a shamanic trance in Hungary wrote: "[E]yes rolling . . . countenance distorted . . . arms and legs flailing around and his entire body shaking . . . he throws himself down and remains there seemingly lifeless for three or four hours. . . ."[72]

In the shamanic rituals observed here, at one stage the shaman appears to fall into a sleeplike state of unconsciousness. Among the Tungus, Shirokogoroff noted that it was standard procedure before a séance for the shaman to "fall asleep."[73] He interpreted this as not a real sleep, but a ritualized aspect of the shaman's performance, recognized as such by the audience. Nevertheless, from within the Tungus tradition, it is understood that sleep can be used as a method of entering into an altered state of consciousness or alternate reality mode in which the shaman acts—the battles fought between shamans were said to take place during sleep and dream. The following story describes an encounter between two such rival shamans.

> One night the shaman was hunting on the salt-marsh; sitting there, he saw in the night some glittering fire. As soon as he noticed it, he pulled out his knife. The fire descended lower. Then he remained sitting quietly. Thereafter he returned home, reported the happening and said: "So *Saŋγuni* [name of another shaman] has come! Keep quiet and let me fall asleep." Then he fell asleep and became a shaman;[74] while he was sleeping, he began to follow the aggressor-shaman and reached *Saŋγuni 's* wigwam. *Saŋγuni* was sitting at the entrance. He sat down and began to scold *Saŋγuni*: "You see, I nearly caught you when you were asleep. You are a bad man. Why did you go in the form of fire?" *Saŋγuni* was sitting silent with his head hung down. When the shaman ceased to speak, *Saŋγuni* told him: "From now on I shall never do so."[75]

Although somewhat confusing, the passage above is illuminating for its use of sleep in a double context: that of shamanic sleep, powerful and magical, and that of ordinary sleep—the sleep of unconsciousness and powerlessness. The first shaman encounters his rival Saŋγuni in the salt-marsh appearing in the form of fire. The shaman then uses the ordinary state of sleep to access his spirit power; and in a shamanic dream state, he follows Saŋγuni and finds him dozing in front of his tent. The shaman then chastises Saŋγuni, pointing out how easily he could have caught him in the powerless state of ordinary sleep. Yet, how are we to understand the encounter? The narrative seems to say that the shaman, hunting in the waking world, perceives some kind of fiery phenomenon that he recognizes as a rival shaman. However, in his dream state, does he travel to a dreamworld tent or a real-world tent? Is Saŋγuni dozing in the shaman's dreamworld, or would someone in the waking world also see him sleeping there? Such questions, however, will not lead anywhere, because the answer to the question of how the dreamworld of the shaman interacts with the waking world is not found in the categories of dreaming and waking, but in their nature as transitional states. In accordance with a shamanic worldview, the ambiguity of the narrative expresses the idea of distinct realities that, nevertheless, are capable of taking on each other's characteristics due to the liminal qualities inherent in both dreaming *and* waking states of mind.

In shamanic systems, the functions and operations of life belong to the visible waking world; upon death, some aspect of the person joins the ancestors and the invisible spirit world. Trance, sleeping, and dreaming are states in which the invisible world with its geography and inhabitants becomes available to the senses of living people. When one is dreaming, falls sick, falls asleep, or falls into trance, it is a sign that some spirit or soul dimension has separated from the person, even while another spirit may join the person. Therefore, all forms of nonwaking conditions—unconsciousness, sleeping, dreaming, trance, and illness (which brings about lethargy, sleep, dreams, and semiconsciousness)—are associated with death and the separation of the animating spirit from the body. They are all inherently dangerous states during which the person's soul wanders about in the spirit world and from which it must take care to return to the living. When he shamanizes, the Inuit *angakkoq* reminds the spirits of the dead, "I am still of flesh and blood."[76]

The shaman is not always successful, however, in his attempt to negotiate the world of dream and death. A twelfth-century Lapp chronicle recounts a story in which the shaman's soul traveling across the ocean in the form of a whale encounters his adversary in the form of sharp poles at the bottom of the ocean that cut open the stomach of the spirit whale. According to the story, this accident in the spirit world results in the shaman's death.[77] Shamanic power and activity are intimately associated with sleep and dream, which in turn are linked with the realm of spirits and death. This is not to say that sleep or dream is the same as trance, but it does emphasize that they are fluid and interrelated states, supposedly brought about by the temporary departure of the soul, and thereby related to death (the permanent loss of soul), and to the power that is associated with death and the spirit world. To sleep is to put oneself into spirit mode, so to speak. The following description of a shaman's activity during sleep comes from a "big shaman" of the Australian Worora. It speaks precisely to the relationship between sleep, dream, trance, and soul travel shared by many shamanic traditions around the world:

> If a shaman speaks with the spirits of the dead, this takes place by his soul leaving him while he is asleep. . . . At sunset the shaman's soul meets somewhere the shadow of a

> dead ancestor. The shadow asks the soul whether it shall go with it. The shaman's soul answers yes. The shadow of the dead ancestor then becomes his helping spirit. Then they go on together, either at once into the kingdom of the dead or to a place in this world at which the spirits of the dead have gathered. . . . The spirits begin to sing and dance. . . . When the dance is over the spirits release the shaman's soul and his helping spirit brings it back to his body. When the shaman wakes his experiences with the spirits seem to him like a dream. . . . Then he will first explain the dances to his wife and sing them to her, and after that he will teach them to everyone else. That is how the magnificent pantomimic dances of the aborigines come into being.[78]

The themes touched upon here are characteristic of many shamanisms:

- sleep as a state during which the soul leaves the body
- helping spirits (ancestors, animals, or any kind of phenomena can act as spirit guides)
- agreement established between the soul and helping spirit
- sleep and dream as a space/time dimension in which the shaman's soul can travel either to the realm of the spirits (in this case, the kingdom of the dead) or to another place in this world
- firsthand knowledge brought back and shared with the community

Compared to the experiences of the ordinary waking world, the experiences of the spirit world that take place during sleep can only be described as "like a dream."

DREAM, INITIATION, AND POWER

For many peoples, the beginning of the shaman's ability to heal lies in the shaman's own experience of sickness and the initiatory dream or vision in which he encounters the spirits who are responsible for his condition and who will become his allies. In one type of visionary experience recounted by Siberian and Inuit peoples, the shaman-to-be is stripped to the bone and his body is dismembered or reduced to a skeleton and subsequently reconstituted and refleshed. Vilmos Diószegi recorded just such a Siberian initiatory dream: "I have been sick and I have been dreaming. In my dreams I had been taken to the ancestor

and cut into pieces on a black table. They chopped me up and then threw me into the kettle and I was boiled. . . . When I came to from this state, I woke up. This meant that my soul had returned. Then the shamans declared: 'You are the sort of man who may become a shaman. You should become a shaman, you must begin to shamanize!'[79]
The dream itself is the manifestation of the fledgling shaman's power to see the spirits and navigate the invisible world. As well, the dream is the bestower of that power and a sign that the power must be used; otherwise, the shaman is in danger of incurring the anger of the spirits who have summoned him. A common theme in shamanism is the difficulties of both obeying and disobeying the call of the spirits. Basilov reports the complaint of an Uzbek shamaness:

> [First] I didn't want to take [shaman's role]
> Let your name vanish, you infidels [i.e., helping spirits]
> I didn't want to go your way . . .
> You gathered [the spirits] and put [them] on me.
> You gave an apple into my hand [as a sign of selection]
> You neglected my reluctance.[80]

In my research, I heard similar complaints from a contemporary Bhutanese shaman who expressed the desire to be free of the spirits and lamented that the Buddhist lamas could do nothing to release him.

Since shamanic power is allied with the ability to communicate with the spirits through chanting, singing, or speaking the language of the spirits, initiatory dreams are frequently known to play a part in the lives of traditional singers and musicians, who by virtue of their skill possess shamanlike qualities. Basilov notes the close relationship between bard and shaman among many Central Asian groups. Among the Uzbeks, the word *bakhshy* can mean either singer or shaman; and the Kirghiz believe that a man could be an authentic performer of the "Manas" epic only with the blessing of the hero himself given in a dream or a vision.[81] Basilov recounts the following paradigmatic dream of Allashukur, who was forty years old when he was stricken for six months with a type of paralysis.[82] In a dream, he embarks on a journey to a sacred mountain shrine. On his way home, he encounters a retinue of spirits and their chief.[83] He is invited to join their feast and is given musical instruments; he is told to play by the women, and although he has no musical knowledge, he is able to play. It is determined that he fell ill because six months earlier the troupe had stopped to rest near his village and a sick spirit had drunk water from a jar in his house. When Allashukur subsequently drank water from the same jar, the spirit's sickness adhered to him. The chief of the spirit troupe destroys the offending spirit of sickness, and Allashukur is told, "You are free from your illness now. We have killed your illness."[84] Upon waking from his dream, Allashukur recovers, and mysteriously—without formal lessons, and although none of his ancestors were musicians—is able to sing and play the violin with skill. This dream follows a familiar formula in which the initiatory illness is engendered by the same spirits who heal and assist. The one who has the control or assistance of that power is able to inflict illness and death as well as to heal. In a shamanic worldview, there is no escape from the ambivalence of power.

Initiatory dream reports can be very simple, like the dream of a particular mountain or animal, or extremely detailed. A well-known example of the latter is Popov's report of the initiatory dream of the Samoyed Nganasan shaman Djaruoskin, which begins like this:

> When I was a young man I used to dream all sorts of insignificant things just like any other man. But once, I saw myself going down a road until I reached a tree. With an axe in my hand, I went round the tree and wanted to fell it. Then I heard a voice saying: "(Fell it) later!" and I woke up.
>
> Next day the neighbours said to me: "Go and fell a tree for the *kuojka* sledge [a special sledge for transporting sacred items]!" I set out, found a suitable tree and started to cut it down. When the tree fell, a man sprang out of its roots with a loud shout.[85]

The man tells Djaruoskin that the root of the tree only looks thin in his eyes, but in reality is thick enough to pass through. Djaruoskin follows the man into the root of the tree, and the dream story continues at great length with his adventures in the spirit world and his shaman training. It ends with the statement, "Suddenly I recovered my senses: I must have been lying for a considerable time, near the root of the tree."[86] In this account, the distinction between ordinary dreams and shaman dreams is quite clear. The shaman-to-be is also directly introduced to the nature of the dreamworld where what appears to be in waking reality a thin tree root, not as thick as a man, proves, in this alternate reality, to be a wide tunnel entrance to another world. It is a common feature of dreams that the dreamer experiences mysterious transformations or metamorphoses. The shaman-dreamer, however, learns to use the power of this ordinary aspect of dream, and learns to extend that quality into the waking reality of the group, where it can become the basis for the extraordinary transformation called healing.[87]

ENVISIONING THE INVISIBLE

Shamanic systems distinguish between the world of dream and spirits and the world of waking consciousness. However, they also believe that the solid world of waking reality can be made malleable, subject to the shaman's manipulations; and conversely, that in the nebulous dream/trance/spirit world, the shaman takes hold of invisible spirit things in a very physical way. Bogoras recorded that the most powerful songs or magical incantations among the Chukchee were those invested with material shape by the shaman. His song can take the form of an animal or group of animals, a part of a carcass like a fox head without a body, or a person, or any inanimate object. The materialized incantation or "spell" can then be sent to attack the enemy.[88] Similarly, among the Dene Tha, shamanic power is constituted concretely and individualistically as "a power," a particular gift from an animal that can materialize in many different ways in the phenomenal world—often in the form of the animal. The one who possesses it can also send the power gift to assist another.[89]

Although the interaction between this world and the spirit world might appear to juxtapose different realities, the division of the universe into discrete categories such as natural/supernatural, this world/other world is not helpful in understanding the shamanic perspective. Jean-Guy Goulet tells the story of an encounter in a cemetery between a deer and relatives visiting the grave site of a family member. Because the dead man's animal helper had been a deer, the deer in the cemetery was immediately perceived as the spirit power of the dead brother sent to communicate with the family. As Goulet notes, the deer was not first appropriated as a deer and then understood to be the dead man's power; it was in itself that power.[90] In other words, the symbolic continuum that is the physical deer, animal helper spirit, and gift of power manifests in the waking experience shared by deer and human.

The shaman's ability to communicate with the spirits is most called upon for rituals of healing. However, based on the belief in the interconnectedness of things, healing in shamanism extends much beyond the matter of individual illness. As the Daur elder quoted earlier indicated, the shaman must fight to restore the balance of good and evil, to restore the harmony of life to the person, to the community, and to the environment of which the person is an inseparable part. To do this, the shaman must divine the reason for the illness, discover the "person" responsible for the illness, and determine the method of dealing with the person, be it coercion, ransom, trickery, or out-and-out battle.

Homology is integral to shamanic diagnosis as well as to the healing process. Among the Soyot of Siberia, the pains and symptoms of sickness signify the abuse of the soul captured by evil spirits: "The wicked spirits lie in wait, they capture the roaming soul and torture it. Thereupon the owner of the soul falls sick. If the wicked spirit dips the soul into hot water, the man, whose soul it is, suffers of fever. If it is submerged in cold water, the owner will have the shivers. If the spirit twists the hands and the legs of the soul, then the owner has pains in his limbs."[91] The sick person is not so much cured as rescued from a spirit/dream state in which he is trapped. The principle underlying the passage above operates in both directions; the shaman's activity in the physical world has its effects also in the spirit world. In Sudhir Kakar's study of the healing practices of a Muslim *pir* (wise elder), the pir explains that the "holy water" he gives his patients drives demons away by literally washing the blood so that the demon can no longer drink it and is, therefore, forced to leave.[92] This would imply that the concrete action of drinking/washing extends to the invisible healing process.

Further, because human beings and all aspects of the waking world possess spirit persona, all types of phenomena have the capacity to enter into direct communication with other persons. Phenomena such as a song, a dream, or a disease can also be persons with their own history and agency. Among the Turkish tribes of Siberia, smallpox is called "the spotted guest" and, like humans, has its own ancestors. Diószegi tells the story of Toka, an old man who was stricken with the disease. During a séance while the officiating shaman was conducting Toka's soul to his ancestors, the shaman guide and the soul became separated; Toka's soul followed the road to the father of the "spotted guest" instead of the one that led to his own ancestors. In this way, Toka became a shaman through the power of the ancestor of the smallpox, instead of through his own ancestor.[93] In this narrative, we see again the theme of the shaman being cured, empowered, and assisted by the spirits that caused the disease.

In the dreams and visions of the shaman, all that is invisible or abstract in the waking world takes shape and becomes visible, graspable, and subject to manipulation. Dreaming is often described as the experiences of the spirit-soul wandering about; but as well as being a mental state in which the person acts in the spirit world in spirit form, the dream itself is in some cases identified with soul or spirit. In Hultkranz's study of soul concepts among the Wind River Shoshone, the word *navujieip* signifies both "soul" and "dream," and its activity during sleep is described this way: "*Navujieip* comes alive when your body rests; it acts as a guide and comes in any form: as an insect, an animal or a person, and so on. That is the case when I am dreaming; I see me then in my own shape, or like an animal, a snake, even a tree; I am acting in my *navujieip*. Sometimes it mystifies you: you do the most impossible things in the shape of your *navujieip*."[94]

The mystifying and impossible things that one can do in the spirit mode, or "in the shape of your *navujieip*," is another prominent motif in shamanic dream narratives. A Buryat story tells of a shaman, who, in order to defeat a cattle-stealing demon, ties his horse to a post in the tent, lies down with his ax under his pillow and tells his wife, "Do not let my horse out and do not waken me." As the story goes, "Soon he and his horse were sound asleep, but they were not asleep, it was only their bodies which were so quiet. In reality, the shaman was riding swiftly toward the Angara [River]," where he intercepted the demon driving the cattle over a bridge. "The Shaman turned himself into a bee, made his axe equally small, and, taking it with him, flew under the bridge and hewed the pillars so that the bridge broke in two."[95] The cattle and the demon fell into the river and the shaman called up a terrible storm. The story ends with the shaman returning to his tent. There, he gets up from his bed where his wife thought he had been sleeping, frees the horse from its post in the tent, and drives it out to the pasture. "And all was as if it had not been. But the cattle of Olzoni were never stolen again."[96] Interestingly, the dream transformation and activity of the shaman in this narrative is comparable to a certain stage of Tibetan dream-yoga practice in which having recognized the dream as dream within the dream, the yogi practices to change his dream self and the beings of the dream into anything he wishes. He further develops the capacity to transform the external environment of the dream into whatever he likes, and to produce a variety of dreamscapes.[97] The dream state, then, is one in which the creative power of the shaman or the yogi is at its peak. The aim of Tibetan dream yoga is ultimately soteriological, however, whereas the shaman's dream practice is firmly grounded in the needs and practicalities of everyday life.

Dreams that signify the shamanic vocation are not ordinary dreams; they are recognizable dreams with repeated themes,[98] familiar to the social group and invested with shared interpretation. Beginning with this foundation, the shaman learns to explore, control, and interpret the dreaming and visionary process. Although spontaneity and creativity are notable aspects of the way in which shamans do their work, the methods of training in dream or learning the landscape of the other world that result in the shaman's power can be strict and exact.[99] Knowledge of dream and knowledge of the spirit world go hand in hand. Invisible dimensions become perceivable and controllable by virtue of the innate qualities of the dream state. Trances and visions can be achieved through various methods—fasting, alcohol, hallucinogenics, tobacco, drumming, dancing, chanting, or simply going to sleep. The world of dreams, commonly regarded in post-Freudian Western culture as the ultimate private reality, functions in shamanism as a crucial element in the shared reality of the group. By "shared reality" I mean not only that private dreams can be shared with or influence others, but that the very characteristics of dreams and dreaming—permeable, personal, symbolic, and unfixed—are equally the characteristics of a shamanic view of, and approach to, the world and human existence. Whether or not a particular culture uses the phenomena of dream extensively in its shamanizing, a common worldview can be recognized in diverse communities—one in which "fish are transformed women, animals may speak, shed their skins and become human. The sea and stones may cause pregnancy."[100] The shamanic world, then, allows for a system in which, whether awake or asleep, reality—what "is"—is of the nature of dream, and dreams participate in the concrete reality of what "is."

Chapter 2

Dream in the Ancient Indian Matrix

Having examined the approach to sleep and dream within a shamanic context, I turn now to Buddhist thought on the nature of dream as it is situated within the broader Indian worldview that forms its matrix. This chapter explores some commonalities between shamanic and ancient Indian perspectives and examines the genesis of certain dream-related themes that continue into the Buddhist context. First, I wish to highlight the concepts of correspondence and homology present in the ancient Indian matrix as comparable to the principles that underlie shamanic rituals and beliefs. This will be important later in showing how Vedic and shamanic views of the fundamental interconnectedness of a universe of beings relate to the Buddhist theory of cause and effect, as well as the way in which that theory was interpreted in Tibet in relation both to philosophic discourse and to shamanic practices of divination and omenology. Further, my purpose in examining the Vedic emphasis on vitality and materiality as well as the psychological attitude of the Upaniṣads is to show that although Buddhism upheld a psychological approach to dream, the more vitalistic stance of the early Vedas, consonant with a shamanic worldview, was never entirely displaced. When Indian Buddhism arrived in Tibet, it carried concepts of dream and dreaming that in some ways opposed, and in some ways resonated with, the indigenous shamanic system.

RITUAL AND HOMOLOGY IN THE VEDAS

The four Vedas are among the world's oldest religious writings. Including the later works known as the Upaniṣads, they were composed in their entirety ca.1500–600 BCE. Collectively known as the Veda, they are the authority and foundation of all Hindu religious thought that came after, yet their earliest texts do not reflect the central religious concerns of classical Hinduism (belief in continuing rebirth, belief in an eternal metaphysical Soul (*ātman*) as the essence of the individual, and belief in the idea of ultimate spiritual liberation or release (*mokṣa*) from the round of rebirth (*saṃsāra*). The worldview that emerges from the hymns and chants of the Vedas is one dedicated to life and vitality in all its forms. Religious life as portrayed in the Ṛg Veda focuses on pragmatic concerns of maintaining and augmenting individual life force and concomitant prosperity through "food" of all kinds. This concern was extended to dead ancestors, whose continued identity or body (*tanū*) was nourished by the ritual offerings of the sacrifice, as well as to the immortal gods, whose *tanū* was equally sustained by the sacrifice.[1] All these forms of support depended on the efficacy of ritual. The Vedic sacrificial rituals honored a large pantheon of gods who embodied the various powers inherent in the universe—not only the physical powers of nature, but also the powers of mind and thought characteristic of human beings. The primary religious emphasis in the Vedic period was on ritual as the way to connect with, and thereby influence for one's practical benefit, the divine and natural forces that constitute the cosmos. As in a shamanic worldview, power manifests through ritual; and in the Vedic world, the prime ritual was the sacrifice.

The cosmos in which the Vedic sacrifice takes place consists of the sky or celestial realm above, the middle realm of air or space, and the earthly realm below. In this hierarchy, the gods are superior to humankind in their power and immortality, but gods, humans, nature, and the entire cosmos are kin, related in essence and genesis.[2] The universe itself is conceived of as a person. In the famous *Puruṣa Sūkta*, gods, humans, nature, and the entire cosmos comes into being from the ritual sacrifice of the supreme "Person."[3] Gods, humans, and the spirits of the dead all depend on the ritual of the sacrifice for their nourishment and well-being. The power of the ritual is the power of creation, the power of bringing-into-being. As in shamanism, belief in the power of ritual to reveal, create, or transform reality depends on a particular view of the fundamental nature of the universe—that it consists of innumerable interconnections, and that knowledge of those hidden relationships is power.

Walter Kaelber lists homology (Skt. *nidāna* or *bandhu*) as one of the principal concepts that define the Vedic worldview.[4] The Sanskrit words meaning connection, correspondence, or association have two connotations, both of them related to the concrete imagery of "rope," "tie," or "bond." One meaning implies being bound or fastened together as things are tied together by rope. The second meaning implies causation, composition, or construction—to join, unite, put together, and thereby produce something.[5] This understanding of homology, then, has both connective and creative aspects. The complex exchange carried out in Vedic sacrificial rituals depended on a series of correspondences by which the sacrificer identified himself with the sacrificial animal, the animal with the universe, and the universe with the Supreme Being (*puruṣa*); thereby re-creating the primordial sacrifice out of which all phenomena arose. Through the ritual, he creates for himself the results of the sacrifice, be that attainment to the immortal worlds of the gods or the earthly material benefits of wealth and victory over enemies.

The entire arena for the sacrifice, the offering spoons, and the sacrificial stake were constructed according to the proportions of a man. The *Brāhmaṇa* texts state, "It [the sacrifice] is made of exactly the same extent as the man: this is the reason why the sacrifice is the man."[6] The sacrifice, however, was not a real man but one or more animals in place of man.[7] Nevertheless, the sacrificer, in some way, must be bound to the sacrificial animal, because in order for the rite to be effective, it must re-create the primordial ritual in which the Supreme Being (*puruṣa*) was sacrificed, and His body and mind became the universe. The Vedic animal sacrifice was called *paśubandha*, the binding (*bandha*) of the animal (*paśu*).[8] The metaphysical connection between man, animal, universe, and divinity was signified by the word *bandhu*, translated variously as "correspondence," "connection," "association," "correlation," or "identity." The sacrificial animal is bound (*bandha*) to the sacrificial pole, and in the same way that the animal is, by homology, the man, so the man is the divine Agni (Supreme Being as Fire, the presiding deity of the sacrifice) by virtue of the bond (*bandhu*) between them.[9] The essential correlation that the ritual affirms is between the sacrificer and the divine nature of the entire universe from its primordial beginnings.

There is danger, however, inherent in the ritual by which an earthly man is connected to the power of the gods. By means of the Vedic sacrifice, the reality of increased life force, physical strength, wealth, and power is obtained, but the path leads through the opposing reality of destruction. The sacrificer must be intimately connected to the animal that is his death substitute, yet his own life force may be polluted or destroyed by association with death—an ambiguous and dangerous situation familiar from shamanic journeys into the spirit world. The problem is resolved by the intermediary presence of two ritual specialists by means of whom the sacrificer is separated from, yet still connected to, the sacrificial animal.[10] The sacrificer is said to touch the animal in an imperceptible (*parokśa*) manner. *Parokśa* also has connotations of "out of sight," "secret," "hidden," "mysterious," and "cryptic." His connection with the sacrificed animal is, therefore, both physically indirect and metaphysical (hidden from the ordinary senses). This physically indirect connection between man and animal mirrors the imperceptible, metaphysical nature of the correspondences between mortality and immortality, gods and men. The ritual reflects the belief that knowledge of the correspondence between seen and unseen penetrates the solidity of disparate things and makes them subject to transformation.

VITALITY AND POWER IN THE VEDAS

In his study of the ancient Indian concept of the human being, Ross Reat concludes that "the Vedic concept of the basis of human life is surprisingly materialistic when considered in relation to later Indian psychology."[11] The emphasis on the vitalistic nature of the gods, the cosmos, human beings, and the power that moves them all is captured in terms such as *vayas* and *vāja*, whose usage connotes the physical and mental vigor necessary both for warriors and for the priests who empower the sacrifice and defeat foes with the power of their ritual chants. In the imagery of the Vedas, this vital power is associated with the wrathful action of the Maruts, the divine riders that represent havoc-wreaking thunderstorms: "With gleaming lances, with their breasts adorned with gold, the Maruts, rushing onward, hold high power of life [*vayas*]."[12]

Further, in the Vedic worldview, an intimate relationship exists between extraordinary vital power and extraordinary power of mind or thought. Mental power is closely associated with the concrete action of the senses, especially with the faculty of perception or vision. Gonda notes the association of the verb *cit* (to think) with meanings such as "appearing, becoming conspicuous" and "to make visible to, or manifest to, to reveal" (in both the senses of "to exhibit to the sight" and "to disclose something not previously known").[13] In other words, thought is mental perception or vision. The ability to see with the mental organs of heart and mind is a power that adheres to those in whom the faculty of insightful thought is developed to a high degree. Gonda describes the "vision" of the Vedic sages as "[t]he exceptional and supranormal faculty, proper to 'seers,' of 'seeing,' in the mind, things, causes, connections as they really are, the faculty of acquiring a sudden knowledge of the truth, of the functions and influence of the divine powers, of man's relations to them. . . ."[14]

The Ṛg Veda refers to mind both as that which creates and the motive force by which things are transported between men and gods. The horses of the Aśvins that carry away the hymns of the singer are said to be "mind-swift."[15] Hymns and prayers are said to be *mano-yuja*, "mind-yoked"—Soma, the god of the intoxicating sacred drink is implored to "set free the song which mind hath yoked, even as thunder frees the rain. . . ."[16] Whether "mind-yoked" refers to the mind as the motive force or as the creative force, the general meaning according to Reat is that visions are "made mobile or functional by the mind."[17]

The Vedas are called *śruti*, "that which is heard," but the ancient seers to whom the songs and chants of the Vedas are traditionally attributed were inspired visionaries who, it is said, *saw* what is heard. Their thought-visions were "materialized" in ritual speech and song to be heard by gods and men. Wayman refers to the story of Kavasa Ailūsa, who saw the hymn called the Aponaptrīya: "The Gods, because able to see the 'silent praise' . . . invisible to the Asuras [titans], were able to defeat their enemy."[18] The ability to perceive the hymn of praise—to envision the invisible, as shamans do—is shared by gods and sages and is a source of power. In turn, for the hymns that are sung on earth to reach the gods, they must again be transformed through mind into mental visions that, by virtue of the mental power generated through the sacrifice, are transported to the heavens. The gods were considered to send actual earthly wealth and earthly cows to the sacrificer induced by the power of their mind-yoked visions, and the sacrificer equally sent the actual heavenly essence of the offerings and praises to the gods by means of the mind-yoked vision expressed in the liturgy of the sacrifice. Gonda notes that in this process of "mentalization," "[m]aking an entity or an idea the object of the process denoted by *man-* one 'realized' it, that is to say: one does not only cause it to appear real to the mind by forming a clear conception of it, one is according to the view of the ancients also able to convert it into actuality."[19] This is what is meant by *dhiyam sādh*, "to accomplish the vision."[20] The ecstatic vision of the sage played out in the ritual songs, therefore, is not to be regarded as something passive that is merely experienced; the vision/song is an entity that is complete only when its purpose is fulfilled and its effects made real, whether those effects be health or strength, magical flight, the acquisition of cows, or the defeat of enemies. In the dynamic and reciprocal flow of power between gods and men actualized through ritual, the Vedic hymns present us with a process of interpenetration between the dimensions of earth and heaven, vital and mental, flesh and spirit that corresponds to shamanic views of the permeability of visible and invisible worlds.

More than any other term in Indian thought, the word that brings together concepts of vital power, occult power, magic, illusion, deception, transformation, wisdom, skill, and mystery is *māyā*. It encompasses meanings such as "art, wisdom, extraordinary or supernatural power," as well as "illusion, unreality, deception, fraud, trick, sorcery, witchcraft, magic."[21] The elusiveness of the term can be seen in the variety of approaches that scholars have adopted in explaining it. O'Flaherty chooses the word "transformation" as a translation that best captures both the early Vedic view of māyā as creative power and the Vedantic appropriation of it as illusion.[22] In his analysis of māyā, Gonda emphasizes the aspects of wonder, mystery, and incomprehensibility over illusion and unreality as defining characteristics of māyā. He puts forth the central meaning of the term as follows: "Incomprehensible wisdom and power enabling its possessor, or being able itself, to create, devise, contrive, effect, or do something."[23]

The concept of māyā in the Vedas has connotations of illusion, not in the sense of unreality, but in the sense of changing appearances through the unfolding and becoming of things. More specifically, the Vedic idea of māyā implies power, the power to create appearances and to transform that which appears. Creation is, in both Vedic and shamanic worlds, a process of magic—that is to say, a process of mysterious transformation; and for both, this process works by virtue of a worldview that perceives seemingly disparate things in terms of a web of interrelations that leaves nothing out.

SLEEP AND DREAM IN THE VEDAS

Among the paradoxes of life, one of the greatest is the paradox of sleep: human beings cannot live without sleep; it renews life, but in sleep, vitality, activity, and all that is characteristic of life, diminish and fade away as in death. Reat notes that in the Vedas, the derivatives of the verb root $\sqrt{}$*jīv* (life) not only meant life as opposed to death, but activity as opposed to sleep. The vital faculties are all associated with wakefulness and activity.[24] The Vedic mind was preoccupied with augmenting life, strength, and vitality; sleep was regarded as a dangerous phenomenon associated with evils such as death and destruction. The following passage gives a good idea of the general Vedic view of the nature of sleep:

> We know thy place of birth (*janitra*), O sleep; thou art son of seizure (*grahi*),[25] agent of Yama (the Lord of Death); ender art thou, death art thou; so, O sleep, do we comprehend thee here; do thou, O sleep, protect us from evil-dreaming. 2. We know thy place of birth, O sleep; thou art son of perdition . . . 3. . . . son of ill-success . . . 4. . . . son of extermination . . . 5. . . . son of calamity . . . 6. We know thy

> place of birth, O sleep; thou art son of the wives (sisters) of the gods, agent of Yama; ender art thou, death art thou; so, O sleep, do we comprehend thee here; do thou, O sleep, protect us from evil-dreaming.[26]

Here Sleep is regarded as a powerful deity associated with death and destruction. Sleep is called upon to protect one from evil dreams as well as to bring the forces of destruction and calamity upon one's enemies. The following passage uses words associated with the nature of sleep to curse the enemy:

> [W]ith ill-success I pierce him; with extermination I pierce him; with calamity I pierce him; with seizure I pierce him; with darkness I pierce him.
>
> Now (*idam*) do I wipe off evil-dreaming on him of such-and-such lineage,[27] son of such-and-such a mother.[28]

In the hymns of the *Atharva Veda*, Sleep is said to have been born among the Asuras and "in search of greatness" turned to the celestial gods, who endowed him with his supreme dominion. But according to the traditional commentary, Sleep (which is unknown to the departed ancestors and to the gods) was banished from heaven because he overstepped his bounds and seized on the gods.[29]

The earliest reference to dream in the hymns of the Ṛg Veda is concerned with protection from evil dreams: "If someone I have met, O king, or a friend has spoken of danger to me in a dream to frighten me, or if a thief should waylay us, or a wolf—protect us from that, Varuṇa."[30] Wendy Doniger notes the ambiguity in this passage regarding whether the thief and the wolf belong to waking reality or the dream.[31] Nevertheless, the appeal makes it clear that protection is needed against dream dangers. Beyond that, the evil dream in itself is associated with wrongdoing and regarded as a danger. Like sin, it is conceived of quasi-materialistically as something to be separated from oneself and to be inflicted on one's enemies: "We have conquered today, and we have won; we have become free of sin. The waking dream, the evil intent—let it fall upon the one we hate; let it fall upon the one who hates us."[32] In the Vedic hymns, psychological conditions such as bad dreams, unfulfilled wishes, fears of poverty, or feelings of hatred[33] are endowed with a vital and material aspect. The gods are petitioned to "loosen and withdraw" sins from the body, to banish evil deeds. Evil dreams and bad intentions can be sent like disease or hailstorms to strike one's enemy. Just as sleep is no protection from sinful deeds that can take place while asleep, so waking is no protection from the demon of evil-dreaming, which can strike while one is awake or asleep.[34] As in shamanic systems, the language of externalization and personification creates a world of complex interactions between humans and a universe of persons.

In Vedic literature, the power of sleep/dream is established by virtue of its fearsome nature. Sleep is the agent of death and far from being "just a bad dream," *duḥsvapna* (nightmare) is among the evils most to be feared and averted, so much so that there is an entire collection of hymns and ritual actions dedicated to the destruction of evil-dreaming,[35] among them the following verses from the *Atharva Veda*:

> Sin of the mind, depart far away!
> Why do you utter improper suggestions?
> Depart from this place! I do not want you!
> Go to the trees and the forests! My mind
> Will remain here along with our homes and our cattle.

> Thou who are not alive, not dead, immortal–embryo of the gods art thou O sleep . . .

> We know thy place of birth (*janitra*), O sleep . . . end-maker art thou; death art thou; so, O sleep do we comprehend thee here; do thou, O sleep, protect us from evil-dreaming.[36]

In these passages, the characteristics of Sleep are highlighted—ambivalent, liminal, and dangerous; Sleep is the bringer of evil, the evil itself, and the protector from evil. The unreliable nature of power and the tension between comfort and anxiety that it produces, is a theme carried through here, as it is in shamanism. As a deity, Sleep, who belongs neither to the wakeful living nor the unconscious dead, is invoked to protect the sleeper from Sleep's own terrifying aspects. The person is enjoined in one ritual to recite these verses while washing his face and, if the dream was very bad, then to make an offering of ritual cakes or deposit such a cake in the territory of an enemy, thereby transferring the evil to the enemy. As George Bolling suggests, the hymns and rituals to get rid of evil dreaming show that, like sin (with which it was associated), it was regarded as a form of quasi-physical contamination[37] that could adhere to cows as well as people and be sent to hang about the neck of one's enemy like an albatross: "What evil-dreaming is in us, what in our kine, and what in our house, that let him, who is not of us, the god-reviler, the mocker, put on like a necklace."[38]

The double nature of Sleep as bearer of evil dreams and protector from evil-dreaming reflects the ur-paradox of life, which is both destroyed and supported by death. Because of life one can know death, and because of death one can conceive of the deathless; the passage of time suggests changeless eternity. In a hymn to the sun, the Ṛg Veda calls immortality the shadow of death: "Giver of vital breath, of power and vigour, he whose commandments all the Gods acknowledge: The Lord of death, whose shade [*chāyā*] is life immortal."[39] Commenting on this passage, Willard Johnson points out that the phrase is based on a double meaning of the word *chāyā* (shadow), which also carries the connotation of "likeness," "reflection," or "image."[40] Death is the shadow that follows a person throughout his or her lifetime, but time and death reveal the likeness or image (*chāyā*) of eternity and immortality. We will encounter this imagery of shadows, reflections, and likenesses again in the Upaniṣadic explorations of the soul and its various associations with the individual—in waking, dreaming, sleeping, and finally in its true state of freedom from all associations.

SELF AND DREAM IN THE UPANIṢADS

The first philosophical treatment of dream in Indian literature appears in the Upaniṣads. These texts, the earliest of which were composed ca. 800–600 BCE, serve as a point of departure for the development of Indian philosophy and psychology. They seek answers regarding the foundation of the world, the essence of human personality, and the path to freedom. One of the grandest themes of Upaniṣadic literature is the search for the basis of individual existence, the search for the self (*ātman*), sometimes interpreted vitalistically as entering or departing the body, sometimes metaphysically as the innermost being or higher self.[41] Dream is explained in the *Upaniṣads* as a condition of the ātman; therefore, the ways in which ātman is associated with various conditions and states of consciousness is of particular relevance to this book in establishing the approaches to dream that were present in the cultural matrix of Buddhism.[42]

The earliest Upaniṣad to discuss ātman in the dreaming state is the *Bṛhadāraṇyaka*, which presents dream as an intermediary condition, a perspective from which the self can perceive both this world and the other. "Now, this person has just two places—this world and the other world. And there is a third, the place of dream where the two meet. Standing there in the place where the two meet, he sees both those places—this world and the other world. Now, that place serves as an entryway to the other world, and as he moves through that entryway he sees both the bad things and the joys."[43] The *Bṛhadāraṇyaka* presents a number of interpretations of the self and its relationship with various worlds or states of being. With regard to dream, one approach is vitalistic, in that ātman is described as leaving the sleeping body that remains behind guarded by the breath. Going forth, he wanders about as he pleases.

> Guarding by breath the lower nest,
> The immortal roams outside the nest;
> The immortal goes wherever he wants—
> The golden person!
> The single goose![44]

Another is more psychological, since the self is understood to create the worlds of the dream and enjoy the experiences of his own creations: "This is how he dreams. He takes materials from the entire world and, taking them apart on his own and then on his own putting them back together, he dreams with his own radiance, with his own light. In that place this person becomes his own light. In that place there are no carriages, there are no tandems, and there are no roads; but he creates for himself carriages, tandems, and roads."[45] Ātman is also described metaphysically, as the ultimate Real from which all realities emanate. "As a spider sends forth its thread, and as tiny sparks spring forth from a fire, so indeed do all the vital functions (*prāṇa*), all the worlds, all the gods, and all beings spring from this self (*ātman*). Its hidden name (*upaniṣad*) is: 'The real behind the real,' for the real consists of the vital functions, and the self is the real behind the vital functions."[46]

The hierarchy of realities and the dynamic between real and more real suggested by this passage is echoed in other Upaniṣadic analyses of the self. In the *Taittirīya*, ātman is associated with five interpenetrating dimensions of a person nested one within another, beginning with the outermost dimension, which is the material self formed from the essence of food. Within that is the vital self formed from the essence of breath, then the self consisting of mind, then the self consisting of perception, and finally the innermost self that consists of bliss.[47] Ātman is also related to four states of consciousness: waking, dream, deep sleep, and an ungraspable transcendental "fourth" state,[48] in which the self "becomes the one ocean, he becomes the sole seer!"[49] According to the *Aitareya Upaniṣad*, in comparison with the true nature of the self, waking is no less a state of sleep than the others; ātman is said to dwell in three conditions of sleep—waking, dreaming, and sleeping.[50]

Drawing on ideas from the Upaniṣads, some Hindu philosophers such as Śaṅkara (ca. 800) emphasized the view that dreams and visions are the ultraillusions of an illusory waking world,[51] and that the true reality of ātman only manifests in the transcendental fourth state, which is unseen, ungraspable, without characteristics, inconceivable, and indescribable, "one whose essence is the perception of itself alone."[52] There is, however, a contrasting, more vitalistic notion of the fourth condition to be gleaned from the earliest Upaniṣads, and it implies that one is *closer* to one's ultimately real nature in dreaming than in any other state.

In the *Chāndogya Upaniṣad*, the sage Prajāpati identifies for his students the immortal ātman as the one who dwells in the waking state in visible form, but one student is dissatisfied with this explanation, since the visible form is subject to sorrow and perishable. Next Prajāpati identifies ātman as "[h]e who moves about happy in a dream." The student remains dissatisfied, because in a dream, a person can experience sorrow and misfortune. The teacher then explains that ātman is truly experienced when one is in deep dreamless sleep, but the student also questions this identification, because in deep sleep there is oblivion and no self-knowledge. Finally, the master proposes a fourth and highest bodiless form, saying, "[T]his deeply serene one, after he rises up from this body and reaches the highest light, emerges in his own true appearance. He is the highest person."[53] In this state, "[h]e roams about there, laughing, playing, and enjoying himself with women, carriages, or relatives, without remembering the appendage that is this body."[54] This description of ātman emerging "in his own true appearance" and roaming about unhindered by the body is very like the dreaming state described in the *Bṛhadāraṇyaka*, where the body is subdued by sleep while the immortal, remaining awake, roams outside the nest, going wherever he wants, creating visible forms, laughing and dallying with women.[55]

The Upaniṣads situate the dream state as a third place, an entryway between this world and the other, between the phenomenal and the transcendent. But beyond that, the liminal nature of dream offers a site where various modes of consciousness interpenetrate and bring their specific qualities to bear on one another. In the Upaniṣads, dream reflects the likeness of the ordinary waking state; the self in dream has the same organs of sense and knowledge as the person in the waking condition.[56] Dream also reveals the nature of the person in the transcendent fourth state who, appearing in his own form, roams about laughing and playing, forgetful of the body. Finally, dream is understood to be a condition of self-illumination with connotations of light and heat as well as bliss. In this it partakes of the bliss and brilliance associated with the state of deep sleep. In deep dreamless sleep, the person is said to enter completely into *tejas* (heat, light, brilliance). "So, when someone is sound asleep here, totally collected and serene, and sees no dreams . . . [n]o evil thing can touch him, for he is then linked with radiance [*tejas*]."[57] The dream state is luminous because it reflects the brilliance of deep sleep, which in turn is both the likeness and shadow of the ultimate self-illumination and bliss of ātman existing in the highest state, in itself. The following passage from the *Bṛhadāraṇyaka* illustrates the confluence of various modes of self in dream.

> Now, when people appear to kill or to vanquish him, when an elephant appears to chase him, or when he appears to fall into a pit, he is only ignorantly imagining dangers that he had seen while he was awake. But when he, appearing to be a god or a king, thinks, "I alone am this world! I am all!"—that is his highest world
>
> Now this is the aspect of his that is beyond what appears to be good, freed from what is bad, and without fear.[58]

In dream, then, all conditions of the self are reflected. From the threshold of dream all realities can be glimpsed; through that passageway one emerges fully into waking, sleeping, or the highest world from which vantage point all other realms are illusory.

The Indian concept of māyā with its varied connotations of creative power, magic, and deception is intimately related to dream. In all of human experience, the most dramatic illustration of the interwoven ideas of creation and illusion are dreams, in which a person, out of the apparent darkness and nothingness of sleep, suddenly enters a bright universe of sensory phenomena, a universe that is later understood to have been wholly self-created and, in contrast to the waking world, seemingly is entirely insubstantial. According to the *Bṛhadāraṇyaka Upaniṣad*, "[i]n that place there are no joys, pleasures, or delights; but he creates for himself joys, pleasures, and delights. In that place there are no pools, ponds, or rivers; but he creates for himself pools, ponds, and rivers—for he is a creator."[59] Just as the dreamer of the Upaniṣad spins a universe from his own mind creating illusory worlds, so in later Indian myths, the phenomenal universe is portrayed as the self-created dream of the god Viṣṇu.

In the vast cycles of evolution and devolution that constitute the ancient Indian understanding of time and the universe, Viṣṇu's sleep represents the dissolution of the universe into its formless state. At that time, the universe remains in a state of potential, waiting to be set in motion again. Viṣṇu is pictured sleeping on the coils of a thousand-headed serpent that represents the potential for a new creation and floating on the waters of nonform; and as he sleeps, he dreams. One of the more famous Viṣṇu myths from the *Matsya Purāna* addresses the external and internal "realities" of dreams and visions. It begins with an account of the dissolution of the universe at the end of the world eon. According to Heinrich Zimmer's rendition, "Vishnu sleeps. Like a spider that has climbed up the thread that once issued from its own organism, drawing it back into itself, the god has consumed again the web of the universe. Alone upon the immortal substance of the ocean, a giant figure, submerged partly, partly afloat, he takes delight in slumber. There is no one to behold him, no one to comprehend him; there is no knowledge of him, except within himself."[60] But within the body of Viṣṇu, the universe unfolds in his dream. One of the players in this dream is Mārkandeya, an ancient sage, who, in wandering over the earth, accidentally falls out of the god's mouth and out of the dream. He finds himself in the dark empty expanse of the cosmic ocean where he sees the immense sleeping form of Viṣṇu and is convinced that he is crazy or dreaming, since this is nothing like "reality." He is, however, soon swallowed up again and finds himself restored to his familiar world, from where he can only think of his former experience as a vision or dream. For Mārkandeya, the Supreme God's dream is reality, and the reality of God merely a confused dream.

The imagery and worldview revealed by such myths is common property in the development of Hinduism and Buddhism, where dream becomes a favored metaphor for the nature of phenomena—that which appears utterly solid and real, yet upon spiritual awakening proves to be devoid of the reality it was mistaken for. Certain Indian thinkers interpreted all ordinary reality as entirely nonexistent, like a dream. Gonda notes that according to the philosophy of the Vedāntin Gaudapada (ca. 700 CE), there is, "in principle, no difference between waking and dreaming."[61] In the context of ultimate reality, appearances and experiences, whether awake or dreaming, are equally false. In non-Mahāyāna Buddhist thought, along with other similes like dewdrop, water bubble, mirage, or magician's show, dream is also used to characterize worldly life. It is not used, however, in terms of reality versus illusion, but to emphasize the impermanent, insubstantial, and fleeting nature of the world, which is described as "transitory as a dream."[62] The pleasures of ordinary life based on sensory satisfaction are also "like the enjoyments of a dream . . . lost in this world in a moment."[63] In Mahāyāna and Tibetan Buddhist writing, the dream comparison (along with others such as the rainbow, the reflection of the moon in water, and images in a mirror) points more directly to the idea of the phenomenal world as a purely illusory and unreal apparition.

To sum up, the ancient Indian worldview, against which both Hindu and Buddhist thought developed, has notable similarities to shamanic concepts and ways of interacting with the environment. For both, the world is a web of hidden relations and correspondences, knowledge of which is power. They share a sensual and vitalistic approach to existence in which mental activity is grounded in the physical senses. The mutual flow of visionary empowerment between men and gods expressed in the sacrificial rituals and the Vedic songs can be noted also in shamanic systems where the shaman's chants and offerings induce the spirits to descend. By offering his body as a vehicle of the spirit, the shaman becomes the spirit, gains the power of the spirit analogous to the Vedic ritual in which the sacrificer becomes Agni, the supreme deity of the sacrifice.[64] With regard to sleep and dream, the Vedic emphasis on the dual nature of sleep as both bringer of evil and protector from evil is echoed in the shamanic view of sleep/dream as a state where real dangers can overtake a person as well as one in which protection from evil can be established. In the Upaniṣads, the ambiguities of the dream state can be seen in the presence of materialistic, psychological, and metaphysical interpretations. Further, the Upaniṣadic literature establishes dream as a place where various "realities" overlap but even more importantly, it offers a perspective on dream as a link to liberation and the experience of the self in its absolute true nature. This aspect of dream eventually takes on crucial importance in the Tibetan context. By the time Buddhism arrived on the Indian scene, a variety of contradictory approaches to dream existed. As well, the very nature of sleep and dream was understood to contain conflict. Finally, the notion of māyā as magical creativity contributed to the view that, compared to unchanging ultimate reality, the phenomenal world is illusion; yet, as the Upaniṣads imply, the illusory dream world may reveal the nature of ultimate freedom. The next chapters follow these themes into Indian and Tibetan Buddhist thought.

Chapter 3

Indian Buddhist Views of Dream

When the Buddha gave his first teaching and founded an order of monks, he joined a number of other heterodox teachers who were questioning the established religious system based on the authority of the Vedas and the ritual activity of the Brahmin priests. This movement was both external and internal to the orthodox Brahmanic religion. From within, the discussions and debates presented in the Upaniṣads represent a certain philosophic discontinuity with the ancient Vedic tradition, and contain many ideas in common with the heterodox systems of that time. Buddhism shared the Upaniṣadic view of existence as an eternal cycle of death and rebirth driven by karma—self-oriented actions of body, speech, or mind. To be "liberated" meant to be free from the exigencies of karma and rebirth by cutting away all desires and attachments. Buddhism, however, rejected the Upaniṣadic idea of ātman, the eternal, essential aspect of a person, as the foundation of individual human existence and the basis for continuity from life to life.

Scholars who study the relationship between Buddhism and indigenous cultures have interpreted this rejection of any continuing essence to be a major point of tension between "normative" Buddhism and indigenous traditions that believe in a separable and continuing soul. In his well-known study of Burmese Buddhism, Melford Spiro states, "[Most Burmese] insist—normative Buddhism notwithstanding—on the existence of an enduring soul which, persisting from rebirth to rebirth, experiences the consequences of karmic retribution. This soul is conceived to be either the pre-Buddhist *leikpya,* or in the case of the more sophisticated, an entity (*nāma*) derived from (but inconsistent with) normative Buddhist metaphysics."[1] It should be noted, however, that Buddhist thought did not reject the established Indian worldview of spirits or the methods of dealing with obstructing spirits; neither did it reject the idea that there are subtle dimensions to the human being beyond the gross physical dimension.[2] For example, the gradual training of a monk included learning how to create and act in a mind-made body separate from the physical.[3] What was rejected was the idea of an essential unchanging aspect to any composite structure, such as the human personality, in either its gross or subtle manifestations. The tensions that exist between Buddhist and shamanic views do not, therefore, lie in the area of belief or disbelief in spirits or in a subtle "soul" form of the person that can separate from the gross physical body. Indeed, in Shirokogoroff's opinion, "Any religion which does not oppose the idea of spirits and the possibility of their independent existence is not in conflict with shamanism."[4]

BUDDHIST DREAM THEORY AND ITS INDIAN CONTEXT

With regard to the investigation of the nature of dreams, Indian authors generally fall into two camps: those who argue that dreams are basically memories or recollections, and those who argue that dreams are direct perceptions. The following summary draws from Jadunath Sinha's comprehensive examination of the subject in his two-volume work *Indian Psychology*.[5] Sinha uses the terms "presentative" and "representative" to classify the Indian positions on dream. The former refers to the position that dreams are direct and immediate perceptions, and the latter holds that dreams are mere recollections of past experience. The representative theory is stated clearly by the philosopher of Advaita Vedānta, Śaṅkara. He says, "Dreams are reproductions of past waking perceptions owing to the revival of their subconscious impressions; so they have the semblance of waking perceptions."[6] In other words, dreams only *appear* to be direct perceptions due to a lapse or obscuration of memory.[7] The representative theory does not allow that dream cognition is the result of the direct presentation of an object, real or illusory, to the senses, even though it may appear so.

According to Sinha, most Indian thinkers advocated the presentative theory that dream cognition is essentially perceptual, not recollective, in nature. The emphasis on dream as sensory perception rather than as memory hearkens back to the Vedic view of mental operations as primarily perceptual rather than psychological in nature. It is argued, according to the presentative theory, that dream perceptions are not apprehended merely as memories arising during the dream state but as direct perceptions "produced at that time and place." The dreamer is conscious during the dream that he "sees" a chariot, not that he "remembers" a chariot, and on waking from the dream that he "saw" a chariot. Further, it is noted that the theory of dream as mere recollection of past waking experience does not explain the objects of the dream experience that were never perceived in the past, such as one's own head being chopped off.[8] In such ways, Indian thinkers distinguished between memory as recollection and dream as perception. What Sinha calls the presentative theory is taken up in Buddhist thought, according to which, although the sense organ of sight is not functioning during sleep and a dream chariot as an object of sight is not present, the mind, which is counted among the sense organs, is functioning and perceives its own objects without the participation of the other senses.[9] The dream is experienced due to the perceptive faculty of the mind alone.

DREAM AND DIRECT PERCEPTION OF THE BUDDHA

The Mahāyāna practice of visualizing the celestial buddhas is related to the understanding of dream as direct perception. Such visualization builds on the earlier Buddhist practice of calling to mind the qualities of Śākyamuni Buddha (*buddhānusmṛti*, "recollection of the Buddha") with some significant differences. In the *Visuddhimagga* (*Path of Purification*), Buddhaghosa's fifth-century commentary on the Pāli canon, the instructions for recollecting the Buddha contain no reference to the image of the Buddha or his physical features. It is an analytical form of meditation in which the meditator brings to mind and contemplates, point by point, each sublime quality of the Buddha. Further, it is said that this practice of recollection of the Buddha does not lead to absorption in a trance state (*jhāna*). The results of this type of meditation are described in psychological terms of fearlessness, happiness, and a feeling of closeness to the Buddha inspired by remembering his extraordinary qualities.[10] There is no indication that the meditator literally sees the form of the Buddha in any kind of vision or dream.

In the development of Mahāyāna Buddhism, however, along with the belief in numerous celestial buddhas and bodhisattvas appearing in the universe for the benefit of beings, the meditation on recollection of the Buddha was taken beyond memory and psychological benefits. It came to be associated with the ability to directly perceive the Buddha (any one of the celestial buddhas or bodhisattvas).[11] A detailed explanation of the Mahāyāna practice leading to direct visual perception of the Buddha, whether waking or sleeping, is found in the *Pratyutpanna Samādhi Sūtra*. This early Mahāyāna sūtra has been translated from the Tibetan by Paul Harrison as "The Samādhi of Direct Encounter with the Buddhas of the Present" with comparative notes on Sanskrit and Chinese versions.[12] In it the practitioner is enjoined not only to recall the special qualities of the Buddha, but also to recall the physical characteristics of a Buddha, "endowed with the thirty-two marks of the Great Man and a body with a colour like gold, resembling a bright, shining, and well-set golden image, and well adorned like a bejewelled pillar. . . ."[13] The Mahāyāna version of this practice, then, emphasizes the role of the imagination in generating a vision of the Buddha. Further, in the *Pratyutpanna Samādhi Sūtra*, dream is used both as a simile for explaining the nature of the meditative vision and as a vehicle for the encounter. Chapter 3 of the *Pratyutpanna Samādhi Sūtra* explains that one can encounter the Buddha Amitāyus through meditation in just the same way that those who are asleep and dreaming can see and converse with family or friends, and further, can remember the experience and relate it to others upon awakening:

> In the same way . . . *bodhisattvas*, whether they be householders or renunciates, go alone to a secluded spot and sit down, and in accordance with what they have learned they concentrate their thoughts on the . . . Perfectly Awakened One Amitāyus; . . . If they concentrate their thoughts with undistracted minds on the *Tathāgata* Amitāyus for seven days and nights, then, when a full seven days and nights have elapsed, they see the Lord and *Tathāgata* Amitāyus. Should they not see that Lord during the daytime, then the Lord and *Tathāgata* Amitāyus will show his face to them in a dream while they are sleeping.[14]

The passage indicates that this meditation leads to an alternate state of consciousness in which the encounter with Amitāyus is direct, immediate, and sensuous, just like one's experience of dreams. Beyond that, the meeting can take place either in a trancelike daytime vision or in nighttime dream. In another dream analogy, the text points out that just as the faculty of sight is not obscured by darkness or walls in a dream, and this not due to any magic power, so in the state of concentration or in a dream arisen due to this meditation, the vision of the Buddha and the hearing of the Dharma is not the result of ordinary magic powers or *siddhis*. Harrison gives the following from a Chinese version.

> Without having obtained divine vision, the *bodhisattvas* see the Buddha Amitābha; without having obtained divine hearing, they hear the *sūtra*/dharma expounded by the Buddha Amitābha; without having obtained magic power, they suc-

> ceed in going to Amitābha's Buddha-field. The *bodhisattvas* also do not die from here to go to be born there. Simply staying in this world as before, they see the Buddha, the *Tathāgata* Amitābha, and hear him expounding the Dharma. As they have heard it they take it up. The *bodhisattvas* then wake from this concentration, and then expound widely to others the Dharma as they have heard it.[15]

Since this practice is advocated for monastics and householders alike, the author makes sure that its marvelous effects are neither mistaken for supernormal powers that take long years of extreme meditative effort to achieve nor understood as the result of rebirth in some other state after death. The above passage also presents the Mahāyāna idea that authentic new teachings can be received and propagated through visionary and dream experiences. Elsewhere, the text states explicitly: " 'Furthermore, for those *bodhisattvas* who preserve this *samādhi, sūtras* which have not [previously] been expounded to or heard by them will be spoken and their uttering heard, even if it is only in their dreams.' "[16]

The *Pratyutpanna Samādhi Sūtra* engages with dream in a variety of ways: as a simile for immediate perception; to show that visionary experiences are not dependent on magical powers; as a mental state that allows for encounters with supernatural beings to take place; and, finally, as a method for realizing the soteriological goal, the liberating truth about the phenomenal world that it is ultimately as illusory as a dream. With regard to the role of dream in attaining liberation, the *Pratyutpanna Samādhi Sūtra* relates a story in which three men dream of three different courtesans whom they had heard of but never met.[17] Due to their lustful thoughts dwelling on the beautiful appearance and lovely qualities of these women, they each encounter the woman of their dreams in a dream and have sexual relations with them. On waking, they relate all that they had experienced to the Bodhisattva Bhadrapāla, who then teaches them the meditation method of the *Pratyutpanna Samādhi Sūtra*. The implication is that the dream experience serves as a basis for realizing the Mahāyāna view of the empty and ultimately unreal nature of all phenomena. The story further underscores the idea that the dream experience is of great significance in the path to Awakening, both as a method of accessing an alternate reality where the Buddhas are encountered face-to-face and teachings are received, and as a method of realizing the ultimate truth that all realities are of the nature of dreams; they appear to the organs of sense, but upon investigation and analysis, no ultimate status can be affirmed about anything.

DREAMING AND PARANORMAL POWERS

The Buddhist view of how dreaming takes place is of importance in establishing the correspondence between dream and paranormal powers, a correspondence that is commonly recognized in shamanic cultures. In *The Selfless Mind*, Peter Harvey explains the dream process relative to the Theravāda Buddhist concept of *bhavaṅga-citta*. Harvey describes *bhavaṅga-citta* as the "natural, unencumbered state of *citta* [mind]."[18] Based on the Pāli texts, he outlines the Theravāda view of the processes of consciousness in waking perception, in meditation, and in sleep.[19] In deep, dreamless sleep, consciousness flows along in its bhavaṅga phase, and all mental activity is at rest. In waking consciousness, moments of mental activity alternate with transitional moments of rest. In the dreaming state, as in the waking state, there is alternation between the bhavaṅga resting mode, when *citta* (mind) is not active, and moments of mental activity that represent a break in the bhavaṅga mode. Mind or consciousness in its natural state of rest is described as radiant and shining. It is considered to be a pure state, undefiled by mental afflictions, but as soon as mental activity takes place, then, in ordinary persons, the afflictions of greed, ill will, anger, pride, desire, and so forth arise.[20]

These afflictions, however, are not inherent to the active state of mind, and when they have been eliminated, the radiance of the natural state of mind pervades all mental activity, and the mind is empowered to develop the higher types of knowledge, which include the overcoming of the restrictions of normal physical laws through supernormal powers. Harvey's study of mind in the Theravāda texts leads him to conclude that the bhavaṅga state is the mind's naturally pure state and that "to unlock the power of this natural purity, the mind must be fully 'woken up' by meditative development, so that its radiant potential may be fully activated."[21] To be clear, one does not experience the mind in its natural state merely by entering into the bhavaṅga mode of deep, dreamless sleep because sleep is a state of unconsciousness. As Harvey emphasizes, it is necessary for the mind to awaken to its own radiance. With regard to dream, his research indicates that the process of dreaming and the process of experiencing the higher (supernormal) types of knowledge are one and the same:

> The mind functions in a parallel way in dreaming and in experiencing the higher knowledges, when the *citta* is free of defilements. In both cases, there is a very rapid alteration between *bhavaṅga* [basic mental continuum] and *javana* [active mind], the mind being "quick to change" in both. The

> difference lies in the fact that, in dreaming, wholesome *cittas* [mind states] are "confused," due to the debilitating effect of dullness-and-drowsiness. In the higher knowledges, the full radiance of *bhavaṅga* is uncovered, and can empower the *javana cittas* [active mind states] with the ability to develop paranormal powers.[22]

This would imply that the mind state that allows for the development of supernormal powers is none other than the dreaming state free from dullness and confusion. In other words, mundane supernormal powers are a function of wakeful or mindful dreaming. This would explain why standard monastic retreat practice is carried out alone, while dream yoga retreat practice requires a partner. It is not only to make sure that no one disturbs or wakes the practitioner suddenly, but more importantly, to ensure that the practitioner remains subtly awake and alert in his or her sleep and does not fall into a deep, unconscious sleep.

The status of the dream state is difficult to reconcile with Buddhist belief and teaching. If it were to be said that one dreams while asleep, that would contradict the *Abhidhamma* teaching that sleep takes place when there is no disturbance of the mind-stream by thoughts. And if it were to be said that dreaming takes place while awake, that would contradict the *Vinaya*, which says that a person is not morally responsible for dream acts.[23] Hence the Buddhist position is that the dreaming person is neither truly asleep nor truly awake but engaged, as the *Bṛhadāraṇyaka Upaniṣad* affirms, in a third place where supernormal powers manifest.

DREAM INTERPRETATION AND CLASSIFICATION

According to Wendy Doniger's study of dream in Indian texts, the first major description of dream theory, typology, and divination in Hindu literature appears in an appendix of the *Atharva Veda* composed around the sixth century CE.[24] In this system, dreams are classified according to the ancient medical divisions of "humors": choleric, phlegmatic, and bilious—in other words, according to the physical and emotional makeup of an individual. Dreams, it is thought, mirror a person's temperament, so that certain dreams are indicative of a particular type of person and, conversely, particular types of people have specific kinds of dreams. Although dreams are also classified as auspicious or inauspicious, it is not at all obvious which dreams would belong to which category. What might appear as the goriest nightmares—

dreams of dismemberment and destruction—are said to bring good luck: "If his ear is cut off, he will have knowledge; his hand cut off, he will get a son; his arms, wealth; his chest or penis, supreme happiness. . . . If someone dreams that his bed, chairs, houses, and cities fall into decay, that foretells prosperity."[25] Conversely, "A dream of singing, dancing, laughing, or celebrating a marriage, with joy and rejoicing, is a sight portending evil pleasure or disaster."[26] The Vaiśesika[27] school of Hindu philosophy recognizes three causes of dreams: (1) pathological disorders (2) subconscious impressions, and (3) unseen agency. Unseen agency is said to be the cause of dreams about things never before experienced in waking life; these dreams are omens—that is, prophetic dreams caused by the "unseen agency" of the merit or demerit, *dharma* or *adharma*, of the dreamer.[28] As we will see, the category of prophetic dreams caused by merit or demerit is prominent in the Buddhist dream theories that developed along with other schools of Indian thought.

The earliest text to offer a Buddhist interpretation of the phenomena of dream is the *Milindapañha*, the oldest sections of which date to the first century BCE. In the conversations between King Milinda and the Buddhist sage Nāgasena, dream is defined as a sign, mark, or image (*nimitta*) "coming across the path of the mind."[29] These images can be either true prognostications or deceptive/false appearances. Nāgasena classifies dreams according to the type of person who is doing the dreaming. These are of four kinds: (1) persons whose physical condition is dominated by wind, by bile, or by phlegm (the three humors that determine the person's disposition or temperament); (2) persons who are under the influence of a spirit; (3) persons who have many dreams due to previous experiences; and (4) persons who receive true prognostications. In this list, the dreams of persons who are suffering from an imbalance of the humors are considered false; so are the dreams of someone whose mind is simply indulging in the play of experience, as well as dreams that arise due to the influence of gods and spirits. The only dreams that are to be trusted are those that come to those who receive true prognostications. This is a crucial point in the foundation of Buddhist dream theory, because it ties the value of the dream to the character of the person dreaming. Other developments in Buddhist dream theory can be found in two commentaries dating to the fourth and fifth centuries CE: the *Samantapāsādikā*, Buddhaghosa's commentary on the *Vinaya*; and the *Manorathapūraṇī*, his commentary on the *Aṅguttara-nikāya*. Both texts enumerate the same four causes of dreams: (1) imbalance or disorder of the physical elements of the body, (2) previous experiences, (3) influence of spirits, and (4) portents.

According to the *Samantapāsādikā*,[30] a person suffering from physical disorders would have dreams such as slipping down a mountain or flying or being pursued by a tiger, a wolf, a lion, or a thief. These dreams, along with those based on previous experiences that simply replay what one has seen or heard previously, whether good or bad, are dismissed as nothing at all. Dreams due to the influence of gods may portend good or evil to come, depending on the disposition of the spirit toward the dreamer. Serinity Young's discussion of these texts indicate that unlike Nāgasena, for whom dreams due to the influence of spirits are entirely false or untrustworthy, both the *Manorathapūraṇī* and the *Samantapāsādikā* classify such dreams as prophecies that are possibly true or possibly not; the important point is that the prognostications drawn from these dreams are not to be trusted. Finally, the fourth type, true or trustworthy prognosticatory dreams (portending good or evil) are those that arise due to the merit or demerit of the dreamer. Examples given by Buddhaghosa include the conception dream of Queen Māyā, the sixteen dreams of the king of Kosala, and the five great dreams of a buddha's awakening.[31] In each case, the dreamer is a person who has accumulated great merit throughout his or her present and past lives, by virtue of which the dream prophecy is especially true.[32] Finally, Young calls attention to a passage in the *Manorathapūraṇī* where Buddhaghosa says that all these types of dreams are seen by ordinary people and that the perfected ones do not dream.[33] The view that enlightened ones do not dream calls to mind the ancient Vedic idea that Sleep/Dream held no dominion over the perfect ones, the gods, and it is also present in Tibetan dream theory. According to one of the foremost contemporary Tibetan exponents of dream yoga, Tenzin Wangyal, the instructions for the final stage of dream yoga practice are the same as the instructions for achieving enlightenment in the *bardo* (the intermediate state between death and rebirth). The practitioner is instructed to remain in the clear light, a state of nonduality in which awareness is fully absorbed in its own natural qualities of spaciousness and luminosity. He says, "When the practitioner fully integrates with the clear light, dreaming stops."[34]

In *Vajrayāna* as well as in Theravāda theory, dreams are understood to arise based on the dualistic play of observer and observed, and although they can portend future awakening, it is agreed that, in themselves, dreams signify that the soteriological goal has not been attained. Therefore, there is a certain denigration of dreams in Buddhism, a denigration that is also linked to the fact that prognostications drawn from dreams, omens, astrology, and the like were thought to be the business of Brahmins and not considered right livelihood for the Buddhist monastic *saṅgha* (community).[35] Further, Brahmin dream interpretation is censured as open to manipulation and superstition involving rituals of animal sacrifice. In the *Jātaka,* the past-life stories of the Buddha, the story of the king of Kosala's sixteen dreams juxtaposes the interpretation of the Brahmin soothsayers with the Buddha's interpretation. The Brahmins predict great evil for the king based on his dreams and propose to sacrifice great numbers of animals and birds to avert the disaster. In the Buddha's interpretation, the dreams are also prognostications of evil, but they are dreams foretelling events of a future degenerate age; the events have no impact on the king's present life and, therefore, require no ritual. In the story, the Brahmins are represented as exploiting the righteous king for the sake of their own gain, and the ethical position of Buddhism is put forward. The story ends with the Bodhisattva exhorting the king: "Henceforth, O king, join not with the brahmins in slaughtering animals for sacrifice."[36]

Another *Jātaka* tale recounts the story of a past birth in which the Bodhisattva retrieves a suit of clothes from the charnel ground, to the horror of the Brahmin who had thrown it away because it had been eaten by mice and was, therefore, an ill-omened thing that would bring bad luck to the wearer.[37] The Bodhisattva denounces the belief in omens and the story closes with advice to renounce belief in dreams and other such omens.

Such narratives indicate that in Indian Buddhist thought, dreams and their interpretation were associated with omenology, superstition, and a concern with ritual purity, all of which were to be overcome through empirical investigation and insight into the truth of how things come into being and pass away. However, this disparagement of dreams needs to be balanced with the great importance granted to the narratives of dream omens that portended the birth of the Buddha and his enlightenment.

THE CONCEPTION DREAM OF QUEEN MĀYĀ

The narrative of the life of the Buddha is situated in the context of incalculable eons of time, the eternal cycles of evolution and devolution of the universe, and the beginningless, endless round of birth and death that characterize the ancient Indian worldview. An ordinary person becomes a bodhisattva (person destined for buddhahood) when the mind is irreversibly committed to that goal and the training required to attain it. In the biographies of the Buddha, his moment of commitment is represented by the vow that he takes in a previous life. Incalculable eons in the past, born a Brahmin ascetic by the name of Sumedha, he encounters the buddha of that period, Dīpaṅkara, and, moved by faith and devotion, vows to achieve the same state of buddhahood. Dīpaṅkara prophesies that Sumedha's aspiration will be fulfilled and that he will be reborn to become Gautama the Buddha.[38] But this does not take place for many hundreds of eons. After many births and accumulation of great virtue, he is reborn in the Tuṣita heaven, from where he descends into the womb of Māyā, wife of the chief of the Śākya tribe, to live out his last birth.

Māyā's conception dream of a white elephant entering her womb is the paradigmatic prophetic dream in Buddhist legend.[39] This dream and its interpretation are preserved, more or less elaborately, in all accounts of the life of the Buddha. The *Nidānakathā* (ca. 2nd–3rd century CE) gives the following description:

> The four Guardians of the world, lifting her up in her couch, carried her to the Himālaya mountains. . . . Their queens then came toward her, and taking her to the lake of Anotatta, bathed her to free her from human stains; and dressed her in heavenly garments; and anointed her with perfumes; and decked her with heavenly flowers. Not far from there is the Silver Hill, within which is a golden mansion; in it they spread a heavenly couch, with its head towards the East and on it they laid her down. Then the future Buddha, who had become a superb white elephant, and was wandering on the Golden Hill, not far from there, descended thence, and ascending the Silver Hill, approached her from the North. Holding in his silvery trunk a white lotus flower, and uttering a far-reaching cry, he entered the golden mansion, and thrice doing obeisance to his mother's couch, he gently struck her right side, and seemed to enter her womb. . . . And the next day, having awoke from her sleep, she related the dream to the rāja.[40]

The conception of the Buddha is always presented in this dream format; however, the narratives of Māyā's dream suggest the possibility of interpreting the dream as a present happening experienced by her as a dream. The *Mahāvastu* (ca. 1st century CE) presents the natal dream as both dream and real event: "When the mighty and mindful one passed away from his abode in Tusita, taking on the form of an elephant of the colour of a snow-white boar, mindful, self-possessed and virtuous he descended into his mother's womb as she lay abed high up in the palace, fasting and clothed in pure raiment. At break of day she said to her gracious spouse, 'Noble king (in my dream I saw) a white and lordly elephant come down into my womb.' "[41]

Similarly, from the *Lalitavistara* (1st century CE): "The Bodhisattva . . . saw that the right time had arrived. Just at the appropriate moment, on the fifteenth of the month when the moon was full . . . the Bodhisattva descended from the Tusita realm, and, retaining full memory and knowledge, entered the womb of his mother. . . . Māyādevī, sleeping softly on her couch, saw this in a dream."[42]

The same difficulty in determining the exact nature of the relationship between dreamworld and real world that was noted in the shamanic dream narrative previously examined appears in these passages. Are we to understand that Māyā, while sleeping, had a prophetic dream of an elephant entering her womb, or that she participated in an actual occurrence in which the Bodhisattva appeared to his future mother in this form—an event that, like Mārkandeya in the Viṣnu story, she could only interpret as being a dream? There were different Buddhist responses to the question. Bhikkhu Telwatte Rahula notes that a philosophical treatise such as the *Abhidharmakośa* dismisses the dream as merely poetic expression;[43] and Alfred Foucher points out that the Chinese annals try to make sense of the elephant descent by portraying the Bodhisattva mounted on an elephant.[44] In most versions of the legend, the account of the Bodhisattva's time spent in the Tuṣita heaven and his discussion with the gods as to which family he should choose to be born into, which place, which time, and in what form he should descend to take birth are both represented as actuality, but the transition from one world to another is couched in the liminal language of dream—a process that resonates with the shamanic understanding of dream *as* event.

As the story continues in the *Mahāvastu*, Brahmin sages are brought in to interpret the dream for the king, who is told that such a dream means that a male child has been conceived in the womb of the queen and, further, that if the child remains in the household life he will become a great world ruler, but if he renounces the household life he will become a buddha. The god Mahā-brahmā is finally brought in to give the definitive interpretation. He puts it to Māyā that a woman who sees a sun or moon will give birth to a universal king, but "the woman who in her dream has seen a white elephant enter her womb will give birth to a being as select as the elephant is among animals. He will be a Buddha who knows the Good and the True."[45] This interpretation links the dream with the prognosticatory certainty that the child to be born will attain the enlightened state of a buddha. This foremost dream in Buddhist history, then, is represented variously as an actual event, as a dream to be interpreted, and as true prophecy.

DREAMS OF AWAKENING

Just as the physical birth of a buddha-to-be is heralded by a dream, so the spiritual birth of a fully awakened buddha is heralded by dream. The link between dream and spiritual awakening can be found in the earliest Buddhist literature. In the *Aṅguttara-nikāya*, the Buddha recounts the five great dreams that appear to a *bodhisattva* signifying the moment of his awakening to buddhahood (see table 1).[46]

These dreams mark the coming into being, the "awakening" of the Three Jewels: the Buddha, the Dharma, and the *Saṅgha*. The *Aṅguttara-nikāya* presents the dreams as the precursors of his full awakening. "When[,] monks[,] to the Tathāgata . . . there came the dream that this great world was his bed of state . . . [then] the unsurpassed full

Table 1. The Five Great Dreams of Awakening

Dream	*Portending*
1. He reclines on the world like a great bed with his head resting on the Himālaya Mountains as his pillow, his left hand plunged in the eastern sea, his right hand in the western sea, and both feet in the southern sea.	Full enlightenment.
2. Sacred *kusha* or *tiriyā* grass sprouts from his navel and reaches to the clouds.	The proclamation of the Dharma (the Four Noble Truths and the Eightfold Way) to gods and men throughout the three worlds.
3. White worms with black heads creep up and cover his feet and legs as far as the knees.	The numbers of white-robed householders (the lay saṅgha) who will take refuge in the Buddha's teaching.
4. Four variously-colored birds come from the four quarters of the world, fall at his feet, and turn white.	People from the four Hindu castes will renounce caste and join the monastic saṅgha.
5. Walking on a mountain of dung without becoming soiled by the filth.	The Buddha's activity in saṃsāra and his nonattachment to the things of the world.

awakening to the highest was wholly awakened [within him]. To him, wholly awakening, this first dream came."[47] The wording suggests that the dreams occur immediately prior to the moment of awakening or even as he was awakening. The close proximity of dream and awakening might suggest a causal relationship,[48] however, such an interpretation would contradict the Pāli Buddhist view that nirvāṇa is unborn, unbecome, uncreated, and unconditioned.[49] Although there are many descriptors for nirvāṇa, both positive (*mutti*, "freedom") and negative (*nirodha*, "cessation"), it is never considered to be subject to any cause or condition.[50] The five great dreams of a buddha can be understood simply as true prognosticatory dreams in accordance with the classifications given by Nāgasena and Buddhaghosa. Young's detailed cross-textual analysis indicates that the timing of the Buddha's awakening relative to the dreams is ambiguous—did they occur before his departure from home, the night before his enlightenment, or moments before his awakening? She points out that the *Aṅguttaranikāya* supports a stronger sense of immediacy, whereas the *Manorathapūraṇī* states that when these dreams occur the bodhisattva will attain enlightenment the next day.[51] Yet, regardless of the timing, the crucial element of the liberation dreams lies in the reliability of their prophetic truth. As the dawn heralds sunrise, these dreams signal the arising of liberation in the mind-stream of the bodhisattva. The implication is that the dreams presage and, more importantly, *authenticate*, the attainment of the final stage in the spiritual life of one destined for buddhahood.

Just as the archetypal and legendary life of a buddha is marked by dream prophecy,[52] so in Mahāyāna literature the career of a bodhisattva includes the dreams or visions that signal the stages of spiritual attainment. From the *Mahāratnakūta Sūtra*[53] comes the following elaborate account of the visions seen by a bodhisattva at the point of attaining each of the ten stages of spiritual development (see table 2).

Although these dreams are very stylized and triumphal in spirit, their presence indicates the persistent theme of dream or vision as an authenticating feature of spiritual attainment within the Buddhist textual tradition. This legitimizing aspect of dream becomes a predominant value in the Tibetan context.

DREAM AND THE MORAL CONDITION OF THE DREAMER

True prognosticatory dreams are karma driven, because they arise on the basis not only of a person's accumulation of merit, but also on the accumulation of demerit. Therefore, dreams portending evil for the

Table 2. The Ten Visions of a Bodhisattva

At the threshold of the stage called:	*The Bodhisattva dreams of:*
1. Great Joy	All the innumerable hidden treasures in the billion-world universe
2. Stainless Purity	The universe flat as one's palm and adorned with countless lotus flowers
3. Illumination	Himself, clad in armor and brandishing a cudgel, repressing enemies
4. Radiant Flames	Rare flowers being scattered over the earth by the wind from the four quarters
5. Invincible Strength	Women wearing ornaments and garlands of flowers on their heads
6. Direct Presence	Himself playing in a beautiful pond with gold sand at the bottom, and jeweled steps on its sides, adorned with lotus flowers
7. Far-Reaching	Himself passing unharmed through hells
8. Immovable Steadfastness	Himself bearing the signs of a lion king on his shoulders
9. Meritorious Wisdom	Himself as a universal monarch teaching the Dharma, surrounded by innumerable kings, shaded by white, jeweled canopies
10. Dharma-Cloud	Himself with a golden body, in a circle of light, showing the thirty-two auspicious signs of a Tathāgata, seated on a lion-throne, and surrounded by countless gods

Source: Garma C. C. Chang, *A Treasury of Mahāyāna Sūtras: Selections from the Mahāratnakuta Sūtra* (London: Pennsylvania State University Press, 1983), 421–22.

dreamer are also considered reliable for the person who has accumulated great demerit. The dreams of Māra, the obstructor of Enlightenment, exemplify this point. On the night before his battle with the Buddha, Māra dreams of thirty-two signs portending evil. Among them, he sees his crown fall from his head, the trees and flowers of his garden withered, his lakes dried up, his favorite garden birds falling to the ground, his women weeping, his clothes and body grimy and filthy, the walls and towers of his palace destroyed, trees and forests uprooted, the world come to an end.[54] Māra himself interprets the dreams to be evil omens, as does his son, who advises that he not do battle with the Buddha. The dream, of course, is proven true in the ensuing battle in which the forces of Māra are routed.

As Young notes, the disturbing motifs recounted in this narrative are similar to those in the dreams of Siddhārtha's wives. Siddhārtha's father as well as his wives have premonitory dreams of his departure from the palace. In the *Lalitavistara*, Gopā dreams that she sees the sun and moon and stars fall from the sky, her crown fall off, her pearl necklaces and jewels become broken and scattered, and herself naked with arms and legs cut off. Her hair is cut off, her bed is broken down, trees are uprooted, and Meru, the king of mountains, is shaken to its foundations.[55] A similar dream is reported by Yaśodharā in the *Abhiniṣkramaṇasūtra*. The different textual versions of Siddhārtha's response to this dream present both the idea of dream as ultimately empty of value and the view that dream holds prophetic significance. In the *Abhiniṣkramaṇasūtra*, the Bodhisattva gives a very philosophic response. He knows the dreams are premonitions of his leaving, but at the same time he dismisses them as not worth considering, as "the empty products of a universal law."[56] In the *Lalitavistara*, the prophetic aspect of the dream sequence is elaborated, and they are described as favorable omens portending good for the dreamer. The images are very similar to those of Māra's negative dream, but these omens are interpreted positively.

> Be happy—these dreams show nothing wrong.
> Beings who have formerly practiced good works
> are the ones who have such dreams.[57]

Specifically, among the omens are signs of her spiritual progress:

> Since you have seen trees uprooted,
> And your hair cut off with your left hand,
> soon, Gopā, you will cut the net of the fettering passions;
> you will remove the veil of false views
> that obscures the conditioned world.[58]

In her comparison and analysis of these dreams, Young suggests that the positive interpretation of negative imagery represents "an attempt to establish a new dream terminology that reverses the world-affirming values of Brahmanical Hinduism."[59] Her interpretation accords with other ways in which Buddhism invested Brahmanic practices, motifs, and ideas with new meaning. For example, the practice of the *brahmavihāras* as meditations on loving-kindness, compassion, sympathetic joy, and equanimity reinterpreted Brahmanic ritual practices focused on attaining the heaven of the god Brahmā. The interpretation of negative dream images in a positive way, however, can also be found in the Brahmanic tradition, as mentioned: "Whoever, in a dream, has his head cut off or sees a bloody chariot will become a general or have a long life or get a lot of money. If his ear is cut off, he will have knowledge; his hand cut off, he will get a son; his arms, wealth; his chest or penis, supreme happiness. . . ."[60] Both Buddhist and Brahmanic texts provide similar dream interpretation and imagery, but regardless of the direction of influences, Buddhist dream theory in Indian literature is not distinguished by classification methods, or the reinterpretation of motifs, or the view of dream as illusion. What is peculiarly Buddhist is the emphasis on the role that karma—merit and demerit—plays in the interpretation and validity of the dream. The interpretation of Gopā's dreams in the *Lalitavistara* concludes with this speech from the Bodhisattva:

> Because, Gopā, you have always honoured me
> and surrounded me with the greatest respect,
> there are for you neither unfortunate rebirths nor sorrow;
> soon you will rejoice, filled with great joy.
>
> In times past, I gave in abundance,
> I guarded my conduct and always acted patiently.
> That is why those with faith in me
> Will all be filled with pleasure and joy.
>
> For tens of millions of kalpas in the world,
> I purified the path of Enlightenment.
> That is why, for all who have faith in me,
> The paths to the three unfortunate rebirths
> Will be no more.
>
> Be happy and do not give in to sadness;
> be joyous and give yourself over to cheer.
> Soon you will obtain joy and contentment.
> Sleep, Gopā; the omens are favourable for you![61]

It is clear that the omens are favorable due to her virtuous actions of devotion and faith toward one who is supremely virtuous. It is not the content of the dream but the moral condition of the dreamer that is the determining factor in whether or not the dream is of positive or negative value.

This leads to an important question for the monastic community whose aim is to live an ethically pure life—that is, whether or not the actions one performs in dreams generate merit or demerit. This is a different question from whether or not the dream itself is a good dream, portending good for the dreamer, or bad, portending evil. The *Vinaya* takes up the problem of a monk who emits semen during a dream. The intentional emission of semen is an offence requiring a formal confession and probation for the monk in question; however, according to the text, "there is no offence if he was dreaming, if there was no intentional emission, if he was mad, unhinged, in pain, a beginner."[62] Again, this pronouncement places the emphasis on the mental and physical condition of the person;[63] the judgment acknowledges the effect that every state of mind has on a person's ability to form and carry out intentions. Commentaries on the Pāli *Vinaya* such as the *Kathā-vatthu* make the further point that dreams in general may be ignored precisely because the mental actions of dreams do not have the strength to create consequences: "Although a dreamer may entertain evil thoughts of murder, etc., no injury to life or property is wrought. Hence they cannot be classed as offences. Hence dream-thoughts are a negligible quantity and for this reason, and not because they are ethically neutral, they may be ignored."[64] In other words, a person cannot commit sins in a dream, because although the mental processes are the same in dreaming as in waking, in dreaming one does not have volitional control over the dream thought or act, and hence one is not morally responsible for it. Nevertheless, it is also understood that dreams are related to the character of the person and can have an effect on the personality. There is the sense that even though one is not morally responsible for one's dreams, they can, to some degree, be controlled and, further, that they both reveal and mold the character of the dreamer. The tension and ambiguities of the dream state can be observed in the contradictory notions that dream thoughts and actions are negligible, yet carry ethical value, indicate spiritual progress, and are enshrined in the spiritual career of a buddha or bodhisattva.

Although many of the dream images and motifs found in Buddhist texts are common to the wider Indian culture, Buddhist narratives are marked by a soteriological subtext. The practical approach to dream, as a method of predicting and achieving this-worldly happiness, health, and prosperity, is combined with the use of dream and vision as a way of promoting Buddhist ethics and furthering the goal of liberation. Indeed, in the Pāli sūtras, this approach is brought to bear on any kind of success or power that a practitioner wishes to obtain. Whether the desired result is understood in terms of material benefits, spiritual benefits, or supernormal powers, the necessary conditions are the same: one should be "possessed of moral habit . . . possessed of right conduct and resort, seeing danger in the slightest faults. . . ." He or she should be "one who fulfills the moral habits, who is intent on mental tranquillity within, whose meditation is uninterrupted, who is endowed with vision [*vipassanā*, "insight"], a cultivator of empty places."[65] Success of all kinds, then, for the Buddhist practitioner is primarily linked with the accumulation of merit/virtue and wisdom/insight.

The *samaṇa* "counterculture" movement, to which the Buddha belonged, emphasized individual experience, renunciation, solitude, prolonged meditation, and the realization of supernormal powers on the path to liberation. These are characteristics of what Geoffrey Samuel would call "shamanic Buddhism," in contradistinction to the "clerical" Buddhism of monastic organization, text study, rituals, and the pursuit of virtue. Ironically, however, the shaman or charismatic religious specialist in classical shamanic complexes, such as those of the Siberian Tungus, would regard the practical use of dreams as of the highest value, whereas the "shamanic" Buddhist is one who regards dreams as empty of ultimate value. The dreams of the shaman signify his supreme accomplishment as a shaman; the dreams of the Buddhist signify that the supreme goal still eludes him. The distinction is very important from the Buddhist perspective, because although Buddhism accepts and works with the relationship between dream and mundane psychic powers, there is no attaining to the supramundane power of liberation through ordinary dream consciousness, because of its association with sleep as a state of dullness or unconsciousness, the antithesis of mindful awareness. Contrary to those who believe that liberation can be attained in the dream state (due to the supernormal powers experienced in dreams), Buddhaghosa argues that there can be no penetration of the Dharma "by one who is asleep, or languid, or blurred in intelligence, or unreflective."[66] Nevertheless, throughout Buddhist history, dreams continue to appear as signposts of ethical and spiritual progress, and to function as alternate states of consciousness by means of which other worlds and other beings become accessible. Finally, in the Vajrayāna development of Buddhism, there is a new movement to explore the possibility of "mindful awareness" in the dream state.

To sum up, Buddhism accepts the idea that dreams represent direct perception, and in Buddhist psychology the process of dreaming is closely related to the process of developing supernormal or magical powers. These are ideas that resonate with a shamanic perspective in which dreams are realities and dreaming itself is a power. The conception dream of the Buddha's mother highlights the role of dream as a liminal place of transition and communication between the heaven world where a bodhisattva waits to take birth and the earthly beings among whom he will be born. Mahāyāna Buddhism teaches that through the power of concentration and recollection one can attain direct perception of the Buddhas and visit the Buddha paradises, either as waking visions or nighttime dreams. Through such visionary encounters, one can receive authentic spiritual instruction, as shamans do through their dreams and trance states. Furthermore, in Buddhist literature the state of buddhahood and the stages of the bodhisattva path are preceded by stylized dreams whose presence both announces and authenticates the state that has been attained, in much the same way that shamanic cultures accept certain special dreams as the authenticating mark of a shaman's calling.

Buddhist dream theory developed in concert with Indian systems of interpretation and classification. The Upaniṣadic view of dream as a psychological phenomenon was retained, but from its earliest period onward Buddhist thought included the more ancient idea that certain dream events and dream acts share the same reality value as the waking state. The ancient Vedic emphasis on the concrete sensory nature of mental phenomena, the efficacy of ritual, and the necessity of the mediating activity of specialized ritualists continued throughout Hindu and Buddhist traditions. Such characteristics, which were part of the Buddhist heritage as it was transmitted to Tibet, would have been amenable to the worldview of an indigenous shamanic culture.

The Buddhist emphasis on merit or demerit in the interpretation of dreams mediates between the view of dream as providing valid cognition or trustworthy prognostication and the view of dream as illusion, exemplary of the transitoriness and unreality characteristic of all phenomena. According to Buddhist theory, one who has attained great merit is one whose prophetic dreams are to be trusted. At the same time, the accumulation and perfection of virtue is a crucial factor in achieving the goal of liberation from illusion. The concern with merit in dream interpretation takes on special emphasis in Tibetan Buddhism, where it becomes the primary factor in distinguishing Buddhist from shamanic activity.

Young notes in her comprehensive treatment of this subject that conflicting messages about the nature of dream are prominent in Tibetan biographies; she, however, interprets the conflict primarily in terms of the elite versus the popular view of dreams.[67] Yet, as previously noted, ordinary lay Tibetans are as likely as monastics or tantric practitioners to pronounce on the illusory nature of dream, and as Young's work shows, the use of dream for its prophetic value proliferate in the biographies of the spiritual elite. This makes it difficult to ascribe conflicting views on dream specifically to elite or popular traditions, since they would seem to hold both views quite indistinguishably. Furthermore, the elite philosophical tradition in no way denigrates prophetic dreams, and the popular view of dream includes the understanding that the world is like a dream. The elite/popular division is, therefore, not inherently contradictory.

We know that opposing views of dream coexisted from the earliest days of the Buddhist tradition, but in the Tibetan cultural and philosophical environment the polarities were accentuated; a heightened interest in the practical prophetic use of dream was matched by an equal emphasis on the view of all phenomena as ultimately illusory. In addition, it is reasonable to consider that the Tibetan approach to dream would have been affected by the interaction between Buddhism and an indigenous religious system, which would also privilege dreams as a mode of spiritual communication. In the encounter between Buddhism and shamanism, the need for Buddhist authorities to establish and maintain the superiority of the soteriological goal would constitute a crucial factor in the contradictory attitudes toward dream in Tibetan Buddhism. Conflicting statements regarding the value of dream imply some deeper tension than merely the difference between the textual and folk traditions. The nature of that tension, I would argue, can be more clearly understood in terms of the Buddhist struggle to uphold the preeminence of universal liberation while adapting to the local Tibetan worldview.

Chapter 4

Dream in the Tibetan Context

The past chapters have dealt with dream in shamanic complexes and in Indian thought. As we have seen in Harvey's analysis of waking and sleeping states of mind in the Pāli tradition, dream is closely related to supernormal powers; and in Mahāyāna Buddhism dream is a means by which one can communicate directly with a deity. These are points of comparison with a shamanic perspective according to which dream is both a method of contacting the spirits and an arena for action. However, in Buddhism, precisely because dream is a mental state, it is subject to affliction, and its truth or benefit is therefore suspect and unreliable. In this chapter, I wish to clarify the strands of thought that constitute the Tibetan worldview and indicate the ways in which Tibetan attitudes to dream represent a continuation and elaboration of their Buddhist heritage.

The Buddhism that eventually flourished in Tibet was Mahāyāna Buddhism in its tantric form called Vajrayāna, the Diamond Vehicle. From the first millennium CE onward, the spread of Buddhism in India and the development of the Mahāyāna emphasis on the universality of the bodhisattva path and the "emptiness" of all phenomena created an all-embracing philosophic atmosphere, regarding which Snellgrove comments: "As a pan-Indian religion Buddhism was now ready to adopt any religious practices whatsoever, so long as they might be used as a means towards the perfection of enlightenment, and since the decision about what was usable or not depended upon no recognized authority, but upon those practicing the religion, there was no form of Indian religious practice that did not now have some Buddhist equivalent."[1]

This opened the way for a new religious trend to be incorporated into Buddhist theory and practice. From about 500 CE, texts called tantras appear in both Hindu and Buddhist versions. Tantric systems focus on rituals of identification with a deity by means of which a practitioner can come to exercise ultimate control over the processes of mind and matter. Their unorthodox methods are regarded as the fast but dangerous route to liberation. Friedhelm Hardy summarizes the general tantric approach as follows:

> Man lives in a universe which is pervaded by all kinds of forces. Many of them are destructive and threatening, others relate in a more positive manner to his life. What conventional society has on offer as the means of controlling these forces is believed to be limited and restrictive as to the realisation of man's full potential; there is, however, a knowledge available which the more adventurous and mature person can draw on and thereby improve that realization radically. But it is esoteric, well guarded by a secret tradition. With the help of this esoteric knowledge it becomes possible to expose oneself to even the most dangerous and powerful of such universal forces and not just survive, but actually control them and absorb them for one's own fulfillment.[2]

Regarding the transmission of tantra to Tibet, Hardy further makes the important point that "the Tibetans adopted Tantric Buddhism not as an already fixed system, but as a still dynamic affair, and they actively continued the conceptualization of the Tantric approach in terms of Mahāyāna thought."[3]

The amalgamation of Mahāyāna doctrine and tantric methods formed an entirely new vehicle, the Vajrayāna, which took as its prime symbol the *vajra,* originally a symbol of the scepter or thunderbolt of Indra, the ancient Vedic king of the gods. In Vajrayāna Buddhism, the vajra (also translated "diamond" to indicate strength and clarity) represents the indestructible, indivisible union of the "phenomenal" (things that appear to the senses) and the "absolute" (the indeterminate, ineffable nature of all appearances). The vajra further signifies the diamond-like clarity of the mind that penetrates all seeming solidities and perceives their dreamlike, empty nature. Another name given to the tantric way was Mantrayāna, the Mantra-vehicle. This refers to the primary method by which the devotee connects and identifies with the deity through repetition of the mantra. Repeating the mantra hundreds of thousands of times, the devotee eventually becomes one with the deity and its power. Incantation and ritual have been an aspect of Buddhist practice from its earliest period. However, it is only in the Mahāyāna and, subsequently, the Vajrayāna development that these methods became a dominant means of attaining the goal of liberation. The ideal spiritual person in the Vajrayāna is the *siddha*, the "spiritual adept," described by Snellgrove as the one who "gains power over beings in other spheres of existence, either dominating them, so that they may do one's will, or identifying . . . with them, so that one may enjoy their higher states of existence."[4] The Buddhism that interacted with the shamanic culture of ancient Tibet was established informally via peripatetic tantric Indian yogis, as well as formally through state-sponsored visits by respected Buddhist monks. It incorporated both monastic and tantric modes, the one focused on control or restraint of the senses and the other on working with sensory stimuli in the practice of self-transformation.

The first record of Buddhism in Tibet is of a legendary royal family who revered Buddhist texts but did not know what they meant. According to traditional Tibetan history, the "Beginning of the Holy Doctrine"[5] took place during the reign of King Lha Thotori Nyentsen (twenty-eighth in the line of Tibetan kings beginning with Nyatri Tsenpo), when a casket mysteriously fell from the sky onto the roof of the palace. It contained Buddhist texts dedicated to the celestial Bodhisattva Avalokiteshvara and a golden stūpa. Although the king could not read them and had no idea what they contained, he felt they were auspicious and worshipped them, calling them, the "Awesome Secret."[6] Tibetan historians like Gos Lotsawa and Bu-ston consider this event a point of demarcation between the religion of the old kings, dominated by priests called Bön, and the new religion represented by the miraculous appearance on the roof of the palace.[7] Traditional records relating to King Lha Thotori Nyentsen also tell us that the advent of Buddhism in Tibet was foreshadowed by a dream in which the king is told that five generations after him there will be one who will understand the meaning of the texts.[8] This prophecy is considered to have been fulfilled in the reign of King Songtsen Gampo, the fifth monarch after Thotori and the first Tibetan king to formally accept Buddhism.

CONFLICT AND COMPETITION

A distinctively Tibetan Buddhist worldview emerged from the interplay between adopted Buddhist ideals, tantric practices, and the pre-Buddhist indigenous shamanic culture. In Tibet, Buddhist authority came to dominate the religious landscape not only in terms of ethics, philosophy, and soteriology, but also in terms of the magic and ritual on which the Tibetan people depended to keep them safe in a world of unreliable and often hostile spirits. This preeminence, however, was not gained without resistance. During the reign of King Songtsen Gampo (618–50 CE), when the early Tibetan empire was a rising force, Buddhism was flourishing in the surrounding regions of Nepal, China, and Central Asia. Two of the king's wives from Nepal and China were said to have brought with them Buddhist images and were active in supporting the building of Buddhist temples, including the twelve "limb-binding" temples that were built to suppress the great demoness that was Tibet.[9] This was the first significant step in the development of Buddhism as a state religion. However, it was not until the reign of Trisong Detsen (ca. 740–98 CE) that Buddhism was firmly established as the religion of the Tibetan kings, and the full-scale dissemination of Buddhism as a religious institution was put in place. The dissension that King Trisong Detsen faced over the new religion is reflected in certain inscriptions set up during his reign. According to one: "This practice of the Buddhist religion is to be held in affection and in no way for no reason whatsoever is it to be destroyed or abandoned, whether because people say it is bad, that it is not good, or by reason of prognostication or dreams. Whoever, great or small, argues in that way, you are not to act accordingly."[10] In another edict regarding his conversion he stated, "That [Buddhism] was not the old religion. Because it did not accord with the propitiations and rites of the tutelary deities, all suspected it to be no good. They suspected it would harm [me, His Majesty]. They suspected it would threaten governance. They suspected [that it brought about] epidemics and cattle plagues. They suspected it, when famine suddenly fell upon them."[11]

The intense rivalry resulting from the conversion of the Tibetan court to Buddhism is captured in a Bön-po curse that reads:

King Trhi-song-de-tsen is a foolish fellow.
His ministers are monstrous rogues.
Our blazing light is now withdrawn.
Now is the time of these Buddhist monks.
The princes have great faith in gold
And our haloed *Bön* declines.
May the king be a village beggar
And his ministers be shepherds!
May the land of Tibet break into pieces
And these Buddhist monks lose their law!
May these nuns bear children
And these Buddhist priests lead fighting gangs!
May their monasteries be filled with battle
And their temples set on fire!
May the princes sift their own gold

O may my curse be effective
And may these books of mine be found by someone worthy![12]

The first dissemination of Buddhism continued throughout the regimes of subsequent Tibetan kings and reached its peak under the reign of Relbachen (815–36 CE). The royal patronage of Buddhism during the eighth and ninth centuries notwithstanding, the old religion was not easily displaced. The kings continued to be buried as their forefathers were, according to the ancient pre-Buddhist rites. And in the affairs of state, the presence of Buddhist monks did not eliminate the non-Buddhist sacrificial rituals accompanying the conclusion of treaties. According to Snellgrove: "The Chinese accounts [of the 821 CE treaty] confirm that the principal ceremony was non-Buddhist and accompanied by animal sacrifices. It is, however, made clear that on this occasion the Buddhist participants abstained from smearing their lips with blood and that they afterwards moved into a temporary chapel for Buddhist rites."[13]

The early competition between Buddhist and non-Buddhist religious authorities that was played out in the political rivalries and intrigues of court ministers oscillated between periods of compromise and coexistence and periods of conflict on both sides.[14] Later, it took the form of rival displays of magic and sorcery. From the biography of the eleventh-century saint Milarepa comes a famous account of the shamanlike battle of magic between a Bön-po priest called Naro Bhun Chon and the Buddhist yogi Milarepa (1040–1123). In several contests, Milarepa defeats his opponent. The final contest is a race to the top of the snow mountain called Di Se. The text relates that very early in the morning while Milarepa sleeps, the Bön-po is seen flying through the air on his drum, playing a Bön musical instrument on his way to the peak. Milarepa's students are worried that he might be beaten, but Milarepa, unconcerned, waits until daybreak and proves himself master of the mountain: "[He] snapped his fingers, donned a cloak for wings, and flew over toward Di Se. In a second he arrived at the summit of the mountain. . . . Meanwhile Naro Bhun Chon had reached the neck of the mountain. When he saw the Jetsun [Milarepa] . . . sitting at ease on the summit, he was dumbfounded and fell down from the heights, his riding-drum rolling down the southern slope of Di Se."[15] The closing words of Milarepa attribute his magical abilities and his victory to the blessings of a spiritual lineage, devotion to the guru, virtue in observing the moral precepts, proficiency in meditation, and the nature of enlightened mind. These elements serve to distinguish Buddhist magic from Bön-po magic and to provide the Buddhist soteriological rationale for his miraculous powers.[16]

As Snellgrove has argued, Buddhism originally came into conflict with the cults of local deities and shamanistic pre-Buddhist ritualists known as Bön, but the rivalry really became consolidated between the developing Bön religion and the developing Buddhist religion. In that relationship, both Bön and Buddhism competed for control over the indigenous deities and both propagated a path to liberation; however, from the traditional Buddhist perspective, Bön remained a version of the pagan indigenous element it had always struggled to defeat.[17]

Variants of the storied battle between the lama and other shamanlike figures are also found among the Tamang people of Nepal. According to Holmberg's study, Tamang society recognizes three ritual specialists: the lama who presides over the death rituals and guides the soul to a good rebirth, the *lambu* who performs the sacrificial offerings and exorcisms, and the shaman/*bombo* who calls back lost souls and mediates between humans and spirits while in trance. Their versions of the ancient conflict between the lama and the bombo are not resolved as neatly as in Milarepa's story. In the Tamang version, the lama and the bombo were brothers. In that competition, the lama was also victorious, but the bombo who was banished to the bottom of a lake continued to dance there and managed to throw a spell on the eyes of the lama's daughter. The lama, unable to cure her, was forced to return to the bombo and make a deal with him. In addition to payment for his services, the lama promises the bombo, "I will take care of the dead and you will take care of the living."[18] In this way, the narrative legitimizes the division of ritual roles in Tamang society and allows the lama and bombo their distinctive spheres of influence. In the Milarepa story, the Bön-po does not convert to Buddhism and there is no deal between them; he simply leaves, accepting his defeat. In the Tamang version, the shaman figure is defeated, but even the victorious lama is shown to be in need of his services. The stories imply that Buddhist rivals were defeated but not eliminated and that accommodations were made for both to coexist.[19] In contemporary Tibetan Buddhism, the tradition of the *sung-ma* or *ch'ökyong*—oracle mediums through whom the protector deities speak directly with humans—provides a possible link with pre-Buddhist shamanic rituals of spirit possession and divination.[20] Indeed, the evidence points to a dynamic in which Buddhism with its soteriological concerns must struggle to maintain its foremost position within the Tibetan context.

The wrathful and horrific deities for which Tibetan Buddhism is famous bear witness to the powerful forces of Tibet that were said to be conquered by the superior magic of the eighth-century tantric yogi Padmasambhava.[21] According to legend, he defeated them and bound them by oath to become protectors of the Dharma; nevertheless, they are ever to be treated with caution, and in daily religious practice they are continually reminded of their defeat and their sworn promises. Each ritual invocation recalls the past struggle, renews the oath, and most importantly enacts, in the present, the victory of the Dharma over the obstructing forces of indigenous loyalties.

THE LAMA, THE SHAMAN, AND THE YOGI

The relationship between Buddhist lamas and shamans has been the focus of a number of studies dealing with the relationship between Vajrayāna Buddhism and indigenous traditions.[22] Many scholars have noted the correlation between these two types of ritual specialists in providing such pragmatic services as rainmaking, exorcism, healing, demon suppressing, divination, or guiding the dead. The title of Geoffrey Samuel's study of Tibetan societies—*Civilized Shamans*—captures his thesis that the literate lamas of Tibet function as shamans and that Vajrayāna techniques serve as a sophisticated means of training shamanic practitioners. Barbara Aziz relates the phenomena of spirit possession to the idea of the *tulku* (Tib. *sprul sku*, "reincarnate lama") and suggests that a tulku could be regarded as possessed from birth by a deity—in other words, possessed for life.[23] William Stablein makes a similar comparison in his study of the ritual dedicated to the tantric deity Mahākāla. He states, "[I]f a shaman can say, 'I am possessed by a spirit,' the Vajramaster, after the invitation phase of the ceremony, can say 'I *am* Mahakala.' "[24] Certainly, in these ways lamas can be compared to shamans. However, it is also important to take into account the differences that allow tantric Buddhist lamas to distinguish themselves entirely from shamans and their practices. Tibetan Buddhism recognizes the state of possession,[25] whereby an oracle is taken over by a spirit, and exactly as in shamanic forms of possession, the spirit speaks through the oracle-medium. And although a tulku may well be someone who can enter into a state of possession, to propose that the tulku is, by virtue of his or her reincarnated status, "possessed" is to ignore the basic notions supporting the concepts of possession and reincarnation. Reincarnation implies the continuation of a single mind-stream; possession suggests a second. Shaman and spirit are two distinct entities; the tulku line is one.[26] Similarly, the comparison between the shaman who identifies himself with a spirit and the lama who identifies himself with Mahākāla does not take into account that the identifications would arise from completely different premises within the shamanic and Buddhist traditions, and signify opposing ideologies. The shaman's statement of identity confirms his own reality and that of the spirit who speaks through him. The lama's statement signifies his realization of the ultimately empty and unreal nature of all phenomena, including self and deity. With regard to the relationship between Tibetan Buddhism and shamanism, Stablein makes the observation that "Vajrayāna Buddhism as practiced by the Tibetans offers us an example of how shamanism may have evolved from a preliterate to a literate stage of development."[27] However, the strong affiliations between Vajrayāna Buddhism and shamanism can be recognized without recourse to a theory that sees one as a development or adaptation of the other. At the dawn of Buddhism in Tibet, there were many competing religious orientations, and the development of a unique form of Buddhism in Tibet cannot be captured in a single evolutionary story. The rituals and self-transformation theories of Indian tantrism, distinguishable from "clerical" Buddhism as well as from any indigenous religions, were also present.[28] As Buddhism settled among the Tibetan people, it absorbed and transformed for its own soteriological purposes aspects of the shamanic tradition that were familiar to its Indian and tantric heritage. This acculturation process enriched the Buddhist tradition, generating new ideas and new forms of expression. In turn, it is not difficult to imagine that Buddhist views filtered into the folk practices of the people and generated new ideas that were used to further shamanic goals.[29]

The tantric tradition is set apart from shamanism by its yogic emphasis on what Matthew Kapstein terms "perfectabilism."[30] The Buddhist monk is one who ideally aims for moral perfection. Similarly, the Buddhist tantric yogi or adept aims for perfect realization. He is called a siddha, an accomplished, perfected, or completed one. The striving for perfection relates to a central concern of classical Indian religious thought: the concept of *mārga*, the "path" to liberation, perfect accomplishment of which is the religious goal. Regardless of similarities that may exist between Buddhist tantric siddhas and shamans, the emphasis on attaining to perfection of all kinds,[31] including perfect liberation from the suffering that ensues from ignorance and delusion, is a mark of the yogi that is not present in shamanism. The idea of exiting the world entirely, based on a mode of behavior in life, as a positive religious goal has not been shown to play a part in shamanic systems. Mumford's study of the relations between shamans and lamas shows that the Tibetan Buddhists of Gyasumdo distinguish themselves as spiritually superior to their shaman neighbors based on their perception of the shaman's lack of concern with merit and the goal of universal freedom from rebirth. The shamans in turn point to the hypocrisy of the Buddhists, remarking, "They say we are sinning by killing the animals, but after their fast they come to our village and buy the meat for food."[32] In such ways, the shamans point to the conflict in Buddhism between the practical orientations of lay life and the moral obligations of religious life—a struggle that Sherry Ortner describes in her study of the Sherpas as both manifested in, and mediated by, shamanistic rituals.[33]

In examining the Tibetan Buddhist worldview, various strands of influence emerge: the Buddhist goal of the cessation of suffering (*nirvāṇa*), the ancient Indian concepts of karma and rebirth, tantric rituals of self-transformation, and elements of the shamanic complex that predated Buddhism. The distinctive religious dynamic of Tibet emerged from the particular way in which the shamanic elements were incorporated into the elite religion of the monks and from the way in which the popular folk religion absorbed the teachings of Buddhism. In his study of Tibetan societies, Samuel organizes these influences into three types of overlapping religious activity found among Tibetans: the "Bodhi Orientation," activity oriented toward the ultimate goal of enlightenment; the "Karma Orientation," activity aimed at securing a good rebirth; and the "Pragmatic Orientation," activity specifically directed toward obtaining good fortune or defending against misfortune in this life.[34] These three sum up the Tibetan religious worldview in which Buddhist ethics and soteriological aims, tantric rituals, and shamanic methods of dealing with spirits have been inseparably interwoven. The following pages will examine the Tibetan approach to dream using Samuel's categories as a framework.

DREAM AND LIBERATION: THE BODHI ORIENTATION

Dreams exemplify the nature of the phenomenal world—fleeting, changeable, insubstantial, not ultimately valuable or reliable. At the same time, they are accorded a significant role in terms of prophecy and prognostication. However, it was not until the assimilation of Buddhism into Tibet that dreaming came to be regarded as a path to liberation. In Tibet, an entirely new approach to dream developed in the form of dream yoga. This method of dealing with dream is concerned neither with the prophetic aspect nor with the philosophic. It is a method of conscious engagement with the dream process such that the dreamer comes to exercise power over the dream perceptions, transforming them at will. The dreamer then learns to recognize all mental states, including his perceptions of the passage from life to death, as dreamlike and insubstantial, and subject to transformation. This practice is part of a set of six yogic practices most closely linked with the teachings of the Indian yogin Tilopā, his student Nāropa, and, concerning dream, especially with Nāropa's wife, Niguma.[35] Tilopā tells his student, "Look into the mirror of your mind, the place of dreams, the mysterious home of the dakini [female wisdom guide for tantric practitioners]."[36]

The story of the meeting between the yogini Niguma and her student Khyung-po Naljor is couched in the language of a dream/vision in which she initiates him into the practice of dream yoga. In his vision, Khyung-po is spirited away to a golden mountain where he participates in the dakini's feast and witnesses their dancing. Not knowing where he is, Khyung-po questions Niguma: "Where in India is such a mountain as this to be found, or is this too the dakini's magical creation?" The answer is her quintessential instruction on the fruits of dream yoga through which the practitioner comes to realize the insubstantial nature not merely of thoughts but of all that is taken to be real—even buddhahood:

> These varied thoughts, full of passion and hate,
> Stirring samsāra's ocean,
> Are insubstantial; when you realize that
> All's a golden isle, my son.
> As for apparitional dharmas,
> Like apparition contemplate them to be;
> You'll become an apparitional buddha—
> By the power of devotion it will come to be.

> And she added, "Now I will bless you. Grasp your dreams!" Having grasped my dreams, I journeyed to the land of gods and demigods, where a gigantic demigod just swallowed me whole. The *ḍākinī* appeared in space and said, "Do not try to wake up, my son." It was at that time that she taught me the six doctrines in their entirety.[37]

It is not difficult to see in this Buddhist account of a yogi's travel in a dream state similarities with shamanic soul travel to other worlds, stories of the shaman's ability to transform himself into various animals or other phenomena, or the shamanic idea of dreams and visions as the activity of the soul separated from the body. In a discussion on dream yoga, the Fourteenth Dalai Lama explains that in the Vajrayāna understanding, the ability to travel in dream is the result of a "special dream state" in which the person has created a "special dream body" that is capable of dissociation from the gross physical body. He further notes a difference between ordinary dreams that take place "within the body" and those that constitute the external activity of the subtle or dream body:[38] "The subtle self does not manifest in all dreams, only in a special dream in which one has a special dream body that separates from the gross body. That's one occasion when the subtle body and the subtle self manifest. Another occasion is during the *bardo* or intermediate period between two lives."[39]

One can recognize in these comments the Upaniṣadic theme of the self that creates the dreamworld out of the materials of this world, as well as the shamanic view of a separable dream soul and all the amazing things it can do. The goal of dream yoga, however, is not attained by perfecting the supernormal abilities of the dream body. The culmination of the practice is liberation and the cessation of dreams. The practitioner is enjoined to abandon all conceptualization and enter into "blissful radiance united with non-conceptual thought."[40] The eighteenth-century Nyingmapa yogi Shabkar describes what could be called a visionary soteriology—the liberating experience of the basis of all apparitions, beyond waking and dream states:

> Completely at rest in the natural state of mind—empty, luminous, without taking things as real—I sang this song . . .
>
> Without a center, without a border,
> The luminous expanse of awareness that encompasses all—
> This vivid, bright vastness:
> Natural, primordial presence.
>
> Without an inside, without an outside,
> Awareness arisen of itself, wide as the sky . . .
>
> Within that birthless, wide-open expanse of space,
> Phenomena appear—like rainbows, utterly transparent.
> Pure and impure realms, Buddhas and sentient beings,
> Are seen, brilliant and distinct.
>
> Having seen this for myself, I was ready to sit among the glorious sky-like yogins.[41]

Tantric practitioners are instructed to regard the universe of ordinary waking reality as a dream or illusion. Appearances pose no obstacle to those who have realized and penetrated the utterly illusory, insubstantial, and dreamlike nature of self and other. This view is the basis for the story, well-known in Tibetan circles, of the seventh-century philosopher Candrakīrti milking a painted cow to feed his monks. A similar understanding prevails in the following excerpt from the *Mahāratnakūta Sūtra* where the Buddha explains to the magician Bhadra his ability to miraculously multiply himself:

> If one knows that all dharmas [constituents of existence]
> Are like magic and illusions,
> He is able to produce magically
> The bodies of ten billion Buddhas
> And deliver beings in millions of lands,
> Just as by [ordinary] magic Bhadra can conjure up
> Various things out of nothing.[42]

According to a Mahāyāna perspective, the Buddhist yogi's ability to perform magical deeds is derived, not from being versed in the arts of magic, but from his knowledge and realization of the empty and illusory nature of all things. In the development of dream yoga as a path to liberation, the Tibetan Buddhist tradition expands on relationships hinted at in Indian Buddhism—relationships between dream consciousness and supernormal powers, between the illusory nature of things and the ultimate state of enlightenment, between deception and truth.

DREAMING AND DYING: THE KARMA ORIENTATION

In Samuel's framework, the Karma Orientation of Tibetan religious activity is concerned with death and rebirth, and the accumulation of merit that ensures both good fortune and a good future life. The entire process of death and rebirth is presented as analogous to sleeping, dreaming, and waking. According to the analysis set out in the texts of the *Bardo Thödol* (Tib. *bar do thos sgrol*), a dying person experiences very distinct stages of dissolution, during which gross physical functions cease and mental functions subside until only the most subtle state of pure awareness remains—the "clear light," which, in this context, is called the clear light of death. If the dying person at that point falls into complete unconsciousness and does not experience the clear light awareness as the true nature of mind—in other words, if consciousness does not recognize itself—then the process continues, karmic forces take over, and the person reawakens to experience the dreamlike hallucinations of an intermediate *bardo* state between death and rebirth. Finally, the person once again "falls asleep" into the womb and "awakens" to another life in another form.[43]

The states and stages of death and rebirth correspond to the process by which consciousness enters and leaves meditative states, as well as to the transitions of awareness from waking to sleeping to dreaming, and finally to reawakening. Therefore, one can also experience the luminous mind that manifests at the end of the falling-asleep process just before consciousness "awakes" into the dream state. This is called the clear light of sleep. As in death, if it is not recognized then, consciousness enters into a hallucinatory dream state driven by karma.

In the Tibetan popular imagination, the homologies of death, sleep, dream, and meditation, and their relationship to the merit/demerit system of karma, are most vividly captured in the activity of the *delok* (Tib. *das log*). The intermediate bardo world is accessible not only by those who are destined for rebirth, but also by certain exceptional people who have the ability to enter into states in which they can travel through the bardo. Such a person is known as a delok, one who returns from the dead. Delok narratives are popular accounts that describe a sleeplike, trancelike, deathlike condition during which the person experiences dramatic visionary encounters with the beings traversing the bardo and with the Lord of Death, who pronounces the destiny of each according to his or her own good and bad actions in life. The delok sees directly the joyous results of good actions and the anguish of those whose negativity has brought them to suffering and despair; she returns to life with an emotional message underscoring the Buddhist doctrine on karma and rebirth. In Françoise Pommeret's analysis of delok narratives,[44] she notes that the delok herself is usually one who is intensely religious, and therefore virtuous, a quality that, as we have seen, in Buddhist dream theory confirms the dream or vision as significant and true. It is worth noting that the notion that knowledge gained in dreams or visions is as valid as that gained from waking experience relates to the Buddhist emphasis on dream as direct perception—an attitude familiar to a shamanic worldview.[45]

It is thought that for an ordinary person the various stages of both the falling-asleep process and the dying process pass by extremely rapidly without any knowledge or recognition on the part of the person. However, the one who learns to sleep and dream mindfully, experiencing the luminosity of sleep, is also practising to die with awareness, able to recognize the clear light when it arises at the moment of death. This is the task of the yogi who practices the yogas of dream and sleep.[46] In Tibetan dream yoga the purification of negative karma and accumulation of merit is presented as a crucial element in determining one's success. Tsongkhapa, the fourteenth-century founder of the Gelug school, emphasizes that unless one first trains in both ordinary and extraordinary practices of purification, and keeps all precepts, engaging in any of Nāropa's yogas will lead not merely to failure but to spiritual disaster for both teacher and student.[47] Buddhist tradition holds that actions in a dream are generally involuntary and, therefore, do not have the strength to create karmic results. However, dream actions do reflect and foster habitual tendencies that bear on one's future, hence the injunctions to maintain a virtuous mind when engaging in the dream yoga practice, which has liberation as its goal. By penetrating the nature of what one *takes* to be dream, one penetrates the nature of what one *takes* to be reality. Nāropa's biography states,

> Both Sutras and Mantra-texts assert that the whole of entitative reality is like a dream. By heeding this, the mistaken belief in a Pure Ego is undermined. Moreover, in dreamless sleep one treads the path of death; in dream one passes through the intermediate world between death and (re)birth; and when one awakens one is in the world of concrete patterns. Therefore for undermining the belief in the exclusive reality of what appears during daytime, the fact of dreaming is the most excellent index from among the twelve similes as to the illusory-hallucinatory nature of our world.[48]

Dream, as has always been maintained in Buddhism, is the best simile or metaphor for the fleeting, impermanent, illusory nature of ordinary reality. Life is a dream. In the Tibetan development of dream yoga, however, the metaphor becomes the method by which one can directly experience its meaning. This quality sets dream apart in Nāropa's twelve similes of ordinary reality.

DREAM AND DIVINATION: THE PRAGMATIC ORIENTATION

In the practical day-to-day life of a shamanic culture, the rituals of divination are inextricably linked with the rituals of healing and protection. In her analysis of Siberian and Inner Asian shamanic séances, Anna-Leena Siikala notes that the séance frequently ends with a period of interaction between the shaman and the audience when the shaman is requested to do a divination to answer personal questions and gives further instructions on propitiations to be made.[49] Anisimov describes the procedure at the end of an Evenk séance: "The shaman, at the request of those present, began to divine by means of his rattle and a reindeer scapula. The clansmen, in turn, set forth their desires. The shaman threw his rattle up in the air and, from the way it fell, determined whether or not the desire would be fulfilled. Then he took the shoulder blade of the sacrificed reindeer, laid hot coals on it, blew on them, and predicted according to the direction and character of the cracks in the bone what awaited his clansmen in the future."[50] Divination is also an inseparable part of traditional Tibetan life, and although there are some laypeople who would be recognized as having expertise in this area, Buddhist lamas are frequently the ones called upon to perform divination. Buddhist doctrine does not specifically prohibit divination, but a superstitious concern for lucky and unlucky signs or omens, and attachment to rites and rituals for their own sake, was discouraged among Buddhist monastics. Those who engaged in such practices were generally non-Buddhist ritual specialists regarded by the saṅgha as spiritually inferior to the monks and nuns, who were expected to keep themselves apart from such worldly concerns. The involvement of Buddhist monks and lamas in practices of divination is, therefore, not without tension. The four Tibetan lamas who contributed to Robert Ekvall's early study *Religious Observances in Tibet* confirm such tensions. He states:

> There were much discussion and some disagreement among all four lama collaborators as to what was permissible or proper and what was not. They cited lamas who would divine even for projects of violence and killing, as in the case of blood-feud reprisals, and others who would divine only when the proposed action could be shown to lead to increased religious observance. But it was generally agreed that a lama was under considerable pressure, both from his own sense of obligation and from public opinion, to divine for anyone who requested it.[51]

Regardless of the insecure status of divination within Buddhism, the consensus that such requests should be fulfilled is borne out by its continuing practice in Tibetan Buddhism. In my own research, a Nyingmapa Khenpo commented that on being sent to teach in the West, the instructions from his abbot were that he should fulfill all that was requested of him, even to perform divination, although he was previously quite unfamiliar with such practices.[52]

Within the Tibetan corpus of religious observances such as prostrations, circumambulation, and making offerings, divination occupies an ambiguous and conflicted position. In his study, Ekvall notes the wide divergence of opinion about divination among Tibetan Buddhist authorities.[53] He outlines the following range of practices subsumed under the general heading of "divination." Prognostications can be made by means of rosary beads, dice, arrows, bootstraps, drums, stones (skipping them over a lake or throwing them), pebbles, animal scapulas, religious books, butter-lamps, animal entrails, astrology, songs, lots that are cast, clairvoyant pronouncements, omens that are interpreted, manner of breathing, smoke, phrases, the cries of living creatures (especially ravens and crows), movement of the eyes, humming in the ears, sneezing, pronouncements by oracles and the god-possessed, and dreams.[54] Of this great variety, which is not exhaustive but representative, there are many types—for example, divination performed by means of the drum, scapulas, entrails of animals, the arrow, and dream—that appear in the shamanic complexes of related cultures of Central Asia and Siberia. Within the context of Tibetan Buddhism, however, practices such as clairvoyant perception and dream interpretation are more sanctioned than divination by scapulas, drums, or entrails, which is identified with specifically shamanic systems.

According to the lamas questioned by Ekvall, a dream sign is "the most trustworthy of all the observances and gives the most exact answers.[55] Such a statement continues to remain valid for Tibetan Buddhist authorities, as can be seen in the role that dreams have played in the controversial decision made by the Fourteenth Dalai Lama to ban the worship of a certain contentious spirit called Dorje Shugden.[56] The Dalai Lama reported a series of dreams beginning from the time that he first came into direct contact with the spirit through the mediumship of the state oracle. At that time, he had a very auspicious dream of his teacher dressed in yellow robes pouring out scoops of clarified butter with a golden ladle and surrounded by yellow flowers; however, the dream included the presence of many yaks, a symbol of communal discord. After meditation and prayer on the subject, the Dalai Lama decided to do a divination. He recounts that he questioned a senior and much respected master who was unaware as to the nature of his divination. He asked, "What do you think about my divination—will it be very reliable or not?" The old master answered, "Generally the Dalai Lama's divination should be very reliable, particularly this time, because the preparation including meditation and prayer has been carried out with so much care." With this confidence, the Dalai Lama presented three options for divination: (1) continue the worship, (2) continue, but secretly, (3) immediately stop. The divination fell on number three, and the Dalai Lama stopped his personal worship of the spirit from that day forward. Subsequently, many other dreams indicated to the Dalai Lama that problems of spiritual dissension and discord are associated with this spirit, including one in which the Dalai Lama wrestled with a huge four-armed Mahākāla, a deity associated with Shugden. The Dalai Lama won this battle, breaking two of the four arms of the figure. In another dream, Shugden appears as a small boy beside his bed holding the Dalai Lama's right hand, but the true nature of the boy is revealed when his nails transform into claws. Then, in the dream, visualizing himself as the deity Hayagriva, the Dalai Lama turns the boy into a small dog and swallows him. Finally, after he extended a public ban on the worship of this spirit, the Dalai Lama's tutor appeared to him in a dream, bathed in light, and pronounced his endorsement of the restriction. The Dalai Lama's decision, then, regarding a practical affair of worship affecting the entire Tibetan Buddhist community was definitively influenced and supported by prognostication through dream. However, the most telling aspect of the divination is that its validity, as pronounced by the old master, rests squarely on the virtuous intentions of the Dalai Lama. Following time-honored Buddhist tradition, the dream is trustworthy due to the merit of the dreamer; and from a Buddhist perspective, it is the emphasis on this factor that sets it apart from shamanic forms of divination.

BUDDHIST DISTINCTIONS BETWEEN LAMA AND SHAMAN

Divination, whether shamanic or Buddhist, belongs to the kind of religious activity that generally focuses on questions of prosperity, health, or peace of mind for a particular person or group—where to find a lost son or a lost cow, how to ensure that the rain falls in the rainy season and the sun shines when it should, how to defend against the dangers of the unseen spirit world, and how to prevent premature death. These are the pragmatic concerns that are the business of religious specialists in shamanic cultures around the world. In Tibet, they constitute what Samuel calls the "folk religion." However, as he points out, in contrast with Theravāda communities where "magical and shamanic operations [form] an only partially acknowledged fringe to Buddhist practice, in Tibet they are an integral and fully recognized part of it."[57] Herein lies a major source of tension between Buddhism and the shamanic presence in Tibetan culture. Where the shamanic ritualists are kept distinct, as in Theravāda countries, the spiritual hierarchy according to which Buddhist monks and the Buddhist soteriological way are uppermost can be easily perceived and maintained. In Tibet, where the Buddhist lamas took over the role of shamans as ritual experts engaged in prolonging life, defeating demons, and guiding the spirits of the dead, it would be important that these worldly activities not demean or devalue the superior aim of Buddhist practice. The lama is expected by the community to exhibit his mastery over supernatural forces. At the same time, however, he must take care not to be identified simply as an accomplished shaman. The validation for his power must be based on Buddhist ethical and soteriological concerns; otherwise, there is no basis for claiming spiritual superiority. This concern is evident in one of the most widely revered texts of Tibetan Buddhism, *Words of My Perfect Teacher*, written in the nineteenth century by Patrul Rinpoché. Throughout the text, he castigates those who perform the rituals without any true understanding. Here is what he has to say about their methods: "For example, when they practice Chö for a sick person, they work themselves into a furious display of rage, staring with hate-filled eyes as large as saucers, clenching their fists, biting their lower lips, lashing out with blows and grabbing the invalid so hard that they tear the clothes off his back. They call this subduing the spirits, but to practice Dharma like that is totally mistaken."[58] He is not impressed either with tantric or shamanlike supernormal powers: "Even someone who can fly like a bird, travel under the earth like a mouse, pass through rocks unimpeded, leave imprints of his hands and feet on rocks, someone who has unlimited clairvoyance and can perform all kinds of miracles—if such a person has no bodhichitta [mind of compassion], he can only be a tirthika [non-Buddhist] or possessed by some powerful demon."[59] For Patrul Rinpoché, the true Buddhist practitioner is set apart from other wonder workers by virtue of *bodhicitta*, the bodhi mind that is oriented toward the ultimate soteriological goal of Buddhahood; this was also Milarepa's explanation for his defeat of the Bön-po magician. Their attitudes belong to a well-established Buddhist tradition that distinguishes between the supernormal powers of a buddha and the magic of illusionists.

While it is argued that lamas in Tibet function as shamans by means of the techniques and practices of Vajrayāna Buddhism,[60] an impassable divide separates the activity of a qualified lama from that of other shamanlike figures. Patrul Rinpoché writes:

> Nowadays householders, announcing that they are going to protect themselves and their flocks from disease for the year, call in some lamas and their disciples—none of whom have received the necessary empowerment or oral transmission, nor practiced the basic recitation—to open up the mandala of some wrathful deity. Without going through the generation and perfection phases, they goggle with eyes like saucers and whip themselves into an overwhelming fury directed at an effigy made of dough. . . . Practices of this sort poison the Secret Mantrayana and transform it into the practices of the Bönpos.[61]

What is at issue here is not the ritual but the qualifications of the so-called lamas. The practitioners are said to be devoid of either outer or inner authenticity. They have not received the initiation into the mandala and, therefore, have no authority to perform the ritual, nor has the inner purification necessary for the efficacy of the ritual been performed.

In response to the question, "How is a lama different from a shaman?" one contemporary Tibetan lama commented that the difference lay in the source of refuge; the shaman relies on worldly deities, whereas the lama takes refuge in the Triple Gem. For another, the difference lay in the lama's compassion. The example given was that if a lama and a shaman both have the power to kill a bird by magic, the lama has the further power, through his immeasurable compassion, to revive the dead bird or to liberate its consciousness. Although Buddhist authorities uphold the difference between shaman and lama, there are instances where the boundary seems so thin as to be nonexistent. For example, Michael Aris comments that the great Bhutanese miracle worker Pemalingpa (1450–1521) should perhaps be thought of as a "Buddhist shaman" rather than as a "Buddhist saint." "Pemalingpa . . . never seems to have spent any time meditating, let alone studying . . . the word "compassion" scarcely forms part of his vocabulary, appearing no more than two or three times in the whole of his autobiography. Nor does he ever voice any concern for issues of common morality. . . . Instead what we find is a constant and heavy insistence on the strength of his supernatural powers."[62] Pemalingpa's numerous recorded dream journeys and trances are replete with many shamanic themes. His autobiography reveals that his visions and ability to receive instruction and guidance from spirit guides began with sickness and periods of unconsciousness. His trancelike experiences are described in language that suggests a state of possession: "a swirling, darkening, burning, inebriated, uncontrollable condition."[63] Other connections with Central Asian shamanic traditions include the dances taught to Pemalingpa in his dreams, where the dancers appear as animal spirits, as well as his reputation for controlling the weather. Regardless of such analysis, however, Pemalingpa considered himself to be firmly within the framework of the Buddhist tradition, as his devotees have up to the present day.

The ancient antagonism between Buddhist lamas and other shamanlike figures is reflected in the life story of one of Tibet's most famous twentieth-century weather controllers, Ngagpa Yeshe Dorje. In 1959, having fled Tibet, he spent nine years in Darjeeling carrying out the rituals of making and stopping rain and hail. During that time, he tells of the jealousy that he aroused in the local ritualists of Darjeeling, who were, in his words, "uneasy that a Tibetan lama was doing what they should have been doing." He describes the ritual of a local non-Buddhist practitioner:

> The priest was half naked, sitting on the ground. His wife was also almost naked. On one side of her head her hair was braided; on the other, her hair hung loose. Their faces were painted red on one side and black on the other.
>
> The woman approached her husband carrying a rooster and a knife in her hands. While she moved around him, the priest continued performing rituals, writhing on the ground and motioning. The priest had a fire burning in front of him. After shouting and hooting for a while, she cut the rooster and killed it. She then drank some blood and offered some to the priest. This is how they performed the hail rites.[64]

Yeshe Dorje considered this to be a "bizarre ritual," but he acknowledged that it was a big success and blamed his subsequent poor health on the terrible climate that ensued. In competition with this same local priest, and angered at the situation, Yeshe Dorje revealed his power. He says,

> One day, in a sudden fury, I decided to so something. I lifted up my *shabten* [ritual worship] cup and, evoking the deities, called out the name of this priest and said, "You want this: you have it!" I visualized throwing the cup to the priest. Sadly, there was a thunder and hailstorm a few moments later. Heavy hail fell near the house of the priest. His wife lay unconscious, in shock for several hours, due to the surprise of the storm. There was loud thunder and lightning, as if pieces of meteorites were landing. The priest's house was flooded, carrying out his belongings, while nothing happened to the other houses.[65]

In such ways, Tibetan Buddhist practitioners, past and present, show themselves proficient in shamanic power while maintaining important distinctions between themselves and other ritual specialists.

SHAMANISM AND SOTERIOLOGY

Since the spiritual goal of Buddhism is liberation or salvation from saṃsāra, the wheel of death and rebirth, it is important for our comparison to consider how, or if, such a concept could fit into an understanding of shamanism. In defining soteriology, Ninian Smart states: "The implication of the idea is that human beings are in some kind of unfortunate condition and may achieve an ultimately good state either by their own efforts or through the intervention of some divine power."[66] This definition ties the concept of salvation to the human condition (characterized as unfortunate) and the utter transcendence of that misery (characterized as "ultimately good"). Willard Oxtoby notes three further aspects that inform the traditional Christian view of salvation: victory over death, victory over sin and evil, and victory over purposelessness.[67] These three aspects relate to the Christian emphasis on resurrection, the final defeat of Satan, and the ultimate goal of human life.

Scholars who apply this concept of soteriology to shamanic complexes often interpret salvation according to Christian themes of resurrection and victory over death and evil. For example, with regard to tribal religions Smart says, "In small-scale societies the figure of the shaman is often important in serving as the expert who provides healing and reenacts the death and resurrection of the person who has experienced evil."[68] Jonathan Smith, however, questions whether soteriological patterns must rely on the theme of triumph over death. He proposes a basic dichotomy of worldviews, between the "locative," and the "utopian." The locative refers to those traditions or currents in a tradition that emphasize one's place in the world, the delineation of boundaries, and the labor of maintaining the fragile balance of the cosmos. The utopian vision of the world stresses the value of no place, the breaking of all boundaries and limits.[69] According to Smith, for locative traditions, to return from the dead is not a sign of salvation: "What is soteriological is for the dead to remain dead. If beings from the realm of the dead walk among the living, they are the objects of rituals of relocation, not celebration."[70] Yet, even in this instance, the use of the word "soteriological" still implies the idea of ultimate good, and to speak of ultimate good from a shamanic perspective can be misleading in light of the shamanic tendency to accord evil its place in the cosmos.

The concept of salvation in shamanism has also been interpreted in terms of themes such as the vision quest. In his study of the encounter between the Tibetan yogi Khyung-po and the yogini Niguma, Kapstein identifies four types of soteriological themes in the story: the soteriology of the shamanic vision quest, of the guru's grace, of yogic perfection, and of Buddhist insight.[71] The latter three all deal with salvation as defined by Smart—the utter transcendence of the unfortunate human condition—accomplished by means of devotion to the guru, the practice of yoga, or insight arising from meditation practice, respectively. The soteriology of the shamanic vision quest, however, is based on Kapstein's recognition of certain shamanic themes in the Tibetan story. He states: "[The] superabundance [of shamanic motifs] in the culminating moments of a pilgrim's quest must be seen above all as authenticating the hero's attainment of a shaman's salvation, through power won from a woman during a dream-flight on a magical mountain of gold."[72] Here, the shaman's salvation is related to the successful completion of, and the power gained from, the vision quest. Yet, it would be important to note that the completion of the vision quest and the attainment of power in a shamanic tradition usually marks the *beginning* of the shaman's career as shaman, and not the *culmination* of the religious path, as the spiritual goal is understood in Buddhist and other salvation-oriented traditions. The idea of personal or universal salvation—in the sense of the ultimate victory of good over evil and the utter transcendence of worldly life as the goal of religious behavior—has not been shown to play any significant role in the ritual way of shamans. According to Jonathan Smith's typology, the salvation question is one that has been addressed from the perspective of either a locative or a utopian map of the cosmos. However, he notes that there are traditions that follow a third map. These traditions, he claims, "neither deny nor flee from disjunction, but allow the incongruous elements to stand. . . . They seek, rather, to play between the incongruities and to provide an occasion for thought."[73] In examining the ambiguities inherent in the Tibetan approach to dream, one can point to this tradition as an example of Smith's third type of map.

To summarize, the spread of Buddhism to Tibet met with resistance on the part of those who represented the old religion, but royal patronage of the monastic institution provided a strong base for Buddhist activity and eventual domination. Kapstein argues that among the factors contributing to the "conversion" of Tibet and the cultural dominance of Buddhism by the eleventh century were "the association of Buddhism with the old monarchy and its successors, its mastery of literacy and learning in this world and of one's destiny hereafter."[74] On an unofficial level, however, Buddhist yogis entered into competition with other ritualists with enthusiasm and did not hesitate to display their own brand of magic based on penetrating the nature of dream and illusion. Eventually, as Kapstein notes, a synthesis prevailed that saw spiritual accomplishment in terms of both ritual mastery and philosophic learning.[75] The use of dream as a method of divination and prognostication was familiar to pre-Buddhist Tibetans as it was to Indian Buddhism, and since the establishment of Buddhism in Tibet it has continued to be a prominent aspect of divination rituals right up to the present day. The development of dream yoga further established a new role for dream in Tibetan Buddhism in that dreaming became a practice entered into not merely for its prophetic value but as a method leading to liberation. The Tibetan synthesis of Buddhist and shamanic themes resulted in a new approach to salvation—one that plays between the place-orientation of shamanism and the freedom-from-place of the Buddhist nirvāṇa, between dream as reality and dream as empty of all reality.

Chapter 5

Tibetan Dream Theory, Imagery, and Interpretation

In Buddhist theory, dreams, like all ordinary mental processes, are associated with desire, hatred, and delusion (the three "poisons"). These negative influences are regarded as adventitious afflictions originating from and perpetuating the fundamental error of reifying the data of the senses into a universe of fixed entities. The task of the Buddhist meditator is to purify the mind of this tendency.

The relationship between dream, sense experience, and the three poisonous mental states is illustrated in a Mahāyāna sūtra entitled "The Meeting of the Father and the Son."[1] According to the classification outlined in this text, a dream of anointing one's body with a fragrant substance indicates a dominant mental state of desire manifesting through the sense of smell, a dream of seeing oneself fighting with an enemy indicates hatred manifesting through sight, a dream of hearing unintelligible words indicates delusion manifesting through hearing, and so forth. The organizing framework is based on the ancient Indian medical analysis of dreams interpreted according to the three humors—bile, wind, or phlegm—replaced in this text by the three mental poisons.[2] In a way, the medical metaphor persists, since the arrangement offers a method of diagnosis through dream by which the dominant mental affliction can be determined. Such a classification of dream offers a pragmatic tool through which the practitioner can come to understand the relationship between the sense faculties and mental states as well as directly perceive the effect of mental states on the personality by means of the dream images. This typology, however, relates only to the view of dream as produced by negative and deluded mental states. In Tibetan literature, dream is also presented as a method through which one can attain the highest goal of awakening from ignorance and delusion. In the practice of dream yoga, by actively engaging with the essenceless and conditioned ("empty") nature of dream images, the practitioner comes to realize and actualize the empty nature of the mental states that evoke them. These two aspects of dream, then—as a function of deluded mind and as a method of attaining liberation—underscore, on the one hand, that the mental afflictions, the poisons obstructing liberation, are to be abandoned or purified, and, on the other, that through direct realization of the illusory nature of the very same afflicted mental states, one can recognize all phenomena as mere appearance, empty of any ultimate substance or reality.

In order to explore the relationship between dreaming, delusion, and the goal of awakening, this chapter will examine dream as it relates to ordinary lay life and to religious practice. I will first outline general Tibetan dream theory and then present a selection of various types of dreams and their interpretations found in the oral and written culture of Tibet. Dreams to be examined are those recorded in medical texts, in folklore, and in biography, and those related by contemporary lay and monastic Tibetans. Finally, the Tibetan approach to dream will be considered in terms of the encounter between an indigenous shamanic perspective and the Buddhist soteriological worldview that was adopted by Tibet.

GENERAL DREAM THEORY

In Tibetan literature, dreams are interpreted according to their association with a complex set of contributing factors, including the time the dream occurred, the frequency of the dream, the health of the person, the mind state or daily life of the person, and the degree to which the mind of the person is dominated by the afflictive emotions. Further, dreams are considered significant only to the degree that they are dreams of clarity as opposed to confused "karmic" dreams that arise from psychological imprints or latent predispositions that are the results of previous intentions or actions. As explained by a renowned contemporary lama, Namkhai Norbu, dreams can be classified broadly into two types: those based on karmic traces (Tib. *bag chags*, "habitual tendencies created by karma"), and those based on the natural clarity of the mind.[3] Karmically influenced dreams are further subdivided into two types: those related to the body/mind condition of the dreamer, and those based on past experiences (whether in this life or in past lives). Dreams of clarity are also related to mental conditions and previous experience, but their quality is vivid and clear, indicating the attenuation of obscuring mental factors. As a Nyingmapa Khenpo commented, "[S]ome *bag chags* [habitual tendencies] are better than others."[4] Dreams of clarity are associated with a mind that is relaxed and relatively free of self-oriented emotional disturbance, and with the even flow of psychic energy through the body. Such dreams are said to occur in the early morning hours just before waking, when sleep is light, and are especially significant if recurring.

For purposes of dream interpretation, Tibetan works divide the night into three watches or periods: dreams influenced by karma take place in the first watch; dreams influenced by spirits in the second watch; and prophetic dreams in the third period.[5] Drawing from the writing of Longdol Lama (b. 1719), Norbu Chophel identifies the three periods as dusk, midnight, and dawn.[6] Dreams occurring before midnight are usually ignored as nothing more than confused recollections resulting from the leftover imprints of prior thoughts and actions, which themselves were based on a deluded apprehension of reality. To dwell on such dreams is merely to contribute to further confusion and delusion. Dreams occurring in the second period after midnight arise due to the influence of external spirits, gods, or other nonhuman beings. They can be taken as auguring events that could come to pass in the future, but cannot be entirely relied upon. Dreams occurring in the last period, just before waking, indicate the immediate future of the dreamer or of others. If they are frequent and clear, it is considered that the prediction will definitely come to pass. Norbu Chophel echoes Buddhaghosa and the earliest Buddhist theories of dream interpretation when he notes, "Only dreams during this period call for interpretation."[7] Tibetan dream theory follows the fourfold arrangement of the *Milindapañha*: dreams arising due to pathological disorders, previous experiences, spirit influences, and prophecy.

THEORY AND IMAGERY FROM MEDICAL TEXTS

In Tibetan medical theory, the mind/body organism is understood to exist as an interrelated complex of material, mental, and psychic dimensions ranging from the gross to the extremely subtle. The physical channels of energy in the body such as veins and arteries and their centers of conjunction are thought to have subtle counterparts.[8] The same word, *tsa* (Tib. *rtsa*), designates both the physical system of connecting muscles, tendons, and veins and the psychic flow of energy.[9] The various operations of the physical senses are also correlated with what Dr. Tenzin Tsephel (of the Tibetan Medical and Astrological Institute of the Dalai Lama, Byla Kuppe Branch Clinic) described as the "innermost sense or innermost consciousness" (Tib. *gnyid rnam shes pa*) situated in the center of energy at the heart. Because of this innermost sense, the subtle sensory experiences of dreams are displayed according to the flow and distribution of energy in the body.[10] The innermost consciousness is specifically related to the creative process of conceptualization through which sensory experience is transformed into the phenomena of dreams and waking reality.

The Four Tantras (*Gyu-Zhi*) is the collective name for the texts that constitute the fundamental work on which Tibetan medicine is based: the *Root Tantra*, the *Exegetical Tantra*, the *Instructional Tantra*, and the *Subsequent Tantra*.[11] The information below on the Tibetan medical view of dreams is drawn from chapter 7 of the *Exegetical Tantra*, translated by Dr. Yeshe Dhondhen and Jhampa Kelsang as *The Ambrosia Heart Tantra*.[12] In this review, I have consulted the summaries accompanying the illustrations of the *Blue Beryl*, a seventeenth-century commentary on the *Four Tantras*,[13] and I have taken into account the explanations of Dr. Tenzin Tsephel.[14]

The *Four Tantras* identifies seven classes of dreams: dreams that arise based on previous visual, auditory, or mental/emotional experiences; on aspirations made in prayer; on desires and other mental conceptions; on future possibilities (i.e., prognosticatory dreams); and on the humors or some ailment or imbalance of the humors.[15] Of these, as was the case in earlier Buddhist dream analysis, only prognosticatory dreams are of significance.[16] Recurring dreams that arise toward dawn and are clearly remembered upon awakening are examined for signs of recovery or deterioration. Other dreams can assist in the diagnosis of the illness.

Traditional Tibetan medical diagnosis requires the doctor to conduct a thoroughly holistic investigation encompassing all aspects of the patient's mental and physical behavior, condition, and external surroundings. The fundamental Buddhist principle of interdependent causality and conditionality[17] is the basis for an approach that takes into consideration the total cosmic, psychic, and physical environment. Such an understanding of the radical interconnectedness of all phenomena underlies the instructions in the medical tantras dealing with the auspicious or inauspicious signs encountered by the doctor on the road to the patient's house as well as those that are noticed in the immediate vicinity or entrance to the house. It is incumbent on the physician to take note of the auspices of decay or recovery that are contributing factors to the total situation in which diagnosis, assessment, and treatment of the patient's condition takes place. Table 3 lists some auspicious and inauspicious signs that would have a bearing on the patient's condition.

Significant dreams of the patient also function as omens of recovery or decay. Since the Tibetan medical texts follow the Indian classifi-

Table 3. Omens of Recovery or Decay from the *Blue Beryl* Treatise

Auspicious sights	*Inauspicious sights*
a basket full of grain, a vessel full of curd	at the house of the patient, grain or curd being carried out of the house
a jar full of ale	a broken clay jar
a burning butter-lamp, a burning fire	an expired butter-lamp
flowers being offered in a religous ceremony	An even-numbered gathering of animals like foxes and dogs
fried rice or jam	
an image of a deity	
a cow with a calf/a woman with a child	

Source: Gyurme Dorje and Fernand Meyer, ed. and trans., *Tibetan Medical Paintings: Illustrations to the "Blue Beryl" Treatise of Sangye Gyamtso (1653–1705)* (New York: Harry N. Abrams, 1992), 1:49.

cation of humors, dream images further indicate what humoral dispositions predominate in the patient. It is believed that a predominance of the wind (air) energy results in images that are black, green, or blue and sensations of flying or riding. Those in whom bile (fire) predominates perceive yellow and red images, and their dreamworld is sluggish and solid. Phlegmatic (water) temperaments perceive white images like snow, white flowers, white garments, or pearls and have dreams of physical contact and sensory pleasure. Dreams influenced by phlegm are said to occur late in the evening, those by bile in the second part of the night (midnight or later), and those by wind toward dawn.[18]

According to the *Blue Beryl*, dreams originate "when consciousness is carried in the directional movement of the energy channels and the wind during sleep."[19] Subtle energy moving upward toward the head results in images of ascension and flying that are cosmologically related to the god realms. Energy moving through the ophthalmic channels results in rapturous sensations, and energy moving downward in the body results in images of darkness, fear, and bestiality that are associated with the animal and hell realms. Sick people are said to have bad dreams precisely because the pathways of energy flow, especially the central channel at the heart, are blocked by imbalances in the various types of energy circulating in the body.

As Table 4 indicates, there is a wide range of dream images, some more understandable than others, listed in the *Blue Beryl* that

Table 4. Dreams Portending Death or Recovery from the *Blue Beryl* Treatise

Dreams portending serious illness or death	*Dreams portending recovery*
riding a cat, a monkey, a tiger, a fox, a human corpse	riding a lion, elephant, horse, or bull
riding naked on a buffalo, horse, pig or a camel	wearing white garments
a thornbush sprouting from the center of the chest	a holy man or a famous person
a bush with a bird's nest growing from the crown of the head	a great conflagration like a forest fire
lotuses emerging from the heart	a pure lake
falling into an abyss	being smeared with blood
sleeping in a cemetery	a great buffalo (leader of the herd)
breaking one's skull	raising a Buddhist flag of silk or an umbrella or victory banner
being surrounded by tormented spirits, ravens, or villains	finding or receiving apricots, apples, or walnuts
having the skin peeled from one's limbs	climbing a mountain, the roof of a house, or a walnut tree
reentering the womb of one's mother	dreams of the gods, such as Brahmā, Indra, Varuna, or other sacred beings
being swept away by water	swimming across a river, traveling northeast
being swallowed by a giant fish	escaping from danger
sinking into a swamp	defeating an enemy
finding or receiving iron or gold or silver	being praised or worshipped by a deity or one's parents
losing at a business venture or in a quarrel	one's body being ablaze
being prosecuted for tax evasion	fainting and getting up again
taking a bride	
sitting naked	

Source: Gyurme Dorje and Fernand Meyer, ed. and trans., *Tibetan Medical Paintings: Illustrations to the "Blue Beryl" Treatise of Sangye Gyamtso (1653–1705)* (New York: Harry N. Abrams, 1992), 1:51.

indicate serious illness or, as the text says, that the patient has been "ensnared by the lasso of the Lord of Death."[20] Alternately, auspicious dreams foretell the return of health and longevity.

Still other types of dreams signify the presence of a particular disease. For example, dreams of drunken dancing or being carried off by a dead person are linked with epilepsy, a thorny plant or bamboo or palm tree growing from the heart indicates tumors, and receiving an oil massage or dreaming of lotuses growing from the heart mean leprosy.[21]

POPULAR DREAM IMAGES

Informal conversations with members of the older generation of Tibetans resident in one of the refugee camps of South India yielded the examples of auspicious and inauspicious dream symbols shown in table 5.[22] In general, Tibetans do not feel the need to have their dreams interpreted, as the shared symbolism is very clear. Only in cases of dreams where the symbolism is very enigmatic or the dreams indicate a continued decrease in *lung-ta* (personal luck/fortune) would a person seek out ritual interpretation and assistance. The oral folk tradition also recognizes dreams relating to Dharma practice or the spiritual state of the dreamer. Dreams of saying many mantras, of seeing oneself in Buddhist robes or in the company of monks, as well as dreams of stūpas or other images related to the monastery or the deities would all be considered very auspicious, whether or not the person is currently engaged in any specific Dharma practice.

In the list provided by the elderly people of the Tibetan settlement at Camp Four in Bylakuppe, the folk images are notably different from the medical textual tradition. They emphasize practical household concerns, food production, and festivities—in other words, the pragmatic concerns of a folk culture fed by local traditions.

Although ordinary Tibetans recognize many dream symbols, ritual dream interpretation is the province of experts, and the dream to be interpreted is not necessarily dreamed by the person requesting the interpretation. For example, Chophel reports that in order to determine the cause of an illness, a person would give a piece of upper-body clothing to a qualified lama, who would put it under his pillow and "invite a dream to come to him." The dream vision is said to appear in one, three, or five days, depending on the power of the spirit causing the illness.[23] In the Tibetan tradition, even the method of interpreting dreams can be given in a dream. One of the great seventeenth-century visionaries of the Nyingma school, Migyur Dorje, is credited with the account of a dream in which he receives instructions for examining and counteracting

Table 5. Dream Symbols from Lay Tibetans in Bylakuppe, Karnataka, India

Auspicious Dreams	*Inauspicious Dreams*
wearing fine clothes	ragged clothes
burning house	broken-down house
fruit	spoiled meat
lit candles or butter-lamps	candles or butter-lamps extinguished
finding or using needles	finding gold or silver and giving it away
barley—birth of a boy	upper teeth falling out—death of a male
wheat—birth of a girl	lower teeth falling out—death of a female
big guns—birth of a strong boy	big wind blowing the house or tent away
pure water	dirty water
dead body	being naked
lots of falling snow	owls and foxes
going uphill	going downhill
flying	riding naked on a mule
crops growing nicely	
wearing ornaments	
blowing on a conch shell	
holding a knife	
washing oneself	
gathering or loading wood	

negative dreams and omens. In the dream, a three-headed, six-armed wrathful form of Padmasambhava (the archetypal guru of the Nyingma school) appears and gives him these instructions:

> First, visualize yourself as Wrathful Guru. Second, bring to mind what you need to examine. Third, put frankincense (*spos-dkar*) in your mouth and accumulate this mantra. . . . Then remove the frankincense from your mouth. Fourth, hold one mouthful of barley in your mouth and chant this

> mantra . . . then remove the barley from your mouth. Fifth, place some earth in your mouth and chant this mantra . . . then remove the earth from your mouth. Then visualizing oneself as Wrathful Guru, examine the dream. Whoever the obstacle creators are, imagine that everything dissolves into light and then take that light into your mouth.[24]

In this dream, the deity, appearing in the dream, describes a ritual in which the practitioner, after waking from a dream, in his real-life meditation practice takes on a visionary form as the deity, and using actual substances of frankincense and barley examines his own dream for signs of auspiciousness or inauspiciousness; and as the deity, he is able to immediately counteract any negativity appearing in the dream. The complex interweaving of dream and waking worlds, noted in shamanic accounts, surely stands out in this narrative.

DREAM AND EVIDENCE OF SUCCESS IN RELIGIOUS PRACTICE

Dreams are an integral part of the omenology that traditionally helped to direct life among lay Tibetans. In the religious sphere, however, the role of dream, instead of diminishing, takes on an even greater significance than in ordinary life. One of the most important uses of dream for a religious practitioner is to gauge his or her success in the practice. On this, Stephan Beyer quotes the Master Sahajalalita: "What occur in one's dreams are signs of future practice: a beginner learns in his dream by the strength of the mantra whether or not he will succeed by reciting more."[25] Beyer continues, "Thus signs of success are to dream that the gurus of former times are pleased, that women wearing beautiful clothes prophesy and offer garlands and silk and the three white foods, that one wears beautiful white clothing and ornaments, that the sun and moon rise, that music plays, that one meets the deity's emblem or shrine or person, that one is liberated from terror, and so on. . . ."[26]

Another example of the importance of dreams in portending and gauging success in religious practice comes from one of Tibet's great female saints of the eleventh century, Machik Labdrön. An excerpt from her writings entitled "Categories of Dreams in the Course of the Night" states that those who engage in Dharma practice may have inauspicious dreams of falling off a cliff, climbing up or down a very steep incline, entering a narrow passage, seeing fearful sights, or going in frightening directions.[27] These disturbing dreams are explained as hindrances caused by one's own negative actions, which emerge when one embarks on the path to liberation. However, for a practitioner who is meditating intensively, dreams of finding scriptures, flying through the sky, climbing trees, being successful in debate, seeing beautiful gardens or flowering fruit trees, hearing the music of horns, conches, and drums, and carrying a sword or being beautifully dressed are all signs of progress. Beyond these, the signs of having actually accomplished the meditation practice are to dream of seeing a place or a nice house that one has never seen before, or to be offered fruits, flowers, or nice things to eat and drink by a beautiful boy or girl.[28] This classification emphasizes the correlation between the development of a practitioner's spiritual abilities and the particular dreams that mark the levels of achievement.

Dreams and visionary experiences are a particularly sought-after feature in Machik's tradition of Chöd, the practice of severing ego fixation by offering one's body as nourishment for demons and harmful spirits. Sarah Harding's masterful translation of *Machik's Complete Explanation* provides, in overwhelming detail, interpretations of the manifold dreams and visions that practioners of Chöd may experience. Such dreams can signify the appearance and activity of the various classes of spirits who appear, among numerous other manifestations, as black spiders and scorpions, white people with blue eyebrows and white hair, eight-year-old children with serpentine bodies, frog bodies with human heads and serpent tails, and children with high noses, sunken eyes, and half their hair bound in buns.[29] The text also lists the dreams that signify a practitioner's success in controlling the spirits, in binding them under oath to uphold the Dharma, in receiving mundane spiritual powers, and in expelling bad spirits and disease. Similarly, a great range of dreams are interpreted as evidence of success along the path to buddhahood; and again, great importance is given to the order in which the dreams appear, since they are thought to correspond to the order in which the stages of the path are achieved. Particular dreams signify successively the purification of mind, the blessing of the deity, attainment of the path of liberation, attainment of supreme spiritual powers, and the achievement of the goal; whereupon the entire dream structure that came before is demolished with the words "Uprisings, apparitions, evidence of success are just mind's labels—they never existed."[30]

GAINING PERMISSION OF THE DEITY

One of the most important roles of dream in the Vajrayāna Buddhism of Tibet relates to the notion of permission to engage in deity yoga. In tantric practice, one aims to actualize in oneself the enlightened and powerful nature of a deity through meditation on, and visualization of, the deity with the correct accompanying mantras. However, before the practitioner can carry out such a practice, he or she must receive permission or empowerment to do so from the guru by means of an initiation. More importantly, tantric texts state that for the initiation to be successful, there should be a sign of agreement or blessing from the deity, a sign that frequently comes in the form of an auspicious dream. The theme of permission and consensus with regard to the spirit world is familiar to shamanic worldviews, and its relationship to dream is, in the Tibetan context, comparable to the shaman's initiation that begins with the call of the spirits manifesting through dreams or visions. With reference to the preparation of a disciple for initiation, Mkhas-grub-rje's (1385–1438) survey, translated by Lessing and Wayman in *Fundamentals of the Buddhist Tantras*, states: "The sign of his mental purity must arise; and there must be the sign that the Initiation is not opposed by the deity. . . . Furthermore, if the permission (*anujñā*) of the gods has been received, one may enter into Initiation and the other acts of the *mandala* even if the [prescribed] amount of service is not completed. That very [permission] substitutes for the measure of service, because that [permission] is paramount."[31] Further, the connection with dream is clearly stated: "However, the one who has already done the service consisting in contemplation and muttering [the mantras], must for the performance of Initiation examine his dreams [and decide that] permission has been granted and that it is not opposed."[32]

These passages highlight the role of dream in relation to the permission that must be granted by the deity before the ritual can take place. Hence, the preparations for a formal tantric initation or empowerment ceremony, such as the grand public Kalachakra rituals regularly carried out by the Fourteenth Dalai Lama, include the distribution of sacred *kusha* grass so that the participants may sleep on it and examine their dreams on the first night before the empowerment. Dreams that would indicate the permission of the deity and the readiness of the disciple include dreams of the Triple Gem, of one's personal deity, bodhisattvas, mountains, elephants, waterfalls, or obtaining riches and clothing.[33] Good dreams and prognosticatory dreams also indicate spiritual success; conversely, bad dreams indicate the departure of the deity. With regard to success in ritual practice, the *Vairocanābhisambodhitantra* states:

> One should examine his dreams and assess them as auspicious when in dreams there occur monasteries, parks, superb buildings, the dome of a residence; a sword, wish-granting

> gem, umbrella, assorted flowers, good women dressed in white, pleasant relatives and children; books, Brahmins, Buddhas, Pratyekabuddhas, disciples of a Jina, eminent bodhisattvas; gain of fruit, seeing a crossing of lakes and oceans; from the sky auspicious entrancing words that mention the desired fruit as arising. And a wise person knows that their reverse is a bad dream.[34]

The emphasis on dreams as signs of spiritual progress or signs of permission and authentification of spiritual attainment is nowhere more prominent than in the numerous accounts of dreams and visionary experiences contained in the life stories of Tibet's great yogis and saints. One of the most prolific sources of dreams and visions is the *terma* (concealed treasure) tradition associated with the Nyingma school.[35] The eighth-century yogin Padmasambhava is said to have concealed various tantric teachings and ritual objects to be revealed at a later time by reincarnations of his spiritually adept disciples. Terma can be physical objects hidden in caves and rocks (earth terma) or teachings and instructions that appear in the mind (mind terma) of the treasure revealer (*tertön*). The instructions and prophecies leading to the discovery of the treasure are understood to arise spontaneously in pure visions during the waking state, in meditative experiences, or through dreams of clarity.[36] The dream instructions regarding the treasure to be revealed, like shamanic dream narratives, often break the boundaries of waking and sleeping, as for example the description recorded by the *tertön* Pemalingpa in his autobiography: "When I was staying at Kun zang trag, in a dream three women in Tibetan dress came to me and said, 'Padma Ling pa, wake up!' When I suddenly awakened, before I could think, they told me, 'In the lower part of this valley, to the east of Thar ling at a place called Cha trag, there is a rocky mountain known as Dor je trag. . . .' "[37] The account begins as a dream, but the sleeping Pemalingpa "awakens" to hear the words of the women. Thus, the narrative presents a moment in which dreams, waking visions, and ordinary waking reality interpenetrate one another. Similarly, from the biography of Terdaglingpa (1646–1714), comes the account of a dream in which a celestial dakini comes to his room and, removing her ring, places it in the cup beside his bed. In the morning he awakens to find a scroll in the cup with the instructions for finding a terma.[38]

To be recognized as a treasure revealer, however, one must also have been appointed and prophesied by Padmasambhava as such. This legitimization is also determined through the dreams and visionary experiences of the tertön. Janet Gyatso describes the process in her study of Jigme Lingpa's secret autobiographies, in which Jigme Lingpa (d. 1798) reports many dreams that he interprets to be signs that he is a tertön, and, therefore, that the teachings revealed to him in his visions are authentic terma.[39] The interpretation is not taken lightly, because Tibetan dream theory posits that most dreams are deceptive hallucinations influenced by external spirits or by one's own deluded mind-stream. As Gyatso points out, Jigme Lingpa struggles with self-doubt over his own visions. She states,

> The ones who display the most doubts are the discoverers themselves. . . . As would be expected, they do not indicate doubts about whether a discovery actually took place; rather they worry about the source of their revelation: did it really come from Padmasambhava? Thus does Jigme Lingpa record his fear that his visions might lack the requisite appointment, benediction, and prophecy of Padmasambhava and might have been blessed instead by gods and ghosts, or represent merely the "natural display-energy of clarified channels" or some other kind of "ordinary" meditative experience.[40]

The ambiguous provenance of dreams and visions are thus a source of spiritual anxiety to those who must rely on them.

THE QUESTION OF *TENDREL*

Underlying any kind of divination by means of dream, whether it signifies permission granted by the deity or the authenticity of a treasure revealer, is the Tibetan concept of *tendrel*—a word that is the contraction of a longer phrase[41] referring to the Buddhist doctrine of dependent origination (Skt. *pratītyāsamutpāda*), according to which all phenomena arise dependent on causes and conditions. *Tendrel* is also used to mean "sign," "omen," or "auspice." In Tibetan, then, the term is used both practically and philosophically. Practically, it refers to auspices and omens of all kinds that can be analyzed to determine the fortune or misfortune of a present or future condition. Philosophically, it refers to the most profound and pervasive of Buddhist principles—namely, the principle of dependent or interdependent origination, and by extension, the twelvefold manifestation of that principle in the cycle of rebirth and redeath, often depicted in paintings around the rim of the "Wheel of Life": old age and death arising dependent on birth, birth dependent on becoming, becoming dependent on attachment, and so on for craving, feeling, contact, the six sense spheres, name and form, consciousness, karmic formations, and ignorance. According to this system, the cessation of suffering, condensed in the condition of old age/death, is ultimately dependent on the cessation of ignorance.

The way in which the practical and philosophical meanings are integrated is important for understanding the nature of dream in Tibetan Buddhism. Samuel explains the word *tendrel,* in its sense of "omen" or "sign," as "connections that are not visible on the surface."[42] In this context, as a practical guide for assessing the future, he further comments: "Dream events, apparently chance combinations of words in conversation, the behavior of animals and other natural phenomena can all supply *tendrel.*"[43] Yet, exactly how are the cries of crows, the cracks in the shoulder blade of an animal, and the multitudes of Tibetan folk beliefs regarding signs and omens related to the central Buddhist teaching of cause and effect? This question was put to a contemporary Nyingma authority, who answered that the relationship rests on the all-pervasive nature of the principle of interdependent arising.[44] In other words, because the principle that all phenomena arise interconnectedly and interdependently applies without exception to every existent, linking them throughout time and space, what appears to be a random or chance occurrence can be analyzed in terms of its connections. One can understand *tendrel,* then, as experiences or events that indicate the principle of interdependence and interconnectivity at work. And, in Buddhist theory, just as a particular experience is not constituted merely of a given set of external conditions but is also influenced by the subjective mind, so the omen or the tendrel becomes what it is through the mental attention and attitude of the experiencer. Crows cry in the trees all day, but when the mind pays attention to a particular event, and a particular feeling arises because of it, then one can speak of tendrel. Further, although one can create auspicious conditions, signs that are to be examined or interpreted are understood to be "signs" precisely because they have occurred spontaneously and without contrivance.[45]

With reference to the philosophic understanding of tendrel, the twentieth-century master Dudjom Rinpoché explains that the twelve links of dependent origination (*tendrel*) have both outer and inner manifestations.[46] The outer tendrel refers to the external world of physical elements and the inner tendrel refers to sentient beings that manifest the twelvefold formula. Ekvall's interview with a Tibetan lama provides the following example of how the philosophic and the practical relate: a bowl of yogurt offered to someone represents an "outer" tendrel (external connection that can be read as an omen), and if that person recognizes it as a good omen, then by virtue of receiving it in that way he brings it into the "inner" tendrel (the twelvefold causation cycle) at the link of "feeling." This positive (or negative) feeling may then produce other tendrel in the future.[47] To give another example: the Nyingma yogi, Shabkar, records in his autobiography that during the night before taking the initiation of the deity Hayagriva, he dreams that his mother gives him a skull cup full of beer, which he drinks. When he reports his dream to the initiating lama, he is told, "This is a good dream. It indicates that you have a [karmic] connection that will enable you to accomplish all the guru's pith instructions."[48] It is not only the dream, but also the positive feeling generated by the lama's pronouncement that augurs well for Shabkar's future accomplishment.

In general, a good feeling indicates a good omen. The relation between feeling and dream interpretation is also recognized in shamanic cultures. In her discussion of the dream practices of the North American Dene, Marie-Françoise Guédon notes that their process of dream interpretation did not begin with questions relating to content but always with the question, "How do you feel now?"[49] Similarly, among the Tibetans, the explanations of Machik Labdrön refer to the feeling or mental state resulting from the dream experience: "In sum, dreaming of any beautiful form or tasty food, or pleasant conversation or meeting close friends or doing any good works whatsoever, and when upon awakening the mind is joyful and the heart is bounding with happiness, then surely happiness will be the result. (One will have) good fortune, long life, be free of disease and one's wealth will increase."[50] The passage above, however, relates to the practical world of health and prosperity. With regard to the religious life, dream interpretation is not so simple. The yogin Milarepa warns his student: "Some evil dreams appear as good— / [But only an expert] sees they presage ill."[51]

From the perspective of Tibetan medicine, dreams are accepted as part of a person's entire mental and physical continuum and can indicate past, present, and future states of health or illness. Folklore and popular traditions emphasize dream in its function as an omen or sign of future good or ill fortune. These approaches to dream do not present any particular contradictions, but the ambiguous nature of dream is of much greater significance for spiritual adepts such as yogis and tantric practioners than for the ordinary person.

DREAM AND THE ILLUSION OF ILLUSION

According to Tibetan Buddhist thought, dreams can be a vehicle for the display of a deluded mind, or they can be a vehicle for the transmission of authentic spiritual teachings and lead to the direct perception of the absolute true nature of mind. The tension inherent in this dichotomy is not merely a matter of true and false or significant versus insignificant dreams, nor can it be entirely understood in terms of elite versus popular views. The conflict relates to the Mahāyāna understanding that saṃsāra and nirvāṇa, suffering and salvation, are, ultimately, not separate realities; and further it relates to the tantric view that the only way to overcome the afflictive emotions is by means of those same afflictive emotions. The deceptive hallucinations of the dream state, *in themselves*, reveal the truth of existence to those who recognize appearances as the essenceless display of their own mental projections. In the words of the *Bardo Thödol*, "Recognition and liberation are simultaneous."[52] The dream is not other than the ultimately real, yet if one should confuse the dream with the real, then the cycle of birth and death is not broken.

According to Mahāyāna Buddhist belief, the nature of *all* phenomena, gross or subtle, ordinary or sublime, is like a dream—perceived by the senses, yet utterly unreal and insubstantial. At the outset of his autobiography, Jigme Lingpa characterizes all that is to follow as a "great lying projection." He quotes from a Perfection of Wisdom sūtra: "All phenomena are like a dream, Subhuti. If there were to be some phenomenon beyond the phenomenon of *nirvāṇa*, even that would be like a dream, like an illusion. Thus have I taught, Subhuti, all phenomena are imperfect, imputed. Although they don't exist, they appear, like a dream, like an illusion."[53] He continues, "If this is so, then even more delusive is the dream, whose apparitions, [the products of] residual propensities, are extremely hollow."[54] This denigration of dream in the process of presenting dream as profoundly valuable to spiritual life is common in the writings of Tibetan visionaries. A similar stance is taken by the Fifth Dalai Lama, who writes in the opening of his secret autobiography:

> "As if the illusions of *Saṃsāra* were not enough,
> this stupid mind of mine is further attracted
> to ultra-illusory visions. . . .
>
> Either due to the traces of karmic action left over from my previous existence which now reemerge or to a deception of the Lord of Illusion, I have had various visions which should never have occurred and which ought to be forgotten. But I being small-minded, talkative and unable to keep my fingers at rest, noted them down.[55]

Janet Gyatso makes the important point that although there is social pressure on the writer to appear self-effacing, the theme of deception and illusion is not merely superimposed for the sake of modesty.[56] The Tibetan Buddhist tradition regards the illusions of saṃsāra as subtle and far-reaching, requiring the utmost skill to penetrate. The following conversation between Milarepa and his student Gampopa presents the conflicting attitudes to dream in even stronger terms. Responding to the request of his student to explain whether his dreams are auspicious or not, Milarepa answers:

> My son you have learned the teaching . . .
> You have mastered and stabilized
> The good Samadhi. I have always thought
> That you were wondrous and outstanding.
>
> But now in your great enthusiasm,
> By your dreams you have been caught.
> Is this due to lack of understanding,
> Or merely a pretense? Have you
> Not read Sutras and many Tantras?
> Dreams are unreal and deceptive, as was taught
> By Buddha himself, in the final truth of Paramita.
> To collect, supply and study them
> Will bring little profit.
> So Buddha used dream as one of the eight parables
> To show the illusory nature of all beings.
> Surely you remember these injunctions?
> And yet, your dreams were marvellous—
> Wondrous omens foretelling things to come.
> I, the Yogi, have mastered the art of dreams,
> And will explain their magic to you.[57]

The philosophy that informs the statements above proposes that dreams, like waking life, are "appearances" that exist dependent on causes and conditions, and are ultimately empty of any independent or inherent reality; therefore, they are called illusions. However, as Gyatso argues, if the illusions of saṃsāra really exist, then there would be no way of awakening from them.[58] What is called "illusion" itself arises based on causes and conditions and is itself empty of any intrinsic reality. When this aspect (the empty nature of things) is fully understood and realized as inseparable from perception (the appearance of things), then all phenomena, including dreams, are, in Gyatso's eloquent phrase, "manifestations of enlightened awareness."[59]

As a yogi who has realized the empty nature of perceptions, Milarepa confirms his power over the apparent illusions of saṃsāra saying, "I am a yogi who has fully mastered this illusory body. With a full knowledge and direct realization of the essence of all dreams as such, I can, of course, interpret as well as transform them."[60] Here Milarepa takes on the shamanic role of the dream-master and interpreter, a role that had been validated long before by the Buddha, who is portrayed as correctly interpreting his own and others'dreams.[61] For the Buddhist, however, as noted above in the writing of Patrul Rinpoché, magic or ritual power is of no ultimate value without the liberating knowledge of the Dharma, hence Milarepa's reminder to Gampopa of the teachings of sūtra and tantra with regard to dream. He then enters into an extensive and detailed interpretation of Gampopa's twenty-four dreams. Milarepa ends the conversation by justifying his action in interpreting the dreams (necessary because Buddhist tradition generally held the practice of divination in low esteem), admonishing Gampopa against becoming attached to illusory dreams, and emphasizing the necessity of the requisite knowledge (such as possessed by the Buddha) to carry out dream interpretation:

> To prophesy by judging signs correctly
> Is a virtue allowed by the Dharma;
> But 'tis harmful to be attached
> And fond of dream interpretation,
> Thereby incurring ills and hindrances.
> Knowing that "dreams" are but illusions,
> You can bring them to the Path.
> How can you explain them
> Without thorough knowledge?
> Some evil dreams appear as good—
> [But only an expert] sees they presage ill;
> Only a master of the art
> Can recognize good dreams
> When they take on ominous forms.
> Do not, good priest, attach yourself
> To either good or evil signs![62]

Kapstein emphasizes the necessity in Tibetan soteriography for religious authority to be authenticated in both shamanic and Buddhist terms.[63] However, this is a tension-filled situation in the cultural dialogue between shamanism and Buddhism. From a shamanic perspective, the shaman's ability to work with the world of the spirits is measured, and his authenticity established, by his practical efficacy relative to the demands of his community or clients. For the Buddhist, expertise in delivering individual practical benefits must serve the greater goal of universal liberation. Mumford's study of the relations between Gurung and Tibetan villages in Nepal highlights the fact that the Ghyabrẽ shaman is willing to consciously modify his death rituals, substituting a bird for the traditional sheep sacrifice in response to a scathing denouncement of animal sacrifice by a visiting high lama.[64] In other words, with an eye to efficacy and practicality, the shaman is willing to entertain the possibility that blood sacrifice might have a negative effect on the deceased's ability to find the path to the ancestors. However, the lama, who upholds the Buddhist ethical system, would not be likely to entertain the reverse argument that "the lama's imagined substitutions are . . . mere symbolism which can never become the real offering required in valid gift exchange."[65] The flexibility and range of shamanic activity is a function of an open-ended pragmatic interest in what works; the lama's activity rests on the flexibility and range of the mind, but is circumscribed by a soteriological framework that has already established what works. Serinity Young concludes her discussion on the opposing views of dreaming in Buddhism with the thought that "Buddhism is comfortable with such contradictions."[66] Such a statement, however, rings more true for shamanism than for Buddhism. Shamanism, which promotes the value of balance and harmony, holds that contradictory forces in the world are individually necessary and that each occupies an integral place in the universe. Buddhist philosophy does not accept that positive and negative, truth and deception, are opposing powers to be maintained simultaneously. Nirvāṇa is described as the pacification of all negative states. According to Mahāyāna teaching, such contradictory concepts arise due to a mind that reifies perceptions, and like all conceptualizations, obscure the true nature of reality. For the lama, the ritual, dream, or vision, while true or valid in a practical, conventional sense, must at the same time be seen in a liberation-oriented way and, therefore, be denied any ultimate status or truth. There is, in effect, from the Buddhist perspective, no absolute contradiction, but there is tension—lest the practical use of dream displace or ignore the soteriological aim.

Ordinary people do not dwell much on the tensions related to dream, since, liberation being a long way off, there is no immediacy to the issue, but for the spiritual adept who aims for liberation now, in this life, urgent effort toward resolution is required. From its earliest days, Buddhist thought has distinguished between what is of concern to ordinary people and what is of concern to the one who aims for perfection. In a story from the Pāli canon, a forest spirit accuses a monk of stealing the scent of a lotus whose fragrance he inhales. The monk protests that he has not stolen anything, but the spirit advises him that for one who is committed to the path of purity, the least infraction of the precepts, what appears to others as small as the tip of a hair, should appear to him as large as a cloud.[67] Similarly, the dream narratives of Tibetan saints and yogis bear witness to their struggle to resolve the difference between the concept of dream as true prophecy and the integrity of insight into the deceptive quality of all mental states.

Whether one considers the homely themes related to Tibetan pastoral and agrarian life that appear in popular dream imagery, the traditional religious themes that characterize spiritual life, the strange and wonderful dream images of the medical tradition, or the esoteric practice of dream yoga, concern with dreams and their meaning is manifest in every area of Tibetan cultural life. The yogic, philosophic, medical, and popular traditions merge in archetypal figures such as Milarepa and Gampopa. Gampopa's dreams include popular auspicious imagery such as wearing beautiful clothes and ornaments; the medical imagery of colors (in his case, overwhelmingly white); the tantric imagery of the skull cup and animal pelt; and the religious imagery of a bodhisattva seated cross-legged on a lotus seat (see the appendix). Milarepa interprets all these dreams in terms of Gampopa's spiritual progress and eventual success in attaining the Buddhist soteriological goal. In Tibetan Buddhist religious practice, dreams take on the crucial role of providing assurance for a practitioner that he or she has the approval of and connection with the deity, without which no spiritual practice can be successful. This view is comparable to the shamanic understanding that the success of a shaman depends entirely on his or her direct connection to and relationship with the helper spirits, a relationship manifested in the shaman's dreams and visions. As we have seen, tensions over the role of dream within the Buddhist tradition involve internal factors present from its Indian beginnings, as well as external factors relating to the shamanic layer of Tibetan culture. With regard to the latter, Buddhist and shamanic perspectives agree on the interdependent nature of existence; they share an emphasis on homology and interrelatedness, which provides the conditions for resolution between a shamanic concern with harmony among the worlds and the Buddhist concern with liberation from all worlds.

Conclusion

Tibetan Buddhism regards dreams and visions as a primary vehicle for the attainment and transmission of spiritual knowledge, but without the orientation toward the Buddhist goal of liberation, they are merely deceptive appearances or illusions. This qualification does not apply in shamanism, which regards dream consciousness simply as an alternate modality of life, one that is especially familiar to the shaman in his role of mediator between various dimensions of reality. Further, in Buddhist dream interpretation, the moral character of the dreamer influences the positive or negative interpretation of the dream. Again, this is not a major factor in shamanism, where personal morality is of lesser import than matters relating to the balance of power that creates harmony or disharmony for the community and the universe. The main concern in a shamanic worldview is the capacity to access power. Does one have the ability to "dream"? In some shamanic traditions, almost all members of the community can act as shamans; among others, those who dream are set apart by their aptitude.

Tibetan approaches to dream reflect the encounter between a shamanic understanding of dream as grounded in the world of the senses and the interaction between human and spirit realms, and Buddhist teaching on the impermanent, essenceless nature of mind and phenomena. In this encounter, the Buddhist soteriological perspective is maintained partly by minimizing the importance of dreams. Despite that attitude, however, dreams as portents of the future or as a mode of communication between human and nonhuman beings are employed by Buddhist religious leaders to satisfy the practical needs of the community for spiritual guidance and ritual intervention.

The opportunity for harmony between shamanic and Buddhist worldviews can be found in the Tibetan appropriation of the core Buddhist teaching on cause and effect in the concept of tendrel. The equivalent Sanskrit term, *pratītyasamutpāda* (dependently arising together), emphasizes that all phenomena originate dependent on their unique causes and conditions. This principle manifests in a series of twelve interconnecting aspects that constitute the way in which the psychophysical person and the corresponding cosmic environment arise and continue. As Samuel points out, the latter emphasis on cosmic and personal interconnectedness is taken up in the Tibetan view of tendrel as "connections that are not visible on the surface."[1] The Tibetan interpretation, then, which accentuates the arising together aspect, the "co-incidence" of things, provides the opportunity for the technical translation of a key term in Buddhist philosophy to carry the mundane meaning of "omen" or "auspice." In other words, the basic Buddhist theory of dependent origination allows for an approach to the practical use of omens that does not do violence to fundamental assumptions of Buddhism. Nevertheless, there is a defense to be maintained against the degradation of the soteriological aim. This defense is apparent in the superior spiritual position that Buddhism claims against all forms of shamanism.

As Young has shown, dream narrative proliferated in Tibetan literature far beyond the Indian Buddhist material. Dreams related to mythic themes of conception and liberation continued to appear, but compared with the triumphal dreams of buddhas and bodhisattvas recorded in Mahāyāna texts, dream narratives in Tibetan biographies and autobiographies give the impression of recording the real-life concerns of spiritual aspirants as they struggle to distinguish truth from deception, mundane from supramundane, in their path to liberation. Given the importance of dream in the spiritual lives of Tibetan Buddhists, the purpose of this book has been to determine the significance of the contradictory attitudes toward dream present in Tibetan written and oral traditions—the view of dream as spiritually and materially significant alongside the view of dream as the illusory product of a deluded mind. The contradiction cannot be properly understood or any resolution proposed without taking into account the variety of attitudes and worldviews that inform Tibetan culture. The tensions evident in the Tibetan approach to dream reflect two forces that are themselves manifestations of more complex issues. The first force is the contradictory attitudes to dream that were already present in the Buddhism adopted by Tibet, attitudes that echo even more ancient ambivalencies inherited from the Indian Vedic and Upaniṣadic traditions. The second force is the response of the Buddhist tradition to the indigenous shamanic presence in Tibetan culture, especially in relation to the role of dreams and visions privileged by both shamanism and Buddhism as a means of religious authentification. Conflicting statements in Tibetan Buddhist literature toward dreams are, therefore, in part the inheritance of attitudes already established in Mahāyāna Indian Buddhist texts and, in part, a manifestation of the inevitable tensions arising out of the interface between two systems that rest on very different premises.

What can be gleaned of the indigenous religious worldview and behavior of the Tibetans indicates a strong affiliation with the beliefs and rituals of shamanism as this complex has been provisionally defined in chapter 1. The world and its contents, including the subjective self, are regarded as radically imbued with spirit and capable of intentional interaction. The idea of "spirit beings" that help or hinder one another is not limited to material or quasi-material entities such as stones or souls but can embrace any conceptualization whatever. If it has a name, it can manifest as friend or enemy; a disease, a song, a dream, or a thought can act, communicate, and contribute to the web of interrelationships that constitutes the universe. In this world of persons, dreams are regarded as a particularly effective medium for the interaction and communication between human beings and spirit beings. The shaman's calling is often instigated or confirmed by the spirits through specific dreams; as he learns to relate consciously to his trance and dream states, so he learns to consciously communicate with, and relate to, the spirits and the unseen dimension of all things.

From its Indian Buddhist background, Tibetan culture inherited an overall approach to dream that can be analyzed according to three perspectives: the psychophysical, the philosophical, and the ritual. The *psychophysical* perspective is based on the Indian understanding of mind and how it functions relative to sensory experience. Under this heading comes the view of dream as caused by sickness or the physical condition of the person, dreams influenced by past karma or the moral condition of the person, and dreams related either to negative mental states or to religious practice and liberation.

The *philosophical* perspective has two aspects. One is concerned with the view of dream as recollection (as opposed to dream as direct perception). Buddhist theory accepts dream as direct perception, and based on this understanding Mahāyāna texts proclaim that the accomplished meditator can directly encounter and receive teachings from the Buddhas in a dream. The other entails the Mahāyāna view of the world as mere appearance—compared with the absolute reality of the awakened state, the world of saṃsāra is entirely illusory. From this standpoint, dream, which vanishes upon awakening, is the most suitable metaphor for the illusory nature of all phenomena.

The *ritual* perspective regards dreams as signs and omens to be interpreted. Dream as signifying the activity of external agents such as gods and spirits would come under this heading, as would prognosticatory dreams. Dream as prophecy can be further analyzed into three types: portending worldly fortune or misfortune; disease or health; and spiritual progress. In each of these cases, the dream can signify a future condition or verify a present condition. As we have seen, dreams concerning spiritual progress relate to real-life situations of approval, initiation, and authentification of spiritual success, as well as to the mythic career of buddhas and bodhisattvas.

These three perspectives encompass the varied responses to dream present in the Indian Buddhist tradition as it was taken into Tibetan dream theory and practice. There was already a degree of tension associated with dream, since early Buddhist teaching tended away from an emphasis on the efficacy of ritual and tended toward a devaluation of worldly activity, comparing it to the fleeting insubstantiality and unreality of a dream. In the Mahāyāna and Vajrayāna developments of Buddhism, dream and the world of the senses retain the negative connotation of impermanence and illusion, but that illusoriness takes on a more positive aspect as the very nature of mind and phenomena to be realized, not escaped. It should be noted, however, that this is an emphasis, not an entirely new development, since the Pāli tradition also provides evidence of a positive view of impermanence. According to the *Saṁyutta-nikāya*, "It is owing to the instability, the coming to an end, the ceasing of objects . . . that devas and mankind live woefully." Conversely, "it is owing to the instability, the coming to an end, the ceasing of objects, that the Tathāgata dwells at ease."[2] Throughout the history of Buddhism, liberation is linked with the ability to perfectly comprehend the nature of impermanence and the illusion of identity. Tibetan developments in dream theory and practice took place in the context of the interaction between Buddhism and a shamanistic culture that would have valued dream in its religious life. Yet, from a Buddhist perspective, just as the miraculous acts of a Buddha are not to be mistaken for the magical arts of a sorcerer, a definite divide remains between the Buddhist approach to dream and the shamanic approach, no matter how similar they may appear outwardly.

The contradiction posed by juxtaposing dream as illusion and dream as effective prophecy in Indian Buddhism is primarily philosophic. It reflects the classic split between the world-affirming, ritual-based aspects of Brahmanic religion and the philosophies of traditions that renounced the world and turned away from the values of household life. The contrasting views already present in Indian Buddhism would have been further compounded in the Tibetan context, however, by the pragmatic function of dream as a vehicle of spiritual authentification and a path to enlightenment. Dream authenticates equally the spiritual abilities of the shaman and of the Buddhist lama. In the Tibetan experience, dream further becomes a practical method of attaining the highest goal of liberation, yet while the shaman stands confident in the reality and efficacy of his dreams, the lama must maintain the philosophic view in which dream signifies delusion, incompleteness, and lack of perfection. Ironically, then, the spiritual attainment of the Buddhist adept is authenticated by deception. According to a tantric perspective, the wisdom of the Buddhist sage is achieved by means of the same illusions that keep him bound to ignorance. This paradoxical situation, nevertheless, is grounded in the foundation of Buddhist philosophy, the principle of dependent origination, according to which liberation from suffering is dependent on the very nature of suffering itself.

In Tibetan culture, normative Buddhist, tantric, and shamanic currents have merged to create Tibet's unique religious synthesis. With regard to the status of dreams, the formation of such a continuum has reinforced existing dichotomies within Buddhism as well as created new ones. The tensions delineate important differences that would otherwise be lost, differences that maintain the balance and integrity of the constitutive currents. Forces of resolution, however, must also be present, because without them the continuum cannot hold. In their encounter with Buddhism, Tibetans found a tradition whose tantric practices of deity yoga resonated with shamanic methods of ritual communication with spirits, and whose philosophic emphasis on the interdependent nature of phenomena corresponded to the shamanic view of the world as an interconnected web of beings. Based on this foundation, the practical shamanic arts of interpreting dreams and actively working in and with dream/trance states would have been able to flourish. In turn, the efflorescence of religious interest in dreams and visions infused with the Mahāyāna Buddhist emphasis on the empty nature of all phenomena contributed to the development of a distinctively Tibetan visionary soteriology. Against the ineffable spaciousness and luminosity of mind, the shadow play of dreams and illusions is the only truth to be found. The dichotomies of existence are not resolved in any immutable unity; they appear, but, like rainbows, prove ungraspable, tempting us always with the possibility of discovering where they truly end. In the words of the mistress of dream yoga, the yogini Niguma:

> When we meditate upon the illusion-like nature
> Of all the illusion-like phenomena,
> We attain illusion-like Buddhahood.[3]

Appendix

GAMPOPA'S DREAMS

Gampopa's dreams represent a combination of medical, folk, and religious imagery. They are all interpreted by Milarepa as omens of his supreme success as a Dharma practitioner in achieving the goal of enlightenment and fulfilling the promise of a bodhisattva.

He wears the following:

- A silk and fur-trimmed white hat with the emblem of an eagle on it
- Smart green boots embossed with brass and fastened with silver buckles
- A red-dotted white silk robe, decorated with pearls and gold threads
- A belt embroidered with flowers and decorated with silk tassels and pearls
- A white silk scarf decorated with silver decoration

He holds the following:

- A staff decorated with precious stones and gold work
- A skull bowl of golden nectar for drinking
- A multicolored sack of rice for eating
- The skin of a wild animal with head and claws for a seat

He sees the following:

- On his right a meadow of golden flowers with sheep and cattle
- On his left a jade-green meadow of flowers where women bow to him
- In the center of the meadow, on a mound of golden flowers, a golden bodhisattva cross-legged on a lotus seat
- In front of the bodhisattva, a fountain and a brilliant aura surrounding him like flames and the sun and moon shining from his heart

Notes

PREFACE

1. Barbara Tedlock, "Dreaming and Dream Research," in *Dreaming: Anthropological and Psychological Interpretations,* ed. Barbara Tedlock (Cambridge: Cambridge University Press, 1987), 30.

INTRODUCTION

1. For 24 interpretations of a flying dream provided by contemporary experts, see Anthony Shafton, *Dream Reader* (Albany: State University of New York Press, 1995), 6.

2. For an overview of the major fields and figures involved in modern dream research, see Kelly Bulkeley, *The Wilderness of Dreams* (Albany: State University of New York Press, 1994), 81ff.

3. Ibid., 23.

4. Owen Flanagan, *Dreaming Souls* (Oxford: Oxford University Press), 69. A spandrel is the triangular space between the curve of an arch and the line of the headstone, the architectural side effect of creating an arch.

5. See especially Timothy Knab's account of the dream world and theories of Mesoamerican healers in *The Dialogue of Earth and Sky* (Tucson: University of Arizona Press, 2004).

6. Samten Gyaltsen Karmay, *Secret Visions of the Fifth Dalai Lama,* 2nd ed. (London: Serindia Publications, 1998).

7. The four major schools of Tibetan Buddhism are Nyingma, Kargyu, Sakya, and Gelug. The first two align themselves with the earlier dissemination of Buddhism in Tibet in the eighth and ninth centuries, and the latter two are associated with later reform movements.

8. My interest is in the cultural presentation of these dream images as arising from the mind of one who is regarded as the foremost upholder of

Mahāyāna philosophy and not with whether they were actual dreams of the Dalai Lama or with possible political motivations behind such accounts.

9. Garma C. C. Chang, trans., *The Hundred Thousand Songs of Milarepa*, vol. 2 (Boulder: Shambhala Publications, 1977), 483–84.

10. Nicola Tannenbaum, *Who Can Compete Against the World? Power-Protection and Buddhism in Shan Worldview* (Ann Arbor: Association for Asian Studies, University of Michigan, 1995), 10–12.

11. Sherry B. Ortner, *Sherpas Through Their Rituals* (Cambridge: Cambridge University Press, 1978); Stan Royal Mumford, *Himalayan Dialogue: Tibetan Lamas and Gurung Shamans in Nepal* (Madison: University of Wisconsin Press, 1989); David H. Holmberg, *Order in Paradox: Myth, Ritual, and Exchange among Nepal's Tamang* (Ithaca, NY: Cornell University Press, 1989).

12. With regard to Tibetan religion, the diagram featured in the 1982 edition of Robinson and Johnson's text exemplifies the popular/elite model. Richard H. Robinson and Willard L. Johnson, *The Buddhist Religion: A Historical Introduction*, 3rd ed. (Belmont, CA: Wadsworth Publishing Company, 1982), 145. Seventeen years later, the model appears in Serinity Young's work on dream in Buddhist biographies, *Dreaming in the Lotus: Buddhist Dream Narrative, Imagery, and Practice* (Boston: Wisdom Publications, 1999), 16–17.

13. This, of course, could reflect the education, social status, or simply the inclinations of the people that I interviewed—Tibetans from a refugee camp in South India, not nomads on the high plateau.

14. Karmay, *Secret Visions*, 24.

15. The relationship is examined in detail by Geoffrey Samuel in his study of Tibetan societies, *Civilized Shamans: Buddhism in Tibetan Societies* (Washington, DC: Smithsonian Institution Press, 1993). John Vincent Bellezza also studies the blending of Buddhist and indigenous religion in the practices of the spirit-mediums of upper Tibet. See *Spirit-Mediums, Sacred Mountains and Related Bön Textual Traditions in Upper Tibet: Calling Down the Gods* (Leiden: Brill, 2005).

16. Shamans, however, are also described as foremost in the battle against evil. The issue is one of balance. In his study of Otomí shamanism with the shaman Don Antonio, James Dow writes, "A shaman must firmly declare forever an alliance with the forces of good, with God, and then fight to uphold those forces." James Dow, *The Shaman's Touch: Otomí Indian Symbolic Healing* (Salt Lake City: University of Utah Press, 1986), 8.

17. Johannes Wilbert, "Eschatology in a Participatory Universe: Destinies of the Soul among the Warao Indians of Venezuela," in *Death and the Afterlife in Pre-Columbian America: A Conference at Dumbarton Oaks, October 27th, 1973*, ed. Elizabeth P. Benson (Washington, DC: Dumbarton Oaks Research Library and Collections), 174.

18. David N. Gellner, *The Anthropology of Buddhism and Hinduism: Weberian Themes* (New Delhi: Oxford University Press, 2001), 70.

19. The Bodhisattva Vow, which is the foundation of the Mahāyāna/Vajrayāna Buddhist approach to salvation, ties the liberation of the individual to the liberation of all beings. The bodhisattva vows to delay his or her own complete liberation from suffering until all beings attain that very same state.

20. According to early Tibetan narratives, the Chinese princess of Wencheng, wife of Songtsen Gampo (c. 617–50) established Tibet's most sacred shrine, the Jokhang, to house the statue of the Buddha that she had brought with her from China. A generation later, another royal Chinese wife instituted for Tibetan nobility Buddhist funerary rites in front of that statue. For an intriguing account of the Chinese connection in the construction of Tibet's Buddhist identity, see Matthew Kapstein, *The Tibetan Assimilation of Buddhism: Conversion, Contestation, and Memory* (Oxford: Oxford University Press, 2000), 23–37.

21. Jonathan Z. Smith, *Drudgery Divine: On the Comparison of Early Christianities and the Religions of Late Antiquity* (London: School of Oriental and African Studies, University of London, 1990), 52–53.

22. For a review of the various views of Bön, see Geoffrey Samuel, "Shamanism, Bön and Tibetan Religion," in *Tantric Revisionings: New Understandings of Tibetan Buddhism and Indian Religion* (Delhi: Motilal Banarsidass, 2005).

23. For a discussion of the early culture of Tibet based on Dunhuang documents see David L. Snellgrove and Hugh Richardson, *A Cultural History of Tibet* (New York: Frederick A. Praeger, 1968), 74–78.

24. Per Kværne, *The Bön Religion of Tibet: The Iconography of a Living Tradition* (Boston: Shambhala, 1996), 9–10.

25. David L. Snellgrove, trans., *The Nine Ways of Bön: Excerpts from "gZi-brjid"* (Boulder, CO: Prajna Press, 1980), 21.

26. The Fourteenth Dalai Lama also accepts this view and has publicly acknowleged Bön as a legitimate and distinct Tibetan religion.

27. Here I follow Samuel's argument in "Shamanism, Bön and Tibetan Religion," 116–37.

28. Bellezza, *Spirit-Mediums*. On the basis of a Buddhist text from Dunhuang, another Bön scholar, Samten Karmay, argues for the presence of a native religious system known as Bön, to which Buddhism was opposed, dating back to the time of the ancient kings (seventh to ninth centuries). The text he examines casts Buddhism as the "religion of the gods" and exhorts the reader to turn away from Bön, the non-Buddhist doctrine, whose priests propitiate local and demonic spirits. See Samten Gyaltsen Karmay, *The Arrow and the Spindle* (Katmandu: Mandala Book Point, 1998), 163.

CHAPTER 1

1. Alice Beck Kehoe argues this position in *Shamans and Religion* (Long Grove, IL: Waveland Press, 2000).

2. I. M. Lewis, *Ecstatic Religion: A Study of Shamanism and Spirit Possession* (London: Routledge, 1971); Vladimir Basilov, "Cosmos as Everyday Reality in Shamanism: An Attempt to Formulate a More Precise Definition of Shamanism," in *Shamanic Cosmos: From India to the North Pole Star*, ed. Romano Mastromattei and Antonio Rigopoulos, Venetian Academy of Indian Studies Series, no. 1 (Venice: Venetian Academy of Indian Studies, 1999); Mihály Hoppál, "Shamanism: An Archaic and/or Recent System of Beliefs," in *Studies*

on Shamanism, by Anna-Leena Siikala (Helsinki: Finnish Anthropological Society; Budapest: Akadémiai Kiadó; 1998); and Geoffrey Samuel, *Mind, Body, and Culture: Anthropology and the Biological Interface* (Cambridge: Cambridge University Press, 1990).

3. For a discussion on definitions of shamanism, see Vladimir Basilov, 17–39. For a discussion on the problems of defining shamanism, see Graham Harvey's general introduction to *Shamanism: A Reader* (London: Routledge, 2003).

4. Michel Perrin, "Intellectual Coherence and Constraining Function of Shamanism," *Shaman* 3, no. 2 (1995):160–62.

5. Basilov, "Cosmos as Everyday Reality," 25–37.

6. See Mihály Hoppál's definition of shamanism as a complex system of beliefs that constitutes "a religious configuration *within the religion*" in "Shamanism," 117–31.

7. Peter T. Furst, "An Overview of Shamanism," in *Ancient Traditions: Shamanism in Central Asia and the Americas,* ed. Gary Seaman and Jane S. Day (Niwot: University Press of Colorado; Denver: Denver Museum of Natural History, 1994), 2–3.

8. For an account of the continuing relationship between the spirit world and ecology in the Himalayan kingdom of Bhutan, see Ura Karma, "Deities and Environment," Center for Bhutan Studies, Thimpu, 2001. http://www.mtnforum.org/resources/library/karmu01a.htm accessed on May 4, 2006.

9. For a detailed study of important mountain and lake divinities and their role in the cultural and religious development of Tibet, see John Vincent Bellezza, *Divine Dyads: Ancient Civilization in Tibet* (Dharamsala: Library of Tibetan Works and Archives, 1997).

10. The earliest historical dating for the presence of Buddhism in Tibet is the reign of King Songsten Gampo (ca. 614–50 CE). Tradition holds that he built twelve "boundary and limb-binding" Buddhist temples at the four corners of three concentric squares spreading outward from Central Tibet, each one acting as a great nail to pin down and subjugate the demoness that represented the untamed land of Tibet. See Janet Gyatso, "Down with the Demoness: Reflections on a Feminine Ground in Tibet," *Tibet Journal* 12, no. 4 (1987): 38–53.

11. For a discussion of the various types of *lha,* see Bellezza, *Divine Dyads,* 30–42; Philippe Cornu, *Tibetan Astrology,* trans. Hamish Gregor (Boston: Shambhala, 2002), 245–53.

12. For further discussion on the classes and types of Tibetan deities, see Geoffrey Samuel, *Civilized Shamans: Buddhism in Tibetan Societies* (Washington, DC: Smithsonian Institution Press, 1993), 157–67.

13. John Vincent Bellezza, *Spirit-Mediums, Sacred Mountains, and Related Bön Textual Traditions in Upper Tibet* (Leiden: Brill, 2005), 332.

14. Roger Jackson, "A Fasting Ritual," in *Religions of Tibet in Practice.* ed. Donald Lopez (Princeton, NJ: Princeton University Press, 1997), 289.

15. Yael Bentor, "The Horseback Consecration Ritual" in *Religions of Tibet in Practice,* ed. Donald Lopez (Princeton, NJ: Princeton University Press, 1997), 247.

16. Sudhir Kakar, *Shamans, Mystics and Doctors: A Psychological Inquiry into India and Its Healing Traditions* (New York: Alfred A. Knopf, 1982), 111–13.

17. Lucien Lévy-Bruhl, *How Natives Think*, trans. Lilian A. Clare (New York: A. A. Knopf, 1925), 22–54.

18. For discussion on soul concepts in other northern and central Asian cultures, see V. N. Chernetsov, "Concepts of the Soul among the Ob Ugrians," in *Studies in Siberian Shamanism*, ed. Henry N. Michael, Arctic Institute of North America Anthropology of the North: Translations from Russian Sources, no. 4 (Toronto: University of Toronto Press, 1963), 3–45. Also A. V. Smoljak, "Some Notions of the Human Soul among the Nanais," in *Shamanism in Siberia*, Vilmos Diószegi and Mihály Hoppál (Budapest: Akademiai Kiado, 1978), 439–48. For soul theories in Saami shamanism, see A. Hultkrantz, "Aspects of Saami (Lapp) Shamanism," in vol. 3 of *Northern Religions and Shamanism*, ed. Mihály Hoppál and Juha Pentikäinen (Budapest: Ethnologica Uralica, 1992), 138–45. For Mesoamerican shamanism, see Timothy Knab, *The Dialogue of Earth and Sky* (Tucson: University of Arizona Press, 2004).

19. Giusseppe Tucci, *The Religions of Tibet*, trans. Geoffrey Samuel (Bombay: Allied Publishers Private, 1980), 191–92.

20. Samten Gyaltsen Karmay, "The Soul and the Turquoise: A Ritual for Recalling the *bla*," in *The Arrow and the Spindle* (Kathmandu: Mandala Book Point, 1998), 315.

21. For a description of a 1983 Bön enactment of the *bla bslu* "repurchase of the soul" ritual and related Buddhist text, see ibid., 326–37. An early account of this ritual appears in Ferdinand D. Lessing, "Calling the Soul: A Lamaist Ritual," *Semitic and Oriental Studies* 11 (1951): 263–84.

22. Samuel, *Civilized Shamans*, 186–88.

23. The idea that separate souls inhabit different parts of the body is widely dispersed among shamanic cultures. According to Inuit beliefs, the souls located in the larynx and on the left side of a person are tiny people the size of a sparrow; other souls the size of a finger joint reside in all the limbs of a person. Merete Demant Jakobsen, *Shamanism: Traditional and Contemporary Approaches to the Mastery of Spirits and Healing* (New York: Berghahn Books, 1999), 80. Among the Rungus people of Borneo there is the belief that the joints of the body each have their own soul whose activity in the spirit world results in various aches and pains. George N. Appell and Laura W. R. Appell, "To Converse with the Gods: Rungus Spirit Mediums," in *The Seen and the Unseen*, ed. Robert L. Winzeler (Williamsburg, VA: Borneo Research Council, 1993), 17.

24. Caroline Humphrey, *Shamans and Elders: Experience, Knowledge, and Power among the Daur Mongols* (Oxford: Clarendon Press, 1996), 57.

25. Chernetsov, "Concepts of the Soul," 7.

26. Nurit Bird-David, " 'Animism' Revisited: Personhood, Environment, and Relational Epistemology," in *Current Anthropology*, Supplement (February 1999): 67–91.

27. Ibid., 73.

28. Humphrey, *Shamans and Elders*, 59, 74, n. 93.

29. Jean-Guy Goulet, *Ways of Knowing: Experience, Knowledge, and Power among the Dene Tha* (Vancouver: UBC Press, 1998).

30. Bellezza, *Spirit-Mediums*, 198–99.

31. Ibid., 237.

32. R. A. Stein, *Tibetan Civilization*, trans. J. E. Stapleton Driver (Stanford, CA: Stanford University Press, 1972), 210.

33. Wendy Doniger O'Flaherty uses the image of a Möbius strip to great effect in explaining how the elements in the Hindu mythological universe similarly fold in upon themselves forever. A Möbius strip is formed by joining the ends of a rectangle after twisting one end through 180 degrees to create one continuous surface. See *Dreams Illusion and Other Realities* (Chicago: University of Chicago Press, 1984), 240–45.

34. Gregory G. Maskarinec, *Nepalese Shaman Oral Texts*, ed. Michael Witzel, Harvard Oriental Series, vol. 55 (Cambridge, MA: Harvard University Press, 1998), 13–15.

35. Timothy Knab notes that, in the Mesoamerican context, activity in the world and relationships between persons, either human or nonhuman, are fundamentally tied to the notion of permission and reciprocal benefit. Knab, *Dialogue of Earth and Sky*, 19.

36. Vilmos Diószegi, *Tracing Shamans in Siberia: The Story of an Ethnographical Research Expedition*, trans. Anita Rajkay Babó (Oosterhout: Anthropological Publications 1968), 240.

37. Reinhard Greve, "The Shaman and the Witch: An Analytical Approach to Shamanic Poetry in the Himalayas," in *Shamanism Past and Present: Part 2*, ed. Mihály Hoppál and Otto von Sadovsky (Budapest: Ethnographic Institute, Hungarian Academy of Sciences, 1989), 219.

38. "Recital of the Nine Little Sisters," quoted by Gregory G. Maskarinec in "A Shamanic Semantic Plurality: *Dhāmīs* and *Jhākrīs* of Western Nepal," in *Shamanism Past and Present: Part 2*, Mihály Hoppál and Otto von Sadovsky (Budapest: Ethnographic Institute, Hungarian Academy of Sciences, 1989), 211.

39. Urgunge Onon, in Humphrey, *Shamans and Elders*, 363.

40. Mircea Eliade, *Shamanism: Archaic Techniques of Ecstasy* (Princeton, NJ: Princeton University Press, 1964), 266.

41. Walther Heissig, *The Religions of Mongolia* (Berkeley and Los Angeles: University of California Press, 1980), 102.

42. Walther Heissig, "A Mongolian Source to the Lamaist Suppression of Shamanism in the 17th Century," *Anthropos* 48, nos. 3–4 (1953): 503–5.

43. Tucci, *Religions of Tibet*, 167. For a discussion on the correspondences between the warrior gods (*sgra-lha*) and the mountain deities (*lha-ri*), see Bellezza, *Spirit-Mediums*, 379ff.

44. Thubten Jigme Norbu as told to Heinrich Harrer, *Tibet Is My Country*, trans. Edward Fitzgerald (London: Rupert Hart-Davis, 1960), 24.

45. Ibid., 51–53.

46. For a detailed study of the Buddhist cult of pilgrimage mountains, see Toni Huber, *The Cult of Pure Crystal Mountain* (New York: Oxford University Press, 1999), 23–25; Also Karmay, *Arrow and the Spindle*, 432ff. Bellezza, *Spirit-Mediums*. This study is devoted to tracing the continuity of the mountain cult and its relation to shamanistic techniques of possession in both Bön and Buddhist forms.

47. David L. Snellgrove and Hugh Richardson, *A Cultural History of Tibet* (New York: Frederick A. Praeger, 1968), 23.

48. It is thought that Tibetan peoples likely had their origins in the pastoral and nomadic non-Chinese tribes of eastern central Asia, each tribe having its own sacred mountain, which was considered to be the seat or throne of the tribe's protective deity.

49. The presence of the word *tsen*, "mighty," in the king's name marked his connection to the tsen spirits, who represent the power of the sacred mountains.

50. Although it is beyond the scope of this study to explore the association between the political power of the king and the spirit power of the mountain, that connection plays a part in the appropriation of the cult of the mountain by Buddhism as an instrument of spiritual and political authority. In his comprehensive study of Tibetan indigenous roots, Bellezza notes that both Bön and Buddhist traditions have used the temperamental and wrathful nature of the mountain gods as a mechanism of social control. *Spirit-Mediums*, 263.

51. The Evenks also believe that seven or nine heavens are located between the upper world and the source of the sacred river that connects the three worlds. G. M. Vasilevich, "Early Concepts about the Universe among the Evenks (Materials)," in *Studies in Siberian Shamanism*, ed. Henry N. Michael, Arctic Institute of North American Anthropology of the North: Translations from Russian Sources, no. 4 (Toronto: University of Toronto Press, 1963), 72.

52. George N. Roerich, trans., *The Blue Annals*, 2d ed. (Delhi: Motilal Banarsidass, 1976), 36.

53. Stein, *Tibetan Civilization*, 42–43.

54. Eliade, *Shamanism*, 110–12, 428–31.

55. Stein, *Tibetan Civilization*, 225. Stein notes that the manner in which the body dissolves into light beginning with the feet relates to the Tibetan belief that the soul circulates monthly through the body in a very specific manner from feet to crown. On the thirtieth and first of the month, it resides in the sole of the foot (left for men and right for women), and on successive days it rises higher and higher with the waxing moon to arrive at the crown of the head on the fifteenth, the full-moon day.

56. The idea of the spirit or soul ascending to the sky by means of a rope of rainbow light from the top of the head is echoed in the Tibetan Buddhist rituals called *phowa*, a ritual whereby consciousness, departing from the body through the crown of the head, is transferred to a heavenly buddha paradise.

57. Bellezza, *Spirit-Mediums*, 79; 109

58. Karmay, *Arrow and the Spindle*, 252.

59. Tucci, *Religions of Tibet*, 246

60. Sergei M. Shirokogoroff, *Psychomental Complex of the Tungus* (London: Kegan Paul, Trench, Trübner & Co., 1935) 352.

61. Eliade, *Shamanism*, 118.

62. Jeremiah Curtin, *A Journey in Southern Siberia*. (Boston: Little, Brown and Company, 1909), 108–9.

63. Sarangerel, *Riding Windhorses: A Journey into the Heart of Mongolian Shamanism* (Rochester, VT: Destiny Books, 2000), 13.

64. For example, the use of the metal mirror, the drum, the arrow, raptor feathers in the headdress, juniper incense, zoomorphic helping spirits, and a sucking technique in healing rituals. See Bellezza, *Spirit-Mediums*, 23–34.

65. Goulet, *Ways of Knowing*, 69.

66. Samuel, *Civilized Shamans*, 8.

67. Anna-Leena Siikala, "The Siberian Shaman's Technique of Ecstasy," in *Studies on Shamanism*, by Anna-Leena Siikala and Mihály Hoppál (Helsinki: Finnish Anthropological Society; Budapest: Akadémiai Kiadó, 1998), 26–27.

68. Brian Inglis, *Trance: A Natural History of Altered States of Mind* (London: Grafton Books, 1989), 267.

69. Marie-Françoise Guédon, "La pratique du rêve chez les Dénés septentrionaux," *Anthropologie et Sociétés* 18, no. 2 (1994): 76.

70. Hoppál, "Shamanism," 129–30.

71. Bo Sommarström, "The Sāmi Shaman's Drum and the Holographic Paradigm Discussion," in *Shamanism Past and Present: Part 1*, ed. Mihály Hoppál and Otto von Sadovsky (Budapest: Ethnographic Institute, Hungarian Academy of Sciences, 1989), 127–28.

72. Pál Péter Domokos, *A moldvai magyarság* (Csikszereda, 1931); quoted in Mihály Hoppál, "The Role of Shamanism in Hungarian Ethnic Identity," in *Studies on Shamanism*, by Anna-Leena Siikala and Mihály Hoppál (Helsinki: Finnish Anthropological Society; Budapest: Akadémiai Kiadó, 1998), 169.

73. Shirokogoroff, *Psychomental complex of the Tungus*, 313, 340.

74. Ibid., 371. Shirokogoroff notes that to "become a shaman" means to assume one of the spirit forms that allows him to travel a long way.

75. Ibid.

76. Knud Rasmussen, *Intellectual Culture of the Iglulik Eskimos*, Report of the Fifth Thule Expedition, 1921–24, vol. 7, no. 1 (Copenhagen: Gyldendal, 1929), 129–31.

77. Hultkrantz, "Aspects of Saami (Lapp) Shamanism," 139.

78. Andreas Lommel, "Shamanism in Australia," in *Shamanism Past and Present: Part 1*, ed. Mihály Hoppál and Otto von Sadovsky (Budapest: Ethnographic Institute, Hungarian Academy of Sciences, 1989), 33.

79. Diószegi, *Tracing Shamans in Siberia*, 62.

80. Vladimir N. Basilov, "Texts of Shamanistic Invocations from Central Asia and Kazakhstan," in *Ancient Traditions: Shamanism in Central Asia and the Americas*, ed. Gary Seaman and Jane S. Day (Niwot: University Press of Colorado; Denver: Denver Museum of Natural History, 1994), 276.

81. Vladimir N. Basilov, "Blessing in a Dream," *Turcica* 27 (1995): 238. The relationship between shaman and epic bard surfaced also in my experience with the Bhutanese shaman mentioned in the preface to this book, whose long and beautiful chants called on the epic hero Gesar of Ling.

82. Ibid., 240–44.

83. Ibid., 244. According to Basilov, in Central Asia and Kazakhstan the particular spirits referred to in Allashukur's dream, the *pari*, are commonly regarded as the shaman's helping spirits.

84. Ibid., 242.

85. A. A. Popov, "How Sereptie Djaruoskin of the Nganasans (Tavgi Samoyeds) Became a Shaman," in *Popular Beliefs and Folklore in Siberia,* ed. Vilmos Diószegi, Indiana University Publications: Uralic and Altaic Series, ed. Thomas A. Sebeok, vol. 57 (Bloomington: Indiana University, 1968), 137–38.

86. Ibid., 144.

87. In his study of the *curanderos* of San Martín, Timothy Knab provides an excellent analysis of the metalanguage of dreams and the way in which dreams in that culture function in the context of healing as "an open-ended vehicle for interpretation." Knab, *Dialogue of Earth and Sky,* 133ff.

88. W. Bogoras, "The Chukchee—Religion," in vol. 11, pt. 2, of *Memoirs of the American Museum of Natural History,* ed. Franz Baas (Leiden: E. J. Brill, 1909), 471, 482.

89. See Goulet, *Ways of Knowing,* 75–78.

90. Ibid., 78.

91. Diószegi, *Tracing Shamans in Siberia,* 294.

92. Kakar, *Shamans, Mystics and Doctors,* 50.

93. Diószegi, *Tracing Shamans in Siberia,* 55–56.

94. Åke Hultkrantz, "The Concept of the Soul Held by the Wind River Shoshone," *Ethnos* 16 (1951): 32.

95. The story appears in Curtin, *Journey in Southern Siberia,* 111–12.

96. Ibid.

97. See Glenn Mullin, *The Six Yogas of Naropa* (Ithaca, NY: Snow Lion, 2005).

98. Shirokogoroff notes that the Tungus have different words for two different kinds of dreams: dreams that are "revelation" and dreams that are just "dreaming." *Psychomental Complex of the Tungus,* 362.

99. For Mesoamerican culture, see Knab, *Dialogue of Earth and Sky,* 104–6; for the methods of the Greenlandic *angakkoq,* see Jakobsen, *Shamanism,* 52–65.

100. Lola Romanucci-Ross, "The Impassioned Cogito: Shaman and Anthropologist," in *Shamanism Past and Present: Part 1,* ed. Mihály Hoppál and Otto von Sadovsky (Budapest: Ethnographic Institute, Hungarian Academy of Sciences, 1989), 38.

CHAPTER 2

1. See N. Ross Reat, *The Origins of Indian Psychology* (Berkeley, CA: Asian Humanities Press, 1990), 63, 90–91.

2. Ṛg Veda 8.72.7–8, in T. H. Ralph, trans., Griffith, *The Hymns of the Ṛgveda* (Delhi: Motilal Banarsidass, 1973), 451.

3. Ṛg Veda 10.90.12–14, in Abinash Chandra Bose, trans., *Hymns from the Vedas* (London: Asia Publishing House, 1966), 286–89.

4. The others in his list are heat, sacrifice, and knowledge. Walter O. Kaelber, *Tapta Mārga: Asceticism and Initiation in Vedic India* (Albany: State University of New York Press, 1989), 1.

5. Monier Monier-Williams, *A Sanskrit-English Dictionary,* new ed. (Oxford: Clarendon Press, 1976), 548, 720.

6. *Śatapatha-Brāhmaṇa* 1.3.2.1, in Julius Eggeling, trans., *The Śatapatha-Brāhmaṇa, Parts 1–3,* 2d ed., The Sacred Books of the East Series, ed. Max Müller, vol. 12 (Delhi: Motilal Banarsidass, 1966), 78. The volume number given in subsequent references to this work refers to its number in the Sacred Books of the East Series.

7. The Fire Altar ritual (*Agnicayana*) refers to the sacrifice of five prototypical animals that represent 'all the animals'—man, horse, bull, sheep, and goat. However, the goat is taken to represent all five based on physical comparisons (e.g., the goat is hornless and bearded and man is hornless and bearded). *Śatapatha-Brāhmaṇa* 6.2.2.15, in Eggeling, *Śatapatha-Brāhmaṇa,* 41:177.

8. Herman Tull indicates that this binding could have referred either to the fact that the animal was strangled with a rope or to the fact that it was tied to the stake. Herman Tull, *The Vedic Origins of Karma: Cosmos as Man in Ancient Indian Myth and Ritual* (Albany: State University of New York Press, 1989), 74.

9. *Śatapatha-Brāhmaṇa* 2.6.4.8, in Eggeling, *Śatapatha-Brāhmaṇa,* 12:450–51.

10. This ambiguous and dangerous situation is addressed in the *Śatapatha Brāhmaṇa*: "10. As to this they say, 'That (victim) must not be held on to by the sacrificer, for they lead it unto death; therefore let him not hold on to it.' But let him nevertheless hold on to it; for that (victim) which they lead to the sacrifice they lead not to death; therefore let him hold on to it. Moreover he would cut himself off from the sacrifice, were he not to hold on to it; therefore let him hold on to it. It is held on to in a mysterious [imperceptible] way. By means of the spits the Pratiprasthātṛ (holds on to it); to the Pratiprasthātṛ [holds] the Adhvaryu, to the Adhvaryu the Sacrificer; thus then it is held on to in a mysterious [imperceptible] way." *Śatapatha-Brāhmaṇa* 3.8.1.10, in Eggeling, *Śatapatha-Brāhmaṇa,* 26:188. The argument here is that the sacrificial ritual, despite its association with death, does not lead to death; nevertheless, the sacrificer is protected by two ritual specialists situated between himself and the sacrificial animal.

11. Reat, *Origins of Indian Psychology,* 90.

12. Ṛg Veda 5.55.1, in Griffith, *Hymns of the Ṛgveda,* 267. The image of a high-spirited, sky-borne horse or horsemen representing health and vitality appears also in the Tibetan concept of *lung-ta,* literally "wind-horse," where it encompasses such meanings as life force, energy, personal charisma, and luck. When it is "high," one is full of mental and physical energy and succeeds in everything.

13. Jan Gonda, *The Vision of the Vedic Poets* (The Hague: Mouton & Co., 1963), 99–100.

14. Ibid., 68.

15. Ṛg Veda 6.62.3, in Griffith, *Hymns of the Ṛgveda,* 324.

16. Ṛg Veda 9.100.3, in Griffith, *Hymns of the Ṛgveda,* 521.

17. Reat, *Origins of Indian Psychology,* 113.

18. Alex Wayman, "The Significance of Mantras, from the Veda down to Buddhist Tantric Practice," in *Buddhist Insight: Essays by Alex Wayman,* ed. George Elder, Religions of Asia Series, ed. Lewis R. Lancaster and J. L. Shastri, no. 5 (Delhi: Motilal Banarsidass, 1984), 425.

19. Gonda, *Vision of the Vedic Poets,* 146.

20. Reat, *Origins of Indian Psychology*, 134. This terminology is still used in contemporary Tibetan Buddhist practice, where to "accomplish" the practice of a certain deity means making the mental transformation of oneself into the deity an actuality.

21. Monier-Williams, *Sanskrit-English Dictionary*, 811.

22. Wendy Doniger O'Flaherty, *Dreams Illusion and Other Realities* (Chicago: University of Chicago Press, 1984), 118.

23. Jan Gonda, *Change and Continuity in Indian Religion* (The Hague: Mouton & Co., 1965), 166.

24. Reat, *Origins of Indian Psychology*, 86.

25. "Grahi : a she-demon who seizes and kills men." Ralph T. H. Griffith, trans., *The Hymns of the Atharvaveda*, vol. 2 (Varanasi: The Chowkhamba Sanskrit Series Office, 1968), 203.

26. Atharva Veda 16.5.1–6, in William Dwight Whitney, trans., *Atharva-Veda-Saṃhitā*, vol. 2, Harvard Oriental Series, ed. Charles Rockwell Lanman, vol. 8 (Delhi: Motilal Banarsidass, 1971), 798.

27. The name and lineage of the person against whom the curse is to be sent would be inserted here.

28. Atharva Veda 16.7.1–8, in Whitney, *Atharva-Veda-Saṃhitā*, 800.

29. Atharva Veda 19.56.1–6, in Griffith, *Hymns of the Atharvaveda*, 313–14, n. 4.

30. Ṛg Veda 2.28.10, in Wendy Doniger O'Flaherty, trans., *The Rig Veda: An Anthology* (Penguin Books, 1981), 218.

31. Doniger O'Flaherty, *Dreams Illusion and Other Realities*, 15.

32. Ṛg Veda 10.164.3–5, in Doniger O'Flaherty, *The Rig Veda*, 287–88.

33. Atharva Veda 16.6.7–11, in Whitney, *Atharva-Veda- Saṃhitā*, 799.

34. Atharva Veda 16.6.9, Ibid.

35. George Melville Bolling, "Dreams and Sleep (Vedic)," in *The Encyclopaedia of Religion and Ethics*, ed. James Hastings, vol 5 (Edinburgh: T & T clark, 1913), 39, col. a.

36. Atharva Veda 6.46.1–3, in Whitney, *Atharva-Veda-Saṃhitā*, vol. 1, 314–15.

37. Bolling, "Dreams and Sleep (Vedic)," 39, col. b.

38. Atharva Veda 19.57.5, in Whitney, *Atharva-Veda- Saṃhitā*, vol. 2, 998. The Vedic view of sleep as linked with disintegration and destruction finds its mythological expression in Rudra-Śiva, the terrifying lord of sleep and lord of tears. The double nature of Sleep as both the bearer of evil dreams and the protector from evil-dreaming is reflected in the double nature of Rudra-Śiva—bearer of the deadly arrows of disease and death and lord of healing balms and plants, he who represents the terror of annihilation and the bliss of total peace.

39. Ṛg Veda 10.121.2, in Griffith, *Hymns of the Rgveda*, 628.

40. Willard Johnson, *Poetry and Speculation of the Ṛg Veda* (Berkeley and Los Angeles: University of California Press, 1980), 165.

41. Patrick Olivelle notes the varying usage of this term. In the Upaniṣads, *ātman* refers to the physical body as well as to the innermost self, and serves also simply as a reflexive pronoun. Patrick Olivelle, Upaniṣads (Oxford: Oxford University Press, 1996), xiix.

42. In general, this section concentrates on the earlier *Upaniṣads* believed to predate Buddhism.

43. *Bṛhadāraṇyaka Upaniṣad* 4.3.9, in Olivelle, *Upaniṣads,* 59.

44. *Bṛhadāraṇyaka Upaniṣad* 4.3.12, in Olivelle, *Upaniṣads,* 59.

45. *Bṛhadāraṇyaka Upaniṣad* 4.3.9–10, in Olivelle, *Upaniṣads,* 59.

46. *Bṛhadāraṇyaka Upaniṣad* 2.1.20, in Olivelle, *Upaniṣads,* 95.

47. *Taittirīya Upaniṣad* 2.1–6, in Olivelle, *Upaniṣads,* 184–87.

48. Although this fourfold analysis is most clearly laid out in the later *Māṇḍūkya Upaniṣad* 1–7, in Olivelle, *Upaniṣads,* 289, the discussion of the self related to waking, dream, sleep, and an ungraspable state of supreme bliss in which ātman is the sole seer can be found in the much earlier *Bṛhadāraṇyaka Upaniṣad* 4.2–4, in Olivelle, *Upaniṣads,* 57–68.

49. *Tattirīya Upaniṣad* 4.3.32, in Olivelle, *Upaniṣads,* 62.

50. *Aitareya Upaniṣad* 1.3.12, in Olivelle, *Upaniṣads,* 197. In this *Upaniṣad,* the ātman, conceived vitalistically, is said to enter into man through the crown of the head. Olivelle links the three dwelling places to a verse in the *Ṛg Veda* in which the crown of the head (sky) is associated with deep sleep, the middle region of the navel (atmosphere) with dream, and the feet (earth) with the waking state. In his translation, R. E. Hume comments that some philosophers link the three dwelling places to specific parts of the body: in the waking state, the soul dwells in the right eye; in the dreaming state, in the throat; and in deep sleep, in the heart. Robert Ernest Hume, trans., *Thirteen Principal Upanishads,* 2nd ed. (London: Oxford University Press, 1931), 297.

51. According to Śaṅkara, "We only maintain that the world connected with the intermediate state (i.e., the world of dreams) is not real in the same sense as the world consisting of ether and so on is real. On the other hand we must remember that also the so-called real creation with its ether, air, etc., is not absolutely real; for as we have proved before . . . the entire expanse of things is mere illusion. The world consisting of ether, etc., remains fixed and distinct up to the moment when the soul cognizes that Brahman is the Self of all; the world of dreams on the other hand is daily sublated by the waking state." George Thibaut, trans., *Vedānta Sūtras of Bādarāyana with the Commentary by Śankara, Part II* (Reprint, New York: Dover Publications, 1962), 137. Eliot Deutsch elaborates, however, that "the world is an illusion only on the basis of an experience of the Absolute. The world cannot be an illusion to one who lacks that experience. Empirical reality . . . is transcended only absolutely." Eliot Deutsch, *Advaita Vedānta: A Philosophical Reconstruction* (Honolulu: University of Hawaii Press, 1985), 32 n. 11.

52. *Māndūkya Upaniṣad* 7, in Olivelle, *Upaniṣads,* 289.

53. *Chāndogya Upaniṣad* 8.12.3, in Olivelle, *Upaniṣads,* 175.

54. Ibid.

55. *Bṛhadāraṇyaka Upaniṣad* 4.3.11–14, in Olivelle, *Upaniṣads,* 59.

56. *Māndūkya Upaniṣad* 3–4, in Olivelle, *Upaniṣads,* 59.

57. *Chāndogya Upaniṣad* 8.6.3, in Olivelle, *Upaniṣads,* 170.

58. *Bṛhadāraṇyaka Upaniṣad* 4.3.20–21, in Olivelle, *Upaniṣads,* 61

59. *Bṛhadāraṇyaka Upaniṣad* 4.3.10, in Olivelle, *Upaniṣads,* 59.

60. Heinrich Zimmer, *Myths and Symbols in Indian Art and Civilization*, ed. Joseph Campbell, Bollingen Series, vol. 6 (Princeton, NJ: Princeton University Press, 1974), 37.

61. Gonda, *Change and Continuity*,180.

62. *Buddhacarita* 6.48, E. H. Johnston, trans. *The Buddhacarita or Acts of the Buddha: Part II*, 2d ed. (New Delhi: Oriental Reprint, 1972), 87.

63. *Buddhacarita* 11.29, in Johnston, *Buddhacarita*, 155.

64. In his research, Bellezza notes that Tibetan spirit-mediums regard their entire body as a sacrifice, an offering, sometimes ritually chopped up and offered to appease the harmful spirits. John Vincent Bellezza, *Spirit-Mediums, Sacred Mountains and Related Bön Textual Traditions in Upper Tibet: Calling Down the Gods* (Leiden: E. J. Brill, 2005), 90. The question of the relationship between shamanism and the ancient Indian tradition is the subject of debate. Some scholars have seen in the long-haired space-traveling yogins of the *Ṛg Veda* (RV 10.136.1–7) strong affinities with the classic shamanic complex of Siberia. A Vedic seer is also called *vipra*, literally "the quivering one," possibly indicating the ecstatic shaking characteristic of shamanic possession (see J. F. Staal, "Sanskrit and Sanskritization," *Journal of Asian Studies* 22 [1963]: 261–67). The connection however, is questioned by Gonda, who argues that the word *vipra* can equally refer to poetic inspiration or the "vibrant and exalted speech of moved poets." Gonda, *Change and Continuity*, 208. Other links between the Vedic tradition and shamanism can be seen in the use of hallucinogenics, an area that I have not explored, since my focus throughout the book is on establishing correspondences between worldviews that support the validity of visionary experience, and not on the methods of inducing such visions.

CHAPTER 3

1. Melford Spiro, *Buddhism and Society* (New York: Harper & Row, 1970), 88–89. Spiro uses the term "normative" to refer to the doctrines and teachings of the Pāli canonical texts. Lessing raises the same issue regarding the Buddhist canonical denial of the soul in soul-calling rituals presided over by Buddhist lamas in "Calling the Soul: A Lamaist Ritual," in *Semitic and Oriental Studies* 11 (1951): 265.

2. For a discussion on the *gandhabba* (spirit-being of the intermediary existence) in the Pāli canon, see Peter Harvey, *The Selfless Mind: Personality, Consciousness and Nirvana in Early Buddhism* (Surrey: Curzon Press, 1995), 105–8.

3. *Majjhima-Nikāya* 2.18, in Bhikkhu Ñāṇamoli and Bhikkhu Bodhi, trans., *The Middle Length Discourses of the Buddha* (Boston: Wisdom Publications, 1995), 643.

4. Sergei M. Shirokogoroff, *Psychomental Complex of the Tungus* (London: Kegan, Paul, Trench, Trübner & Co., 1935), 276.

5. Jadunath Sinha, *Indian Psychology*, vol. 1, 2nd ed. (Delhi: Motilal Banarsidass, 1985), 307–24.

6. Ibid., 310.

7. Sinha explains: "Recollection is the apprehension of the previously apprehended and if the element of 'the apprehended' sinks below the threshold of consciousness, then recollection appears as a direct apprehension or perception, or, the *re*-presentation appears as a direct and immediate presentation." Ibid., 310–11.

8. Ibid.

9. In Buddhist psychology, the mind (*manas*) functions in two ways: as coordinator of the data of the five physical sense organs, and as a sixth sense organ that directly perceives its own data, that is, mental objects such as ideas, thoughts and mental images.

10. *Visuddhimagga* 7:67, in Buddhaghosa, *Visuddhimagga: The Path of Purification*, trans. Bhikkhu Ñāṇamoli (Seattle: BPS Pariyatti Editions, 1975), 209.

11. The Mahāyāna Buddhas dwell and teach in their own Buddha fields in all directions of the compass; the cult of Amitābha Buddha and his Pure Land in the West is one of the most prominent.

12. The earliest firm date for the *Pratyutpanna Samādhi Sūtra* is 179 CE, the year it was translated into Chinese. See Paul Harrison, trans., *The Samādhi of the Direct Encounter with the Buddhas of the Present: An Annotated English Translation of the Tibetan Version of the Pratyutpanna-Buddha-Sammukhāvasthita-Samādhi-Sūtra*, Studia Philologica Buddhica Monograph Series, vol. 5 (Tokyo: International Institute for Buddhist Studies, 1990), viii.

13. *Pratyutpanna Samādhi Sūtra*, in Harrison, *Samādhi of the Direct Encounter*, 37.

14. Ibid., 32.

15. Ibid., 33, n. 4.

16. Ibid., 117.

17. Ibid., 34–35.

18. Harvey, *Selfless Mind*, 162.

19. Ibid., 163, for charts demonstrating the sequence of mind moments in sleep and in meditation.

20. According to Buddhahosa's commentary. "Mind also is said to be 'clear' in the sense of 'exceedingly pure,' with reference to the subconscious life-continuum [*bhavanga*]. So the Buddha has said:—'Bhikkhus, the mind is luminous, but is corrupted by adventitious corruptions.' " Pe Maung Tin, trans., *The Expositor: Buddhaghosa's Commentary on the Dhammasanganī, the First Book of the Abhidhamma Piṭaka*, ed. C. A. F. Rhys Davids, Translation Series, nos. 8–9 (London: Pali Text Society, 1921–22), 185.

21. Harvey, *Selfless Mind*, 173.

22. Ibid.

23. For a systematic overview of the Indian Buddhist approach to dream, see the "Seven Questions of Ariyavansa-Ādiccaransī," summarized by Shwe Zan Aung in *Compendium of Philosophy*, ed. C. A. F. Rhys Davids, (London: Luzac & Company, 1972), 46–53.

24. O'Flaherty's summary of *Atharva Veda* 68.1.13–19, 29–37, and 44–47 is from vol. 1 of *The Pariśiṣṭas of the Atharva Veda*, ed. George Melville Bolling and Julius von Negelein (Leipzig: 1910). It gives the following examples: cho-

leric or fiery people will dream of "tawny skies and the earth and trees all dried up, great forest fires and parched clothes, limbs covered with blood and a river of blood, gods burning things up, and comets and lightning that burn the sky." People of watery, phlegmatic temperament dream of "rivers covered with snow—and clear skies and moons and swans; the women in their dreams are washed with fine water and wear fine clothes." People of bilius temperament dream of "flocks of birds and wild animals wandering about in distress, staggering and running and falling from heights, in lands where the mountains are whipped by the wind; the stars and the planets are dark, and the orbits of the sun and moon are shattered." Wendy Doniger O'Flaherty, *Dreams, Illusion and Other Realities* (Chicago: Chicago University Press, 1984), 18.

25. Ibid., 19.

26. Ibid., 20–21.

27. One of six classical schools of Hindu philosophy.

28. Sinha, *Indian Psychology*, 321.

29. T. W. Rhys Davids translates *nimitta* as "suggestion" in *Questions of King Milinda, Sacred Books of the East*, vol. 36 (1894; reprint, New York: Dover Publications, 1963), 157.

30. This comes from the Chinese version of the *Samantapāsādikā*, translated by Bapat and Hirakawa. P. V. Bapat and A. Hirawaka, trans., *Shan-Chien-P'i-P'o-Sha* (Poona: Bhandarkar Oriental Research Institute, 1970), 357.

31. See Serinity Young, *Dreaming in the Lotus: Buddhist Dream Narrative, Imagery, and Practice* (Boston: Wisdom Publications, 1999), 45–46.

32. The *Samantapāsādikā* states that dreams of worshipping the Buddha, reciting scripture, taking vows of good conduct, acts of generosity, or doing any kind of meritorious act also belong in this category—that is to say, they are true signs or omens of the future. Bapat and Hirakawa, *Shan-Chien-P'i-P'o-Sha*, 357.

33. Young, *Dreaming in the Lotus*, 46.

34. Tenzin Wangyal Rinpoché, *The Tibetan Yogas of Dream and Sleep*, ed. Mark Dhalby (Ithaca, NY: Snow Lion Publications, 1998), 140.

35. *Milindapañha* 4.3.27, in T. W. Rhys Davids, *Questions of King Milinda*, 35:247–48.

36. *Jātaka* 1.77, in E. B. Cowell, ed., *The Jātaka or Stories of the Buddha's Former Births*, trans. Robert Chalmers, vol. 1 (London: Luzac & Company, 1957), 194. The same objection to animal sacrifice is raised in the Buddhist encounter with shamanic cultures.

37. *Jātaka* 1. 87, in Cowell, *Jātaka*, 217.

38. T. W. Rhys Davids, trans., *Buddhist Birth-Stories (Jātaka Tales)* ed. C. A. F. Rhys Davids (London: Routledge, 1925), 89–96.

39. As a point of comparison, conception dreams are not unknown in shamanic traditions. Among the aboriginal tribes of central Australia, researchers have identified "conception totemism"—a dream revelation that links the child to be born with the mythic Dreamtime of the original ancestors. Aboriginal belief is that "prior to a child's birth, his or her 'totem' makes itself known to the child's parents or certain other close relatives in a special dream." Ronald M. Berndt, "The Dreaming," in *The Encyclopedia of Religion*, ed. Mircea Eliade (New York: Macmillan, 1987), 13:480.

40. T. W. Rhys Davids, *Buddhist Birth-Stories*, 149–50. Dreams heralding the conception of a great being also appear in Jain literature. Trisalā, the mother of Mahāvīra, the founder of Jainism, is represented as having fourteen conception dreams, and they include many of the motifs found in Māyā's dream. See Jagdish Sharma and Lee Siegel, *Dream-Symbolism in the Śramaṇic Tradition: Two Psychoanalytical Studies in Jinist & Buddhist Dream Legends* (Calcutta: Firma KLM Private, 1980), 10.

41. J. J. Jones, trans., *The Mahāvastu*, vol. 2, Sacred Books of Buddhists, vol. 18 (London: Pali Text Society, 1952), 11.

42. Gwendolyn Bays, trans., *The Voice of the Buddha: The Beauty of Compassion*, Tibetan Translation Series (Berkeley, CA: Dharma Publishing, 1983), 95–96.

43. Bhikkhu Telwatte Rahula, *A Critical Study of the Mahāvastu* (Delhi: Motilal Banarsidass, 1978), 192.

44. Alfred Foucher, *The Life of the Buddha* (Middletown, CT: Wesleyan University Press, 1963), 24.

45. Jones, *Mahāvastu*, 12.

46. *Aṅguttara-nikāya* 5.20.196, in E. M. Hare, trans., *The Book of the Gradual Sayings*, vol. 3 (London: Pali Text Society, 1973), 175–76.

47. Ibid., 176.

48. Serinity Young, for example, interprets this immediacy in terms of a causal relationship between the dreams and the Buddha's awakening. She proposes that the dreams contained signs that caused the Buddha to awaken; the seed of enlightenment and the seed of the eightfold way were lying dormant in the Buddha, only needing to be "stimulated by dreams." Young, *Dreaming in the Lotus*, 26.

49. *Udāna* 8.3, in Peter Masefield, trans., *The Udāna* (Oxford: Pali Text Society, 1994), 166.

50. For a Theravāda view of nirvāṇa, see Walpola Rahula, *What the Buddha Taught*, 2nd ed. (New York: Grove Press, 1974), 35–44.

51. Young, *Dreaming in the Lotus*, 29–31.

52. For a detailed analysis of dream in the biographies of the Buddha, see Young, *Dreaming in the Lotus*, 21–41.

53. The *Maharatnakuta Sātra* is a collection of Mahāyāna sūtras. Selections from it have been translated from the Chinese by Garma C. C. Chang, ed., *A Treasury of Mahāyāna Sūtras: Selections from the "Maharatnakuta Sātra"* (London: Pennsylvania State University Press, 1983).

54. Samuel Beal, trans., *The Romantic Legend of Śākya Buddha* (London: Trübner & Co., 1875), 200–201

55. Bays, *Voice of the Buddha*, 1:293.

56. Beal, *Romantic Legend*.

57. Bays, *Voice of the Buddha*, 1:294.

58. Ibid., 295.

59. Young, *Dreaming in the Lotus*, 36.

60. From *The Pariśiṣṭas*, quoted in O'Flaherty, *Dreams, Illusion and Other Realities*, 19.

61. Bays, *Voice of the Buddha*, 1:296.

62. I. B. Horner, trans., *The Book of the Discipline*, 6 vols. (London: Pali Text Society, 1938–66), 1:197.

63. In this case, the question is whether the condition of the person is one that allows him to form a serious intention to commit an offence.

64. Shwe Zan Aung and C.A.F. Rhys Davids, trans., *Points of Controversy or Subjects of Discourse* (London: Pali Text Society, 1915), 362. The term "negligible" is used here in the context of determining whether a monk has broken the *Vinaya* rules. Although dream thoughts and actions are classified as wholesome or unwholesome, the dream act can be ignored, because through them no actual harm has been done to persons or property and, therefore, it cannot be shown that a monastic rule has been broken.

65. Horner, *Middle Length Sayings*, 41.

66. From the commentary to the *Kathāvatthu* quoted in Aung and Rhys Davids, *Points of Controversy*, 361. The argument here is that "penetration of the Dharma" requires two conditions: the voice of another (i.e., teaching) and wise, systematic attention. Therefore, the attainment of nirvāṇa and the status of an arhat is not possible for one who is asleep, careless, forgetful, or lacking in mindfulness or clear comprehension.

67. Young, *Dreaming in the Lotus*, 16–17.

CHAPTER 4

1. David L. Snellgrove and Hugh Richardson, *A Cultural History of Tibet* (New York: Frederick A. Praeger, 1968), 70.

2. Friedhelm Hardy, "The Esoteric Traditions and Antinomian Movements," in *The World's Religions*, ed. Stewart Sutherland et al., SUNY Series in Buddhist Studies, ed. Matthew Kapstein (Boston: G. K. Hall & Co., 1988), 650. In the Tibetan language, the word for tantra, *rgyud*, has the sense of continuity or a chain of things linked together; it implies teachings transmitted in an unbroken line from authentic master to qualified disciple. The concept of lineage and its purity becomes one of the bulwarks of Tibetan Buddhism against the improper and unauthorized use of tantric practices.

3. Ibid., 654–55.

4. David L. Snellgrove, *Indo-Tibetan Buddhism: Indian Buddhists and Their Tibetan Successors*, vol. 1 (Boston: Shambhala, 1987), 130.

5. George N. Roerich, trans., *The Blue Annals*, 2nd ed. (Delhi: Motilal Banarsidass, 1976), 38. *The Blue Annals*, composed by Gos Lotsawa ca. 1476–78 CE, and Bu-ston's *History of Buddhism*, ca. 1322 CE, are the major sources for traditional Tibetan history. E. Obermiller, trans., *History of Buddhism by Bu-ston* (Heidelberg: O. Harrassowitz, 1931).

6. Dudjom Rinpoche, Jikdrel Yeshe Dorje, *The Nyingma School of Tibetan Buddhism: Its Fundamentals and History*, trans. and ed. Gyurme Dorje with Matthew Kapstein, vol. 1 (Boston: Wisdom Publications, 1991), 508. Bu-ston gives the name "Mysterious Helper" because by worshipping them, the king came to live for one hundred and twenty years. Obermiller, *History of Buddhism by Bu-ston*, 183.

7. Obermiller, *History of Buddhism by Bu-ston*, 183.

8. Ibid.

9. John Powers, *Introduction to Tibetan Buddhism* (Ithaca, NY: Snow Lion Publications, 1995), 125–26.

10. Snellgrove and Richardson, *Cultural History of Tibet*, 38. This inscription also points to the use of dream divination in that period.

11. Matthew Kapstein, *The Tibetan Assimilation of Buddhism: Conversion, Contestation, and Memory* (Oxford: Oxford University Press, 2000), 53.

12. Snellgrove and Richardson, *Cultural History of Tibet*, 107. The period of Buddhist contact and activity associated with the seventh to the ninth centuries is known as the "first dissemination"; after a period of persecution and political chaos, the revival of Buddhism in the tenth century marks the "second dissemination."

13. Ibid., 93.

14. See Helmut Hoffmann, *The Religions of Tibet*, trans. Edward Fitzgerald (London: George Allen & Unwin, 1961), esp. 66–83.

15. Garma C. C. Chang, trans., "The Miracle Contest on Di Se Snow Mountain," in *The Hundred Thousand Songs of Milarepa* (Boulder, CO: Shambhala Publications, 1977), vol. 1, 215–23. In the account of this competition in magic power, Milarepa accuses the Bön-po of a practice familiar to sorcerers of India and the witches of medieval Europe. He says, "I shall not emulate you, the magician who smears drugs on his body in order to deceive others by conjuring up delusive visions." Ibid., 218. For a discussion on the "witch's salve" and its relation to magical flight, see Hans Peter Duerr, *Dreamtime: Concerning the Boundary between Wilderness and Civilization* (New York: Basil Blackwell, 1987), 1–11.

16. The challenge of the magician and the display of magical power in the service of the Dharma also appears in the Mahāyāna texts of the *Mahāratnakuta Sūtra* where the magician Bhadra challenges the Buddha to a contest. That account is also concerned to show that the miraculous power of the Buddha is based on his profound insight into the nature of illusion and not on such things as spells or rituals. See Garma C. C. Chang trans. and ed., "The Prophecy of the Magician Bhadra's Attainment of Buddhahood," in *A Treasury of Mahāyāna Sūtras: Selections from the Mahāratnakuta Sūtra* (London: Pennsylvania State University Press, 1983), 3–21.

17. Bellezza recounts a Bön legend in which the famous Buddhist tantric master, Padmasambhava, is defeated in a magic competition by the Bön deity Targo—originally an autochthonous mountain protector brought under Bön control. See John Vincent Bellezza, *Spirit-Mediums, Sacred Mountains, and Related Bön Textual Traditions in Upper Tibet: Calling Down the Gods* (Leiden: E. J. Brill, 2005), 157. See also idem, *Divine Dyads: Ancient Civilization in Tibet* (Dharamsala: Library of Tibetan Works and Archives, 1997), 293–95.

18. David H. Holmberg, *Order in Paradox: Myth, Ritual, and Exchange among Nepal's Tamang* (Ithaca, NY: Cornell University Press, 1989), 218–19.

19. In the Bön regions of upper Tibet, a similar compromise allows both Buddhist and Bön-po to claim the power of the sacred Targo mountain. It is predominantly under Bön jurisdiction, but Buddhist claims on it have been

accommodated by dividing the mountain's sphere of influence into two realms, an inner Bön circle and an outer Buddhist circle. Bellezza, *Divine Dyads*, 295.

20. Bellezza gives much evidence for this argument in *Spirit-Mediums*. See also Joseph F. Rock, "Contributions to the Shamanism of the Tibetan-Chinese Borderland," *Anthropos* 54 (1959), 796–817. The most famous of the present-day oracle-mediums is the state oracle of Tibet, the Nechung, who embodies, in trance, the protector deity Pehar.

21. Padmasambhava was a legendary eighth-century tantric yogi known for his skill in magic. He is said to have come from the region of Swat and was invited to the court of King Trisong Detsen to defeat the Bön magicians and prepare the way for the establishment of the Dharma. See Snellgrove and Richardson, *Cultural History of Tibet*, 78.

22. See Holmberg, *Order in Paradox*; Stan Royal Mumford, *Himalayan Dialogue: Tibetan Lamas and Gurung Shamans in Nepal* (Madison: University of Wisconsin Press, 1989); Sherry B. Ortner, *Sherpas Through Their Rituals* (Cambridge: Cambridge University Press, 1978); Geoffrey Samuel, *Civilized Shamans: Buddhism in Tibetan Societies* (Washington, DC: Smithsonian Institution Press, 1993).

23. Barbara Aziz, "Reincarnation Reconsidered—or the Reincarnate Lama as Shaman," in *Spirit Possession in the Nepal Himalayas*, ed. John T. Hitchcock and Rex L. Jones (Warminster, England: Aris and Phillips, 1976), 347.

24. William Stablein, "Mahākāla the Neo-Shaman—Master of the Ritual," in *Spirit Possession*, ed. John T. Hitchcock and Rex L. Jones (Warminster, England: Aris and Phillips, 1976), 368.

25. "God-fallen-on" (*lha babs*) or "god-seized" (*lha adzin*).

26. Further, according to Buddhist thought, all beings have been reincarnated, and by that logic, everyone is possessed for life by the spirit of past lives.

27. Stablein, "Mahākāla the Neo-Shaman," 373.

28. In his research on Bön, Per Kværne notes, "Both Bön-po and čhos-pa [Buddhist] sources suggest that Buddhist siddhas, i.e. tantric adepts, and possibly also Śivaist yogins, established themselves in what is now Western Tibet.... This happened prior to—or at least independently of—the official introduction of Buddhism in Tibet in the form of čhos [Dharma]. Siddhas... established themselves in Tibet where they, as all sources agree in stating, became violently opposed to those Buddhist groups who enjoyed the particular favour of the royal house and who designated their doctrine as čhos." Kværne, "Aspects of the Origin of the Buddhist Tradition in Tibet," *Numen* 19 (1972): 38–39.

29. For an insightful study of the influences of Buddhist lamas on shamanic practice and vice versa, see Mumford, *Himalayan Dialogue*.

30. Matthew Kapstein, "The Illusion of Spiritual Progress: Remarks on Indo-Tibetan Buddhist Soteriology," in *Paths to Liberation: The Mārga and Its Transformations in Buddhist Thought*, ed. Robert E. Buswell, Jr., and Robert M. Gimello, Studies in East Asian Buddhism, no. 7 (Honolulu: University of Hawaii Press, 1992), 199.

31. The bodhisattva path in the Mahāyāna tradition consists in developing six major *pāramitās* (perfections): the perfections of generosity, virtue, patience, energetic effort, meditative concentration, and wisdom.

32. Mumford, *Himalayan Dialogue*, 113–14.

33. Ortner, *Sherpas Through Their Rituals*, 157–69.

34. Samuel, *Civilized Shamans*, 26.

35. The six practices are the yogas of inner heat, illusory body (which includes dream yoga), clear light, consciousness transference, forceful projection, and the *bardo* (intermediate-state). See Glenn Mullin, *The Six Yogas of Naropa*, 2nd ed. (Ithaca, NY: Snow Lion Publications, 2005).

36. Herbert Guenther, trans., *The Life and Teaching of Nāropa* (London: Oxford University Press, 1963), 67.

37. Shangs-pa gser-'phreng, khyung-po rnal-'byor-pa'i rnam-thar, folios 15b–17a; quoted in Kapstein, "Illusion of Spiritual Progress," 196.

38. Francisco J. Varela, ed., *Sleeping, Dreaming and Dying: An Exploration of Consciousness with the Dalai Lama* (Boston: Wisdom Publications, 1997), 38–39. This distinction is somewhat reminiscent of the Upaniṣadic discussion of the dreaming self as either leaving the body or roaming around within it.

39. Ibid., 125.

40. Glenn Mullin, ed. and trans., *Selected Works of the Dalai Lama II: Tantric Yogas of Sister Niguma* (Ithaca, NY: Snow Lion Publications, 1987), 139.

41. Ricard, et al., *The Life of Shabkar*, 174–75.

42. Chang, "Prophecy," 13.

43. For translations of the *Tibetan Book of the Dead*, see Francesca Fremantle and Chögyam Trungpa, trans., *The Tibetan Book of the Dead: The Great Liberation Through Hearing in the Bardo by Guru Rinpoché according to Karma Lingpa* (Boulder, CO: Shambhala, 1975). Robert Thurman, *The Tibetan Book of the Dead: Liberation Through Understanding in the Between* (New York: Bantam, 1994). See also Fremantle, *Luminous Emptiness: Understanding the "Tibetan Book of the Dead"* (Boston: Shambhala, 2003). For a contemporary Tibetan Buddhist view of the process of dying, see Sogyal Rinpoché, *The Tibetan Book of Living and Dying*, ed. Patrick Gaffney and Andrew Harvey (San Francisco: HarperSanFrancisco, 1992). On the relationship between the states of waking, sleeping, and dreaming and the process of death and rebirth, see Varela, *Sleeping, Dreaming and Dying*, 111–30.

44. Françoise Pommeret, "Returning from Hell," in *Religions of Tibet in Practice*. (Princeton, NJ: Princeton University Press, 1997), 503.

45. See Graham Watson and Jean-Guy Goulet, "Gold In; Gold Out: The Objectification of Dene Tha Accounts of Dreams and Visions," *Journal of Anthropological Research.* 48 (1992): 224–27. This article emphasizes that among the Dene Tha, "firsthand" knowledge, the only "true knowledge," is obtained through personal sensory experience of this world and in dreams and visions of the other world.

46. For a contemporary account and instructions by a Bön master of Tibetan sleep and dream yoga practice, see Tenzin Wangyal, *The Tibetan Yogas of Dream and Sleep* (Ithaca, NY: Snow Lion Publications, 1998).

47. Mullin, *Six Yogas*, 112.

48. Guenther, *Life and Teaching of Naropa*, 67–68. "A magic spell, a dream, a gleam before the eyes, a reflection, lightning, an echo, a rainbow, moonlight upon water, cloud-land, dimness before the eyes, fog and apparitions, these are the twelve similes of the phenomenal." Ibid., 63.

49. Anna-Leena Siikala, "Siberian and Inner Asian Shamanism,"in *Studies on Shamanism*, by Anna-Leena Siikala and Mihály Hoppál (Helsinki: Finnish Anthropological Society; Budapest: Akadémiai Kiadó, 1998), 12.

50. A. F. Anisimov, "The Shaman's Tent of the Evenks and the Origin of the Shamanistic Rite," in *Studies in Siberian Shamanism*, ed. Henry N. Michael (Toronto: University of Toronto Press, 1963), 105.

51. Robert B. Ekvall, *Religious Observances in Tibet: Patterns and Function* (Chicago: University of Chicago Press, 1964), 276, n. 29.

52. Personal communication from Khenpo Tsewang Gyatso, senior professor of Buddhist philosophy from Ngagyur Nyingma Institute in Bylakuppe, South India.

53. Ekvall, *Religious Observances in Tibet*, 256.

54. Ibid., 262–73.

55. Ibid., 272.

56. The Dalai Lama's dreams are recounted in an audiotaped interview with freelance journalists Andrew Brown, Madeline Bunting, and Mary Finnigan. Audiotape in the possession of the author.

57. Samuel, *Civilized Shamans*, 31.

58. Patrul Rinpoché, *Words of My Perfect Teacher*, 302. *Chö* or *Chöd* is the practice of offering one's body as food to demons and harmful spirits.

59. Ibid., 257.

60. This is the thesis carried through by Samuel in *Civilized Shamans*.

61. Patrul Rinpoché, *Words of My Perfect Teacher*, trans. Padmakara Translation Group (San Francisco: HarperCollins, 1994), 190. "Bönpo" in this context may refer to common village shamans or sorcerers who are not authentic representatives of either Buddhism or the Bön wisdom tradition. See ibid., 385, n. 115. See also Sarah Harding, trans. *Machik's Complete Explanation: Clarifying the Meaning of Chöd* (Ithaca, NY: Snow Lion Publications, 2003), 307 n. 19.

62. Michael Aris, *Hidden Treasures and Secret Lives* (Delhi: Motilal Banarsidass. 1988), 59.

63. Ibid., 62.

64. Marsha Woolf and Karen Blanc, *The Rainmaker: The Life Story of Venerable Ngagpa Yeshe Dorje Rinpoche* (Boston: Sigo Press, 1994), 50–51.

65. Ibid., 51.

66. Ninian Smart, "Soteriology: An Overview," in *The Encyclopedia of Religion*, ed. Mircea Eliade (New York: Macmillan, 1987), 7:418.

67. Willard G. Oxtoby, "Reflections of the Idea of Salvation," in *Man and His Salvation: Studies in Memory of S. G. F. Brandon*, ed. Eric J. Sharpe and John R. Hinnells (Manchester: Manchester University Press, 1973), 26–27.

68. Ninian Smart, "Soteriology," 421.

69. Jonathan Z. Smith, *Map Is Not Territory: Studies in the History of Religions* (Leiden: E. J. Brill, 1978), 101.

70. Jonathan Z. Smith, *Drudgery Divine: On the Comparison of Early Christianities and the Religions of Late Antiquity* (London: School of Oriental and African Studies, University of London, 1990), 124.

71. Kapstein, "Illusion of Spiritual Progress," 197–201.

72. Ibid., 198.

73. Smith, *Map Is Not Territory*, 309.
74. Kapstein, *Tibetan Assimilation of Buddhism*, 17.
75. Ibid., 19.

CHAPTER 5

1. For a detailed classification chart, see Alex Wayman, "Significance of Dreams in India and Tibet," in *Buddhist Insight: Essays by Alex Wayman*, ed. George Elder (Delhi: Motilal Banarsidass, 1984), 403.

2. This is a good example of Benjamin Kilborne's argument that dream classification expresses worldview and changes with the cultural context. In this case, the substitution of the three afflicted mental states for the three humors reflects a specifically Buddhist worldview. See Benjamin Kilborne, "On Classifying Dreams," in *Dreaming: Anthropological and Psychological Interpretations*, ed. Barbara Tedlock (Cambridge: Cambridge University Press, 1987), 189–91. The Pāli suttas describe nirvāṇa as the destruction of precisely these three afflictions. See F. L. Woodward, trans., *The Book of Kindred Sayings*, vol. 4 (London: Pali Text Society, 1927), 170.

3. Namkhai Norbu, *Dream Yoga and the Practice of Natural Light*, ed. Michael Katz (Ithaca, NY: Snow Lion Publications, 1992), 37–42.

4. Personal communication from Khenpo Tsewang Gyatso.

5. Antonella Crescenzi and Fabrizio Torricelli, "Tibetan Literature on Dreams: Materials for a Bibliography," *Tibet Journal* 22, no. 1 (1997): 61.

6. Norbu Chophel, *Folk Culture of Tibet: Superstitions and Other Beliefs* (Dharamsala: Library of Tibetan Works and Archives, 1983), 91.

7. Ibid.

8. For a discussion on how the Tibetan system of nerves and channels relates to Tibetan medicine, see Tom Dummer, *Tibetan Medicine and Other Holistic Health-Care Systems*, (London: Routledge, 1994), 10–13; and Terry Clifford, *Tibetan Buddhist Medicine and Psychiatry: The Diamond Healing* (York Beach, ME: Samuel Weiser, 1990), 68–76.

9. Keith Dowman, *Sky Dancer: The Secret Life and Songs of the Lady Yeshe Tsogyel* (London: Routledge & Kegan Paul, 1984), 246.

10. Personal conversation with Dr. Tenzin Tsephel.

11. Gyurme Dorje and Fernand Meyer, ed. and trans., *Tibetan Medical Paintings: Illustrations to the "Blue Beryl" treatise of Sangye Gyamtso (1653–1705)* (New York: Harry N. Abrams, 1992), 1:14–15. Dream classification and imagery in the Tibetan medical tradition closely mirrors classical Indian texts such as the *Caraka-Saṃhitā.*

12. Yeshi Dhondhen and Jhampa Kelsang, ed. and trans., *Ambrosia Heart Tantra* (Dharamsala: Library of Tibetan Works and Archives, 1983), 1:51–52.

13. Dorje and Meyer, *Tibetan Medical Paintings*, 1:1–45.

14. Personal interview. Dr. Tsephel was of the opinion that the use of dream in medical prognosis or diagnosis is not common in contemporary Tibetan medical practice, although he noted that he paid attention to his own dreams when sick.

15. A similar sevenfold classification appears in the Indian medical text the *Caraka Saṃhitā*: dreams of objects previously seen, heard, or felt; dreams based on desires; dreams based on imagination; premonitions of future events; and pathological dreams. See Jadunath Sinha, *Indian Psychology* 2nd ed. (Delhi: Motilal Banarsidass, 1985), 1:315.

16. See Dhondhen and Kelsang, *Ambrosia Heart Tantra*, 1:51.

17. The Buddhist theory of interdependent origination (Skt. *pratītya-samutpāda*) is translated by the Tibetan word *tendrel* (Tib. *rten 'brel*) and in Tibetan is also used to mean "auspices," "omens," or "karmic connections." See further discussion on pages 107–109.

18. Dorje and Meyer, *Tibetan Medical Paintings*, 1:49.

19. Ibid., 2:205.

20. Ibid., 1:49.

21. Ibid., 1:51.

22. Tibetan Refugee Camp Four at Bylakuppe in the state of Karnataka. Most participants were from the Kham region of eastern Tibet.

23. Chophel, *Folk Culture of Tibet*, 90.

24. From Khenpo Tsewang Gyatso, trans., *Collection des tresors revélés par Gnam-chos Mi-'gyur-rdo-rje*, vols. 1–13 (Paro Kyichu, Bhutan: Dilgo Khyentsey Rinpoché; Bylakuppe, Mysore, India: Pema Norbu Rinpoché; published under the auspices of Ecole française d'Extrême-Orient, 1983). Thanks to Chris Fynn for drawing my attention to this passage. Although I have not investigated the connection between dream and spirits entering the mouth, the relationship is notable. The imagery of taking the offending spirits into the mouth appears also in the Fourteenth Dalai Lama's dream discussed earlier. In Siberian shamanism, the shaman yawns to indicate the spirits entering him through the mouth. And in Indian literature the account of the fourteen great conception dreams attributed to Trisalà, mother of Mahāvīra, ends with the words, "[T]hese dreams in succession the Mistress [Trisalà] saw entering her mouth." Jagdish Sharma and Lee Siegel, *Dream Symbolism in the Śramaṇic Tradition* (Calcutta: Firma KLM Private, 1980), 10.

25. Stephan Beyer, *The Cult of Tara: Magic and Ritual in Tibet* (Berkeley and Los Angeles: University of California Press, 1978), 466.

26. Ibid., 466.

27. James Mullens and Tsering Mullens, trans., "Categories of Dreams in the Course of the Night," unpublished dream manual manuscript, Dharamsala, 1981.

28. Ibid.

29. Sarah Harding, *Machik's Complete Explanation* (Ithaca, NY: Snow Lion Publications, 2003), 231–52.

30. Ibid., 217–29.

31. Ferdinand Lessing and Alex Wayman, *Introduction to the Buddhist Tantric Systems*, 2nd ed. (Delhi: Motilal Banarsidass, 1978), 279.

32. Ibid., 278 n.12.

33. Ibid., 203.

34. Alex Wayman, trans., "Study of the Vairocanabhisambodhitantra," in *The Enlightenment of Vairocana*, Buddhist Tradition Series, ed. Alex Wayman, vol. 18 (Delhi: Motilal Banarsidass, 1992), 121.

35. There is also a concealed treasure tradition associated with the Bön religion.

36. For information on the *terma* system, see Tulku Thondup, *Hidden Teachings of Tibet: An Explanation of the Terma Tradition of Tibetan Buddhism*, ed. Harold Talbott (Boston: Wisdom Publications, 1997). See also Andreas Doctor, *Tibetan Treasure Literature* (Snow Lion Publications, 2005).

37. *The Autobiography of Padma Ling pa—The Exquisite Ray* (published by Kunsang Tobgay, 1975), quoted in Tulku Thondup, *Hidden Teachings of Tibet,* 75–76.

38. Tulku Thondup, *Hidden Teachings of Tibet*, 74.

39. Janet Gyatso, *Apparitions of the Self: The Secret Autobiographies of a Tibetan Visionary,* (Princeton, NJ: Princeton University Press, 1998), 162–67.

40. Ibid., 162.

41. S. C. Das, *A Tibetan-English Dictionary* (Delhi: Motilal Banarsidass, 1902), 537, gives *tenpar drelwar gyurwa* (*rten par 'brel bar gyur ba*) as the long form. Tsepak Rigzin, *Tibetan-English Dictionary of Buddhist Terminology*, 2nd ed. (Dharamsala: Library of Tibetan Works and Archives, 1993), 109 gives *rten cing 'brel bar 'byung ba*.

42. Geoffrey Samuel, *Civilized Shamans: Buddhism in Tibetan Societies* (Washington, DC: Smithsonian Institution Press, 1993), 448.

43. Ibid.

44. Personal communication with Khenpo Tsewang Gyatso.

45. Ibid.

46. Dudjom Rinpoché, *The Nyingma School of Tibetan Buddhism*, trans. and ed. Gyurme Dorje with Matthew Kapstein (Boston: Wisdom Publications, 1991), 1:228.

47. Ekvall, *Religious Observances in Tibet*, 254.

48. Matthieu Ricard et al., trans., *The Life of Shabkar: The Autobiography of a Tibetan Yogin* (Albany: State University of New York Press, 1994), 44.

49. Marie-Françoise Guédon, "La pratique du rêve chez les Dénés Septentrionaux," *Anthropologie et Sociétés* 18, no. 2 (1994): 81.

50. Mullens and Mullens, "Categories of Dreams in the Course of the Night."

51. Garma C. C. Chang, *The Hundred Thousand Songs of Milarepa* (Boulder, CO: Shambhala Publications, 1977), 1:235.

52. Francesca Fremantle and Chögyam Trungpa, trans., *The Tibetan Book of the Dead: The Great Liberation Through Hearing in the Bardo by Guru Rinpoché according to Karma Lingpa* (Boulder, CO: Shambhala, 1975), 60.

53. Gyatso, *Apparitions of the Self*, 16.

54. Ibid.

55. Samten Gyaltsen Karmay, *Secret Visions of the Fifth Dalai Lama*, 2nd ed. (London: Serindia Publications, 1998), 14.

56. Gyatso, *Apparitions of the Self*, 16.

57. Chang, *Hundred Thousand Songs of Milarepa*, 1:231–32.

58. Gyatso, *Apparitions of the Self*, 199.

59. Ibid.

60. Chang, *Hundred Thousand Songs of Milarepa*, 1:231.

61. See Serinity Young, *Dreaming in the Lotus: Buddhist Dream Narrative, Imagery, and Practice* (Boston: Wisdom Publications, 1999), 26–27; 108–9.

62. Chang, *Hundred Thousand Songs of Milarepa*, 1:235.

63. Matthew Kapstein, "The Illusion of Spiritual Progress," in *Paths to Liberation*, ed. Robert E. Buswell, Jr., and Robert M. Gimello (Honolulu: University of Hawaii Press, 1992), 198.

64. Stan Royal Mumford, *Himalayan Dialogue: Tibetan Lamas and Gurung Shamans in Nepal* (Madison: University of Wisconsin Press, 1989), 192.

65. Ibid., 114.

66. Young, *Dreaming in the Lotus*, 17.

67. Stealing is defined as taking what is not given, so the forest spirit points out that the lotus scent is a thing not expressly given to the monk. See C. A. F. Rhys Davids, trans., *The Book of Kindred Sayings*, vol. 1 (London: Pali Text Society, 1930), 260–61.

CONCLUSION

1. Geoffrey Samuel, *Civilized Shamans: Buddhism in Tibetan Societies* (Washington, DC: Smithsonian Institution Press, 1993), 448.

2. *Saṃyutta-nikāya* 35.3.4.136, in F. L. Woodward, trans., *The Book of Kindred Sayings*, vol. 4 (London: Pali Text Society, 1927), 81–82.

3. Glenn H. Mullin, trans. and ed., *Selected Works of the Dalai Lama II: The Tantric Yogas of Sister Niguma* (Ithaca, NY: Snow Lion Publications, 1985), 97.

Bibliography

TRANSLATIONS

Aung, Shwe Zan, and C. A. F. Rhys Davids, trans. *Points of Controversy or Subjects of Discourse.* London: Pali Text Society, 1915. (Translation of the *Kathā-Vattu.*)

Bapat, P. V., and A. Hirawaka, trans. *Shan-Chien-P'i-P'o-Sha.* Poona: Bhandarkar Oriental Research Institute, 1970. (Translation from the Chinese version of the *Samantapāsādikā.*)

Bays, Gwendolyn, trans. *The Voice of the Buddha: The Beauty of Compassion.* 2 vols. Berkeley, CA: Dharma Publishing, 1983. (Translation of the *Lalitavistara.*)

Beal, Samuel, trans. *The Romantic Legend of Śākya Buddha.* 1875. Delhi: Motilal Banarsidass, 1985. (Translation from the Chinese version of the *Abhiniṣkramaṇasūtra.*)

Bose, Abinash Chandra, trans. *Hymns from the Vedas.* London: Asia Publishing House, 1966.

Chang, Garma C. C., trans. *The Hundred Thousand Songs of Milarepa.* Boulder, CO: Shambhala Publications, 1977.

———, ed. and trans. *A Treasury of Mahāyāna Sūtras: Selections from the "Mahāratnakuta Sūtra."* London: Pennsylvania State University Press, 1983.

Cowell, E. B., ed. *The Jātaka or Stories of the Buddha's Former Births.* 6 vols. London: Luzac, 1957.

Dhondhen, Yeshi, and Jhampa Kelsang, eds. and trans. *The Ambrosia Heart Tantra: The Secret Oral Instructions on the Eight Branches of the Science of Tibetan Medicine.* Vol. 1. Tibetan Medicine, no. 6. Dharamsala: Library of Tibetan Works and Archives, 1983.

Dorje, Gyurme, and Fernand Meyer, eds. and trans. *Tibetan Medical Paintings: Illustrations to the "Blue Beryl" Treatise of Sangye Gyamtso (1653–1705).* New York: Harry N. Abrams, 1992. (Prepared from the summaries of Yuri Parfionovitch.)

Eggeling, Julius, trans. *Śatapatha-Brāhmaṇa,* Parts 1–3, Sacred Books of the East. 2nd ed. Delhi: Motilal Banarsidass, 1966.

Fremantle, Francesca, and Chögyam Trungpa, trans. *The Tibetan Book of the Dead: The Great Liberation Through Hearing in the Bardo.* Boston: Shambhala, 1975.

Griffith, Ralph T. H., trans. *The Hymns of the Atharvaveda.* Varanasi: Chowkhamba Sanskrit Series Office, 1968.

———, trans. *The Hymns of the Ṛgveda.* Delhi: Motilal Banarsidass, 1973.

Guenther, Herbert, trans. *The Life and Teaching of Nāropa.* London: Oxford University Press, 1963.

Gyatso, Khenpo Tsewang, trans. *Collection des tresors revélés par Gnam-chos Mi-'gyur-rdo-rje* (excerpt). Vols. 1–13. Paro Kyichu, Bhutan: Dilgo Khyentsey Rinpoché; Bylakuppe, Mysore, India: Pema Norbu Rinpoché; published under the auspices of Ecole française d'Extrême-Orient, 1983.

Harding, Sarah, trans. *Machik's Complete Explanation: Clarifying the Meaning of Chöd.* Ithaca, NY: Snow Lion, 2003.

Hare, E. M., trans. *The Book of the Gradual Sayings.* Vol. 3. London: Pali Text Society, 1934. (Translation of the *Aṅguttara-nikāya.*)

Harrison, Paul, trans. *The Samādhi of the Direct Encounter with the Buddhas of the Present.* Studia Philologica Buddhica Monograph Series, vol. 5. Tokyo: International Institute for Buddhist Studies, 1990. (Translation from the Tibetan version of the *Pratyutpanna-Buddha-Sammukhāvasthita-Samādhi-Sūtra.*)

Horner, I. B., trans. *The Book of the Discipline* 6 vols. London: Pali Text Society, 1938–66. (Translation of the first selection of the *Vinaya-Piṭaka.*)

Johnston, E. H., trans. *The Buddhacarita or Acts of the Buddha: Part II.* 2nd ed. New Delhi: Oriental Reprint, 1972. (Translation of the *Buddhacarita,* by Aśvaghoṣa. Cantos 1–14 are translated from the original Sanskrit manuscript, supplemented by the Tibetan version, Lahore, 1936.)

Jones, J. J., trans. *The Mahāvastu.* Vol. 2. Sacred Books of Buddhists, vol. 18. London: Pali Text Society, 1952.

Karmay, Samten Gyaltsen, trans. *Secret Visions of the Fifth Dalai Lama.* The Gold Manuscript in the Fournier Collection Musée Guimet, Paris. 2nd ed. London: Serindia Publications, 1998.

Kongtrul, Jamgon. *The Great Path of Awakening: A Commentary on the Mahayana Teaching of the Seven Points of Mind Training.* Translation by Ken McLeod. Boston: Shambhala, 1987.

Lessing, Ferdinand D., and Alex Wayman, trans. *Introduction to the Buddhist Tantric Systems.* 2nd ed. Delhi: Motilal Banarsidass, 1978. (Translation of *rGyud sde spyi'i rnam par gzhag pa rgyas par brjod,* by Mkhas-grub-rje.)

Masefield, Peter, trans. *The Udāna.* Oxford: Pali Text Society, 1994.

Maskarinec, Gregory G., trans. *Nepalese Shaman Oral Texts.* Harvard Oriental Series, vol. 55. Cambridge, MA: Harvard University Press, 1998.

Mullens, James, and Tsering Mullens, trans. "Categories of Dreams in the Course of the Night." Unpublished manuscript, Dharamsala, 1981. (Translation from the *Zap-mo gChod-kyi dMigs-'Bum,* by Machik Labdrönma.)

Mullin, Glenn H., trans. and ed. *Selected Works of the Dalai Lama II: The Tantric Yogas of Sister Niguma.* Ithaca, NY: Snow Lion Publications, 1985.

———, trans. *The Six Yogas of Naropa—Tsongkhapa's Commentary Entitled A Book of Three Inspirations: A Treatise on the Stages of Training in the Pro-*

found Path of Naro's Six Dharmas Commonly Referred to as The Three Inspirations. Ithaca, NY: Snow Lion Publications, 2005. (Previously published as *Tsongkhapa's Six Yogas of Naropa*, 1996.)

Ñāṇamoli, Bhikkhu, trans. *The Path of Purification*. Seattle: BPS Pariyatti Editions, 1975. (Translation of the *Visuddhimagga*, by Buddhaghosa.)

Ñāṇamoli, Bhikkhu, and Bhikkhu Bodhi, trans. and eds. *The Middle Length Discourses of the Buddha*. Boston: Wisdom Publications, 1995. (Translation of the *Majjhima-nikāya*.)

Obermiller, E., trans. *History of Buddhism by Bu-ston*. Heidelberg: O. Harrassowitz, 1931. (Translation of the *Chos-hbyung*.)

Olivelle, Patrick, trans. *Upaniṣads*. Oxford: Oxford University Press, 1996.

Patrul Rinpoché. *The Words of My Perfect Teacher*. Translated by the Padmakara Translation Group. San Francisco: HarperCollins, 1994.

Rhys Davids, C. A. F., trans. *The Book of Kindred Sayings*. Vol. 1. London: Pali Text Society, 1917. (Translation of the *Saṃyutta-nikāya*.)

Rhys Davids, T. W., trans. *The Questions of King Milinda*. Sacred Books of the East, vols. 35–36. 1894. Reprint, New York: Dover Publications, 1963. (Translation of the *Milindapañha*.)

———, trans. *Buddhist Birth-Stories*. 1880. Reprint, London: Routledge & Sons, 1925. (Translation of the *Nidānakathā*.)

Ricard, Matthieu, Jakob Leschly, Erik Schmidt, Marilyn Silverstone, and Lodrö Palmo, trans. *The Life of Shabkar: The Autobiography of a Tibetan Yogin*. Albany: State University of New York Press, 1994.

Roerich, George N., trans. *The Blue Annals*. 2nd ed. Delhi: Motilal Banarsidass, 1976.

Thibaut, George, trans. *The Vedānta Sūtras of Bādarāyana with the Commentary by Śankara, Part II*. 1890–96. Reprint, New York: Dover Publications, 1962.

Thurman, Robert, trans. *The Tibetan Book of the Dead: Liberation Through Understanding in the Between*. New York: Bantam, 1994.

Tin, Pe Maung, trans. *The Expositor: Buddhaghosa's Commentary on the Dhammasaṅgaṇi, the First Book of the Abhidhamma Piṭaka*. Edited and revised by C. A. F. Rhys Davids. Translation Series, vol. 8. London: Pali Text Society, 1920. (Translation of the *Atthasālinī*.)

Wayman, Alex, trans. "Study of the Vairocanabhisambodhitantra." In *The Enlightenment of Vairocana*, 1–208. Buddhist Tradition Series, ed. Alex Wayman, vol. 18. Delhi: Motilal Banarsidass, 1992.

Whitney, William Dwight, trans. *Atharva-Veda-Saṃhitā*. Vol. 2. Harvard Oriental Series, ed. Charles Rockwell Lanman, vol. 8. Delhi: Motilal Banarsidass, 1971.

Woodward, F. L., trans. *The Book of Kindred Sayings*. Vol. 4. London: Pali Text Society, 1927. (Translation of the *Saṃyutta-nikāya*.)

ETHNOGRAPHIES AND OTHER SOURCES

Anisimov, A. F. "Cosmological Concepts of the Peoples of the North." In *Studies in Siberian Shamanism*, edited by Henry N. Michael, 157–229.

Arctic Institute of North America Anthropology of the North: Translations from Russian Sources, no. 4. Toronto: University of Toronto Press, 1963.

———. "The Shaman's Tent of the Evenks and the Origin of the Shamanistic Rite." In *Studies in Siberian Shamanism*, edited by Henry N. Michael, 84–123. Arctic Institute of North America Anthropology of the North: Translations from Russian Sources, no. 4. Toronto: University of Toronto Press, 1963.

Appell, George N., and Laura W. R. Appell. "To Converse with the Gods: Rungus Spirit Mediums." In *The Seen and the Unseen: Shamanism, Mediumship and Possession in Borneo*, edited by Robert L. Winzeler. Williamsburg, VA: Borneo Research Council, 1993.

Aris, Michael. *Bhutan: The Early History of a Himalayan Kingdom*. Warminster, England: Aris & Phillips, 1979.

———. *Hidden Treasures and Secret Lives*. Delhi: Motilal Banarsidass, 1988.

Aziz, Barbara. "Reincarnation Reconsidered—or the Reincarnate Lama as Shaman." In *Spirit Possession in the Nepal Himalayas*, edited by John T. Hitchcock and Rex L. Jones, 343–60. Warminster, England: Aris and Phillips, 1976.

Basilov, Vladimir N. "Blessing in a Dream." *Turcica* 27 (1995): 237–46.

———. "Cosmos as Everyday Reality in Shamanism: An Attempt to Formulate a More Precise Definition of Shamanism." In *Shamanic Cosmos: From India to the North Pole Star*, edited by Romano Mastromattei and Antonio Rigopoulos, 17–39. Venetian Academy of Indian Studies Series, no. 1. Venice: Venetian Academy of Indian Studies, 1999.

———. "Texts of Shamanistic Invocations from Central Asia and Kazakhstan." In *Ancient Traditions: Shamanism in Central Asia and the Americas*, edited by Gary Seaman and Jane S. Day, 273–92. Niwot: University Press of Colorado; Denver: Denver Museum of Natural History, 1994.

Belleza, John Vincent. *Divine Dyads: Ancient Civilization in Tibet*. Dharamsala: Library of Tibetan Works and Archives, 1997.

———. *Spirit-Mediums, Sacred Mountains and Related Bön Textual Traditions in Upper Tibet—Calling Down the Gods*. Leiden: E. J. Brill, 2005.

Berndt, Ronald M. "The Dreaming." In vol. 13 of *The Encyclopedia of Religion*, ed. Mircea Eliade, 479–81. New York: Macmillan, 1987.

Beyer, Stephan. *The Cult of Tara: Magic and Ritual in Tibet*. Berkeley and Los Angeles: University of California Press, 1978.

Bird-David, Nurit. " 'Animism' Revisited: Personhood, Environment, and Relational Epistemology." *Current Anthropology* 40, supplement (February 1999).

Bogoras, W. "The Chuckchee—Religion." In vol. 11, pt. 2, of *Memoirs of the American Museum of Natural History*, ed. Franz Boas, 277–536. Leiden: E. J. Brill, 1909. (Reprinted from *The Jesup North Pacific* Expedition, ed. Franz Boas, vol. 7, part 2.)

Bolling, George Melville. "Dreams and Sleep (Vedic)." In vol. 5 of *The Encyclopaedia of Religion and Ethics*, edited by James Hastings, 38–40. Edinburgh: T. & T. Clark, 1913.

Bulkeley, Kelly. *The Wilderness of Dreams.* Albany: State University of New York Press, 1994.

Chernetsov, V. N. "Concepts of the Soul among the Ob Ugrians." In *Studies in Siberian Shamanism,* edited by Henry N. Michael, 3–45. Arctic Institute of North America Anthropology of the North: Translations from Russian Sources, no. 4. Toronto: University of Toronto Press, 1963.

Chophel, Norbu. *Folk Culture of Tibet: Superstitions and Other Beliefs.* Dharamsala: Library of Tibetan Works and Archives, 1983.

Clifford, Terry. *Tibetan Buddhist Medicine and Psychiatry: The Diamond Healing.* With a foreword by His Holiness the Dalai Lama and an introduction by Lokesh Chandra. York Beach, ME: Samuel Weiser, 1990.

Cornu, Philippe. *Tibetan Astrology.* Boston: Shambhala, 2002.

Crescenzi, Antonella, and Fabrizio Torricelli. "Tibetan Literature on Dreams: Materials for a Bibliography." *Tibet Journal* 22, no. 1 (1997): 3–17.

Curtin, Jeremiah. *A Journey in Southern Siberia.* Boston: Little, Brown and Company, 1909.

Das, Sarat Chandra. *A Tibetan-English Dictionary with Sanskrit Synonyms.* Edited by Graham Sandberg and A. William Heyde. Delhi: Motilal Banarsidass, 1970.

Deutsch, Eliot. *Advaita Vedānta: A Philosophical Reconstruction.* Honolulu: University of Hawaii Press, 1985.

Diószegi, Vilmos. *Tracing Shamans in Siberia: The Story of an Ethnographical Research Expedition.* Translated by Anita Rajkay Babó. Oosterhout: Anthropological Publications, 1968.

Dow, James. *The Shaman's Touch: Otomí Indian Symbolic Healing.* Salt Lake City: University of Utah Press, 1986.

Dowman, Keith. *Sky Dancer: The Secret Life and Songs of the Lady Yeshe Tsogyel.* London: Routledge & Kegan Paul, 1984.

Dudjom Rinpoché, Jikdrel Yeshe Dorje. *The Nyingma School of Tibetan Buddhism: Its Fundamentals and History.* Translated and edited by Gyurme Dorje with Matthew Kapstein. Vol. 1. Boston: Wisdom Publications, 1991.

Duerr, Hans Peter. *Dreamtime: Concerning the Boundary between Wilderness and Civilization.* New York: Basil Blackwell, 1987.

Dummer, Tom. *Tibetan Medicine and Other Holistic Health-Care Systems.* With a foreword by His Holiness the Dalai Lama. London: Routledge, 1994.

Ekvall, Robert B. *Religious Observances in Tibet: Patterns and Function.* Chicago: University of Chicago Press, 1964.

Eliade, Mircea. *Shamanism: Archaic Techniques of Ecstasy.* Translated by Willard R. Trask. Bollingen Series, no. 76. Princeton, NJ: Princeton University Press, 1964.

Flanagan, Owen. *Dreaming Souls.* Oxford: Oxford University Press, 2000.

Foucher, A. *The Life of the Buddha.* Middletown, CT: Wesleyan University Press, 1963.

Fremantle, Francesca. *Luminous Emptiness: Understanding the "Tibetan Book of the Dead."* Boston: Shambhala, 2003.

Furst, Peter T. "An Overview of Shamanism." In *Ancient Traditions: Shamanism in Central Asia and the Americas,* edited by Gary Seaman and Jane S.

Day, 1–28. Niwot: University Press of Colorado; Denver: Denver Museum of Natural History, 1994.

Gellner, David N. *The Anthropology of Buddhism and Hinduism: Weberian Themes*. New Delhi: Oxford University Press, 2001.

Germano, David. "Food, Clothes, Dreams, and Karmic Propensities." In *Religions of Tibet in Practice*, edited by Donald S. Lopez, Jr., 293–312. Princeton, NJ: Princeton University Press, 1997.

Gill, Sam. *Native American Religions: An Introduction*. Edited by Frederick J. Streng. The Religious Life of Man Series. Belmont, CA: Wadsworth Publishing Company, 1982.

Gonda, Jan. *Change and Continuity in Indian Religion*. The Hague: Mouton & Co., 1965.

———. *The Vision of the Vedic Poets*. The Hague: Mouton & Co., 1963.

Goulet, Jean-Guy. *Ways of Knowing: Experience, Knowledge, and Power among the Dene Tha*. Vancouver: UBC Press, 1998.

Greve, Reinhard. "The Shaman and the Witch: An Analytical Approach to Shamanic Poetry in the Himalayas." In *Shamanism Past and Present: Part 2*, edited by Mihály Hoppál and Otto von Sadovsky, 219–24. Budapest: Ethnographic Institute, Hungarian Academy of Sciences, 1989.

Guédon, Marie-Françoise. "La pratique du rêve chez les Dénés septentrionaux." *Anthropologie et Sociétés* 18, no. 2 (1994): 75–89.

Gyatso, Janet. *Apparitions of the Self: The Secret Autobiographies of a Tibetan Visionary*. Princeton, NJ: Princeton University Press, 1998. (A translation and study of Jigme Lingpa's *Dancing Moon in the Water* and *Dākki's Grand Secret-Talk*.)

———. "Down with the Demoness: Reflections on a Feminine Ground in Tibet." *Tibet Journal* 12, no. 4 (1987): 38–53.

Hardy, Friedhelm. "The Esoteric Traditions and Antinomian Movements." In *The World's Religions*, edited by Stewart Sutherland, Leslie Houlden, Peter Clarke, and Friedhelm Hardy. Boston: G. K. Hall, 1988.

Harvey, Peter. *The Selfless Mind: Personality, Consciousness and Nirvàṇa in Early Buddhism*. Surrey: Curzon Press, 1995.

Heissig, Walther. "A Mongolian Source to the Lamaist Suppression of Shamanism in the 17th Century." *Anthropos* 48, nos. 3–4 (1953): 493–536.

———. *The Religions of Mongolia*. Translated by Geoffrey Samuel. Berkeley and Los Angeles: University of California Press, 1980.

Hoffman, Helmut. *The Religions of Tibet*. Translated by Edward Fitzgerald. London: George Allen & Unwin, 1961.

Holmberg, David H. *Order in Paradox: Myth, Ritual, and Exchange among Nepal's Tamang*. Ithaca, NY: Cornell University Press, 1989.

Hoppál, Mihály. "The Role of Shamanism in Hungarian Ethnic Identity." In *Studies on Shamanism*, by Anna-Leena Siikala and Mihály Hoppál, 169–75. Helsinki: Finnish Anthropological Society; Budapest: Akadémiai Kiadó, 1998.

———. "Shamanism: An Archaic and/or Recent System of Beliefs." In *Studies on Shamanism*, by Anna-Leena Siikala and Mihály Hoppál, 117–31. Helsinki: Finnish Anthropological Society; Budapest: Akadémiai Kiadó, 1998.

Huber, Toni. *The Cult of Pure Crystal Mountain*. New York: Oxford University Press, 1999.

———, ed. *Sacred Spaces and Powerful Places in Tibetan Culture*. Dharamsala: Library of Tibetan Works and Archives, 1999.

Hultkrantz, Åke. "Aspects of Saami (Lapp) Shamanism." In vol. 3 of *Northern Religions and Shamanism*, edited by Mihály Hoppál and Juha Pentikäinen. Budapest: Ethnologica Uralica, 1992.

———. "The Concept of the Soul Held by the Wind River Shoshone." *Ethnos* 16 (1951): 18–44.

Humphrey, Caroline. *Shamans and Elders: Experience, Knowledge, and Power among the Daur Mongols*. With Urgunge Onon. Oxford: Clarendon Press, 1996.

Inglis, Brian. *Trance: A Natural History of Altered States of Mind*. London: Grafton Books, 1989.

Jakobsen, Merete Demant. *Shamanism: Traditional and Contemporary Approaches to the Mastery of Spirits and Healing*. New York: Berghahn Books, 1999.

Johnson, Willard. *Poetry and Speculation of the Rg Veda*. Berkeley and Los Angeles: University of California Press, 1980.

Kaelber, Walter O. *Tapta Mārga: Asceticism and Initiation in Vedic India*. Albany: State University of New York Press, 1989.

Kakar, Sudhir. *Shamans, Mystics and Doctors: A Psychological Inquiry into India and Its Healing Traditions*. New York: Alfred A. Knopf, 1982.

Kapstein, Matthew. "The Illusion of Spiritual Progress: Remarks on Indo-Tibetan Buddhist Soteriology." In *Paths to Liberation: The Mārga and Its Transformations in Buddhist Thought*, edited by Robert E. Buswell, Jr., and Robert M. Gimello, 193–224. Studies in East Asian Buddhism, no. 7. Honolulu: University of Hawaii Press, 1992.

———. *The Tibetan Assimilation of Buddhism: Conversion, Contestation, and Memory*. Oxford: Oxford University Press, 2000.

Karma, Ura. "Deities and Environment." Thimpu: Center for Bhutan Studies, 2001.

Karmay, Samten. *The Arrow and the Spindle: Studies in History, Myths, Rituals and Beliefs in Tibet*. Kathmandu: Mandala Book Point, 1998.

Kehoe, Alice Beck. *Shamans and Religion: An Anthropological Exploration in Critical Thinking*. Long Grove, Illinois: Waveland Press, 2000.

Kilborne, Benjamin. "Dreams." In *The Encyclopedia of Religion*, edited by Mircea Eliade, 482–92. New York: Macmillan, 1987.

———. "On Classifying Dreams." In *Dreaming: Anthropological and Psychological Interpretations*, edited by Barbara Tedlock, 171–93. Cambridge: Cambridge University Press, 1987.

Knab, Timothy J. *The Dialogue of Earth and Sky: Dreams, Souls, Curing, and the Modern Aztec Underworld*. Tucson: University of Arizona Press, 2004.

Kværne, Per. "Aspects of the Origin of the Buddhist Tradition in Tibet." *Numen: International Review for the History of Religions* 19 (1972): 22–40.

———. *The Bön Religion of Tibet: The Iconography of a Living Tradition*. Boston: Shambhala, 1996.

Lessing, Ferdinand D. "Calling the Soul: A Lamaist Ritual." *Semitic and Oriental Studies* 11 (1951): 263–84.

Lévy-Bruhl, Lucien. *How Natives Think.* Translated by Lilian A. Clare. New York: A. A. Knopf, 1925.

Lewis, I. M. *Ecstatic Religion: A Study of Shamanism and Spirit Possession.* London: Routledge, 1971.

Lommel, Andreas. "Shamanism in Australia." In *Shamanism Past and Present: Part 1,* edited by Mihály Hoppál and Otto von Sadovsky, 25–42. Budapest: Ethnographic Institute, Hungarian Academy of Sciences, 1989.

Macdonell, Arthur A. *The Vedic Mythology.* Varanasi: Indological Book House, 1971.

Maskarinec, Gregory G. "A Shamanic Semantic Plurality: *Dhāmīs* and *Jhākrīs* of Western Nepal." In *Shamanism Past and Present: Part 2,* edited by Mihály Hoppál and Otto von Sadovsky, 203–18. Budapest: Ethnographic Institute, Hungarian Academy of Sciences, 1989.

Monier-Williams, Monier. *A Sanskrit-English Dictionary.* New ed. Oxford: Clarendon Press, 1976.

Mumford, Stan Royal. *Himalayan Dialogue: Tibetan Lamas and Gurung Shamans in Nepal.* Madison: University of Wisconsin Press, 1989.

Nebesky-Wojkowitz, Réne de. *Oracles and Demons of Tibet: The Cult and Iconography of the Tibetan Protective Deities.* London: Oxford University Press, 1956.

Norbu, Namkhai. *Dream Yoga and the Practice of Natural Light.* Edited by Michael Katz. Ithaca, NY: Snow Lion Publications, 1992.

Norbu, Thubten Jigme. *Tibet Is My Country.* As told to Heinrich Harrer. Translated by Edward Fitzgerald. London: Rupert Hart-Davis, 1960.

O'Flaherty, Wendy Doniger. *Dreams, Illusion and Other Realities.* Chicago: University of Chicago Press, 1984.

Ortner, Sherry B. *Sherpas Through Their Rituals.* Cambridge: Cambridge University Press, 1978.

Oxtoby, Willard G. "Reflections on the Idea of Salvation." In *Man and His Salvation: Studies in Memory of S. G. F. Brandon,* edited by Eric J. Sharpe and John R. Hinnells, 17–37. Manchester: Manchester University Press, 1973.

Perrin, Michel. "Intellectual Coherence and Constraining Function of Shamanism." *Shaman* 3, no. 2 (1995): 159–65.

———. "Quelques relations entre rêve et chamanisme." *Anthropologie et Sociétés* 18, no. 2 (1994): 30–42.

Pommeret, Françoise. "Returning from Hell." In *Religions of Tibet in Practice,* edited by Donald S. Lopez, 499–510. Princeton, NJ: Princeton University Press, 1997.

Popov, A. A. "How Sereptie Djaruoskin of the Nganasans (Tavgi Samoyeds) Became a Shaman." In *Popular Beliefs and Folklore in Siberia,* edited by Vilmos Diószegi, 137–46. Indiana University Publications: Uralic and Altaic Series, ed. Thomas A. Sebeok, vol. 57. Bloomington: Indiana University Press, 1968.

Powers, John. *Introduction to Tibetan Buddhism.* Ithaca, NY: Snow Lion Publications, 1995.

Rahula, Bhikkhu Telwatte. *A Critical Study of the "Mahāvastu."* Delhi: Motilal Banarsidass, 1978.

Rahula, Walpola. *What the Buddha Taught*. 2nd ed. New York: Grove Press, 1974.

Rasmussen, Knud. *Intellectual Culture of the Copper Eskimos*. Report of the Fifth Thule Expedition, 1921–24, vol. 9. Copenhagen: Gyldendal, 1932.

———. *Intellectual Culture of the Iglulik Eskimos*. Report of the Fifth Thule Expedition, 1921–24, vol. 7, no. 1. Copenhagen: Gyldendal, 1929.

———. *The Netsilik Eskimos: Social Life and Spiritual Culture*. Report of the Fifth Thule Expedition, 1921–24, vol. 8, no. 1. Copenhagen: Gyldendal, 1931.

Reat, N. Ross. *The Origins of Indian Psychology*. Berkeley, CA: Asian Humanities Press, 1990.

Robinson, Richard H., and Willard L. Johnson. *The Buddhist Religion: A Historical Introduction*, 3rd ed. Belmont, CA: Wadsworth Publishing Company, 1982.

Rock, Joseph F. "Contributions to the Shamanism of the Tibetan-Chinese Borderland." *Anthropos* 54 (1959): 796–817.

Rockhill, W. Woodville, trans. *The Life of the Buddha and the Early History of His Order: Derived from Tibetan Works in the Bkah-Hgyur and Bstan-Hgyur*. London: Kegan Paul, Trench, Trübner & Co., 1907.

Romanucci-Ross, Lola. "The Impassioned Cogito: Shaman and Anthropologist." In *Shamanism Past and Present: Part 1*, edited by Mihály Hoppál and Otto von Sadovsky, 35–42. Budapest: Ethnographic Institute, Hungarian Academy of Sciences, 1989.

Samuel, Geoffrey. *Civilized Shamans: Buddhism in Tibetan Societies*. Washington, DC: Smithsonian Institution Press, 1993.

———. *Mind, Body and Culture: Anthropology and the Biological Interface*. Cambridge: Cambridge University Press, 1990.

———. "Shamanism, Bön and Tibetan Religion," In *Tantric Revisionings: New Understandings of Tibetan Buddhism and Indian Religion*. Delhi: Motilal Banarsidass, 2005.

Sarangerel. *Riding Windhorses: A Journey into the Heart of Mongolian Shamanism*. Rochester, VT: Destiny Books, 2000.

Shafton, Anthony. *Dream Reader: Contemporary Approaches to the Understanding of Dreams*. Albany: State University of New York Press, 1995.

Sharma, Jagdish, and Lee Siegel. *Dream Symbolism in the Śramaṇic Tradition: Two Psychoanalytical Studies in Jinist & Buddhist Dream Legends*. Calcutta: Firma KLM Private, 1980.

Shirokogoroff, Sergei M. *Psychomental Complex of the Tungus*. London: Kegan, Paul, Trench, Trübner & Co., 1935.

Siikala, Anna-Leena. "Siberian and Inner Asian Shamanism." In *Studies on Shamanism*, by Anna-Leena Siikala and Mihály Hoppál, 1–14. Helsinki: Finnish Anthropological Society; Budapest: Akadémiai Kiadó, 1998.

———. "The Siberian Shaman's Technique of Ecstasy." In *Studies on Shamanism*, by Anna-Leena Siikala and Mihály Hoppál, 26–40. Helsinki: Finnish Anthropological Society; Budapest: Akadémiai Kiadó, 1998.

Sinha, Jadunath. *Indian Psychology*. 2nd ed. Vol. 1. Delhi: Motilal Banarsidass, 1985.

Smart, Ninian. "Soteriology: An Overview." In vol. 7 of *The Encyclopedia of Religion*, edited by Mircea Eliade, 418–23. New York: Macmillan, 1987.

Smith, Jonathan Z. *Drudgery Divine: On the Comparison of Early Christianities and the Religions of Late Antiquity*. London: School of Oriental and African Studies, University of London, 1990.

———. *Map Is Not Territory: Studies in the History of Religions*. Leiden: E. J. Brill, 1978.

Smoljak, A.V. "Some Notions of the Human Soul among the Nanais." In *Shamanism in Siberia*, edited by Vilmos Diószegi and Mihály Hoppál. Budapest: Akademiai Kiadó, 1978.

Snellgrove, David L. *Indo-Tibetan Buddhism: Indian Buddhists and Their Tibetan Successors*. Boston: Shambhala, 1987.

——— and Hugh Richardson. *A Cultural History of Tibet*. New York: Frederick A. Praeger, 1968.

———. *The Nine Ways of Bön: Excerpts from "gZi-brjid."* Boulder, CO: Prajñā Press, 1980.

Sogyal Rinpoché. *The Tibetan Book of Living and Dying*. Edited by Patrick Gaffney and Andrew Harvey. San Francisco: HarperSanFrancisco, 1992.

Sommarström, Bo. "The Sāmi Shaman's Drum and the Holographic Paradigm Discussion." In *Shamanism Past and Present: Part 1*, edited by Mihály Hoppál and Otto von Sadovsky, 125–44. Budapest: Ethnographic Institute, Hungarian Academy of Sciences, 1989.

Spiro, Melford E. *Buddhism and Society: A Great Tradition and Its Burmese Vicissitudes*. New York: Harper & Row, 1970.

Staal, J. F. "Sanskrit and Sanskritization." *Journal of Asian Studies* 22 (1963): 261–67.

Stablein, William. "Mahākāla the Neo-Shaman—Master of the Ritual." In *Spirit Possession in the Nepal Himalayas*, edited by John T. Hitchcock and Rex L. Jones, 361–75. Warminster, England: Aris and Phillips, 1976.

Stein, R. A. *Tibetan Civilization*. Translated by J. E. Stapleton Driver. Stanford, CA: Stanford University Press, 1972.

Tannenbaum, Nicola. *Who Can Compete Against the World? Power-Protection and Buddhism in Shan Worldview*. Ann Arbor: Association for Asian Studies, University of Michigan, 1995.

Tedlock, Barbara. "Dreaming and Dream Research." In *Dreaming: Anthropological and Psychological Interpretations*, edited by Barbara Tedlock, 1–30. Cambridge: Cambridge University Press, 1987.

Thomas, E. J. *The Life of Buddha as Legend and History*. London: Routledge, 1960.

Thondup Rinpoché. *Hidden Teachings of Tibet: An Explanation of the Terma Tradition of Tibetan Buddhism*. Edited by Harold Talbott. Boston: Wisdom Publications, 1997.

Tucci, Giuseppe. *The Religions of Tibet*. Translated by Geoffrey Samuel. Bombay: Allied Publishers Private, 1980.

———. *The Theory and Practice of the Mandala*. Translated by Alan Houghton Broderick. London: Rider & Company, 1969.

Tull, Herman. *The Vedic Origins of Karma: Cosmos as Man in Ancient Indian Myth and Ritual*. Albany: State University of New York Press, 1989.

Varela, Francisco J., ed. *Sleeping, Dreaming and Dying: An Exploration of Consciousness with the Dalai Lama*. Boston: Wisdom Publications, 1997.

Vasilevich, G. M. "Early Concepts about the Universe among the Evenks (Materials)." In *Studies in Siberian Shamanism*, edited by Henry N. Michael, 46–83. Arctic Institute of North America Anthropology of the North: Translations from Russian Sources, no. 4. Toronto: University of Toronto Press, 1963.

Wangyal, Tenzin. *The Tibetan Yogas of Dream and Sleep*. Edited by Mark Dhalby. Ithaca, NY: Snow Lion Publications, 1998.

Watson, Graham, and Jean-Guy Goulet. "Gold In; Gold Out: The Objectification of Dene Tha Accounts of Dreams and Visions." *Journal of Anthropological Research* 48 (1992): 215–30.

Wayman, Alex. "Significance of Dreams in India and Tibet." In *Buddhist Insight: Essays by Alex Wayman*, edited by George Elder, 399–412. Religions of Asia Series, edited by Lewis R. Lancaster and J. L. Shastri, no. 5. Delhi: Motilal Banarsidass, 1984.

———. "The Significance of Mantras, from the Veda down to Buddhist Tantric Practice." In *Buddhist Insight: Essays by Alex Wayman*, edited by George Elder, 413–30. Religions of Asia Series, edited by Lewis R. Lancaster and J. L. Shastri, no. 5. Delhi: Motilal Banarsidass, 1984.

Wilbert, Johannes. "Eschatology in a Participatory Universe: Destinies of the Soul among the Warao Indians of Venezuela." In *Death and the Afterlife in Pre-Columbian America: A Conference at Dumbarton Oaks, October 27th, 1973*, edited by Elizabeth P. Benson, 163–88. Washington, DC: Dumbarton Oaks Research Library and Collections, 1973.

Woolf, Marsha, and Karen Blanc. *The Rainmaker: The Life Story of Venerable Ngagpa Yeshe Dorje Rinpoche*. With a foreward by His Holiness the Dalai Lama and an afterword by Robert A. F. Thurman. Boston: Sigo Press, 1994.

Young, Serinity. *Dreaming in the Lotus: Buddhist Dream Narrative, Imagery, and Practice*. Boston: Wisdom Publications, 1999.

Zimmer, Heinrich. *Myths and Symbols in Indian Art and Civilization*. Edited by Joseph Campbell. Bollingen Series, vol. 6. Princeton, NJ: Princeton University Press, 1974.

Index

Abhiniṣkramaṇasūtra, 64
Ailūsa, Kavasa, 39
Allashukur, 29–30
Amitāyus, 52–53
Aṅguttara-nikāya, 61–62
animal sacrifice, 37–38, 58
animals, contracts and negotiation with, 18–20
animism and animistic societies, 16–17
Anisimov, A. F., 84–85
Aris, Michael, 89
ātman, 43, 44, 49, 133n41, 134n50
awakening
  of Buddha, 138n48
  dreams of, 61–63
    five great, 61–62
Aziz, Barbara, 77

bardo, 57, 81–83
Basilov, Vladimir, 11, 29
Bellezza, John Vincent, 12–13, 140n17
Beyer, Stephan, 103
Bhadrapāla, Bodhisattva, 53
bhavaṅga-citta, 54–55
Bird-David, Nurit, 17
birth, spiritual, 61–62
Blue Beryl treatise
  dreams portending death or recovery from, 99–101
  omens of recovery or decay from, 98–100
Bodhi Orientation, 79–82
bodhisattva vows, 124n19
bodhisattva(s), 52, 53, 60, 62, 65
  ten visions of a, 62, 63
Bolling, George, 42
Bön-po, 7–9, 73–76, 140n17, 140n19
  confusions regarding Buddhism and, 8
  ways of understanding, 8
Brahmanical Hinduism, 64–65
Brahmins, 49, 57–58
Bṛhadāraṇyaka, 43–46
Buddha Amitāyus, 52–53
Buddha (Siddhārtha Gautama), 49, 58, 59
Buddhaghosa, 51, 56, 57, 67
Buddha(s), 58, 59, 63, 64, 82
  dream and awakening of, 138n48
  dream and direct perception of, 51–54
  spiritual birth of fully awakened, 61–62
Buddhism. *See also specific topics*
  overview, 5
Buddhist dream theory and its Indian context, 50–51
"Buddhist" dreams, 2
Bulkeley, Kelly, 1

Chāndogya Upaniṣad, 45
Chöd, 104
Chon, Naro Bhun, 75
Chophel, Norbu, 97, 101